D0065679

The Hidden Encyclical
of Pius XI

The Hidden Encyclical
of Pius XI

Georges Passelecq and
Bernard Suchecky

Translated from the French by Steven Rendall

WITH AN INTRODUCTION BY
Garry Wills

Harcourt Brace & Company
NEW YORK   SAN DIEGO   LONDON

Introduction copyright © 1997 by Garry Wills
English translation copyright © 1997 by Harcourt Brace & Company
© Editions La Découverte, Paris 1995

Library of Congress Cataloging-in-Publication Data
Passelecq, Georges.
[Encyclique cachée de Pie Xi.   English]
The hidden encyclical of Pius XI/Georges Passelecq and
Bernard Suchecky; translated from the French by Steven Rendall;
with an introduction by Garry Wills.
p.   cm.
Includes bibliographical references and index.
ISBN 0-15-100244-4
1. Catholic Church—Relations—Judaism—Papal documents.
2. Judaism—Catholic Church—Papal documents.   3. Pius XI, Pope,
1857–1939.   I. Suchecky, Bernard.   II. Title.
BM535.P2431513   1997
261.2'6'08822—dc21   97-7227

The text was set in Bembo.
Designed by Lori McThomas Buley
Printed in the United States of America
First U.S. edition
A C E F D B

Contents

Acknowledgments

The authors wish to express their immense gratitude to Professor Thomas A. Breslin. Without the microfilmed documentation which he so generously made available to them, this book simply would not exist.

For his part, Georges Passelecq would like to thank Professor Pierre-Maurice Bogaert, O.S.B.; Professor Luc Dequeker; Reverend Father Adrien Nocent, O.S.B.; Reverend Father Jean-Marie Schiltz, S.J.; Monsieur l'Abbé Jean-Marie Schoefs; and Reverend Father Ambroise Watelet, O.S.B.

Bernard Suchecky thanks Gisèle Goldberg, Mélitina Fabre-Matveieff, Francine Thomas, Anne Wijnbelt, Bernard Jenn, Bernard Skowronek, and David Susskind, as well as Nathan Ramet of the B'nai B'rith of Antwerp, Georges Schnek of the Central Jewish Consistory of Belgium, and Israel Singer of the World Jewish Congress.

INTRODUCTION:

Fumbling toward Justice

by Garry Wills

It is the stuff of spy novels. An American priest, traveling in Europe during the Nazi persecutions of 1938, visits Rome, which had not been part of his assignment (he went abroad to write about a eucharistic congress in Czechoslovakia). Somehow the pope, Pius XI, learns that the priest is in Rome and invites him to a private meeting at his summer castle. The priest, who has never met this pope, has no idea what the Holy Father could want with him. As he goes toward the papal chamber, a famous countenance glides by him, all sunken eyes and cheeks—Eugenio Pacelli, the pope's secretary of state—without pausing to tell him why he has been summoned.

Alone with the pope, communing with him in French and German, the priest is given a secret mission, to write a condemnation of the racial policies of Nazi Germany. The pope will issue the text as an encyclical (official "circular letter"), but the priest is to write it out of his own conviction: "Say simply what you would say if you yourself were pope."

This is pretty heady stuff. The pope even tells the priest that God must have sent him to Rome at this opportune moment. Why him of all people? The pope, it turns out, has read a book the priest wrote on racial relations with American blacks. What he liked was that the priest used Catholic theology to show that racial division within the human community is contrary to natural and revealed truth.

Sworn to secrecy, the priest has to contrive a cover for his staying in Europe—he pretends that he is visiting relatives and friends near Paris, where he finds books and assistants for this rush assignment. Then, when he turns in the draft encyclical, it disappears down a black hole, not to reappear for half a century. Was it sabotaged? Did the pope, having acted on impulse, entertain second and soberer thoughts? Or was he simply too old to carry through such a bold initiative, outside the normal channels? (Pius XI was eighty-one when he issued this commission in May of 1938. He died a year later, a year filled with urgent duties carried out as he saw the end approaching.)

What happened to the text, and why, even in our time, have so many efforts been made to keep it suppressed? This book gives what answers are currently available to these questions. To understand the background of this extraordinary episode, it is necessary to look at the characters of the two principal players in it, Father John LaFarge, the American Jesuit, and Achille Ratti, the Lombard scholar who had become Pope Pius XI.

LaFarge came of distinguished families. His mother, Margaret Perry, was on her mother's side a Bache, a descendant of Benjamin Franklin. On her father's side she was one of the seagoing Perrys of Newport. Commodore Oliver Hazard Perry, famous for his 1813 dispatch "We have met the enemy, and he is ours" was her grandfather; Matthew Galbraith Perry, even more famous for his 1854 treaty "opening Japan," was her great-uncle. As a boy, the future Jesuit liked to sail and later roamed the waters of his native Newport.

LaFarge's father, after whom he was named, was the distinguished American painter and stained-glass artist, one of Henry Adams's closest friends, a celebrity in the New York of Edith

Wharton and Stanford White. The La Farge name was brought to America by a Frenchman who had served in Napoleon's navy. Arrived in New York, he married into a prominent Catholic family, the Binnses. The painter was educated in Catholic schools— St. John's (later Fordham) and Mount St. Mary's of Emmetsburg, Maryland. Though he remained a Catholic *en principe* (as his son put it), this John La Farge puzzled sophisticated friends with his combination of sincere Catholicism and worldly wisdom and experience. As Henry James put it: "He was . . . intensely among us but somehow not with *all* of us; he being a Catholic, and apparently a 'real' one in spite of so many other omnisciences, making perhaps by itself the greatest difference. He had been through a Catholic college in Maryland . . . but where and when he had so miraculously laid up his stores of reading and achieved his universal saturation was what we longest kept asking ourselves."[1] La Farge studied art in Paris, where he stayed with his Saint-Victor relatives, including the fashionable author Paul de Saint-Victor. Returned to America, he met Margaret Perry in Newport and, despite family objections to union with a Protestant, married her. Shortly after their marriage, Mrs. La Farge became a Catholic of intense and increasing piety, while her husband's bohemian life drew him, on long absences, to France, Japan, and the South Sea Islands. La Farge maintained his studio and career near Washington Square in New York, visiting his family in Newport less often than their nine children would seem to indicate.

John, the couple's last child, was born after a priest assured his mother that it was still her duty to bear children even in her forties.[2] She kept this final pregnancy secret, so as not to disturb her husband, who was engaged in an acrimonious lawsuit with Louis Tiffany over patent rights to stained-glass techniques. The late-born child was so much younger than most of his siblings that he was given the baptismal name John, which the fourth child had already been given and abandoned as he grew up. (The baptismal register, confused over this duplication, simply did not record the second John's appearance at the font)[3].

As a boy John rarely saw his father, though connections made through his name opened many doors when prominent families came to Newport for the summer. The boy knew Edith Wharton there, and other friends of his father, including the Roosevelts of Oyster Bay. Theodore Roosevelt himself advised the son on going to Harvard, and helped reconcile the father to young John's decision to become a Jesuit.[4] It was family tradition that Henry James loved Margaret La Farge from a distance and slipped her into his tales with characteristic indirection.[5]

In an autobiography written in 1954, the younger John LaFarge is filial and forgiving toward his namesake, whose affairs with other women his mother had confided to him with resignation: "Your father is a genius." The son may not have been judgmental, except in this indirect way: He was determined *not* to be a genius. The choice of title for his autobiography is significant: *The Manner Is Ordinary*. On the surface, this is just a quotation from Saint Ignatius's rules for Jesuits (they are to affect no special clerical status); but it reflected a deeper urge, on the boy's part, to escape the "privileges" of genius that had made his father neglect his mother (and him).

Some of LaFarge's siblings followed their father into the art world (mainly as architects), but John said he was too ill-coordinated to use brushes or drafting instruments. This is a suspect claim. His fingers were nimble enough to play the organ very well. Music was one art his father did not understand, and it was the one art young John worked at, studying harmony and counterpoint at Harvard.

Sharing his mother's piety, John was determined from an early age to be a priest. Clerical friends of the family tutored him in languages, and he made a kind of pilgrim's grand tour of Europe with his mother. After being graduated from Harvard, he studied for the priesthood at Innsbruck and was ordained abroad. With his talent and his family connections, he would have found ecclesiastical preferment in New York easy if not inevitable. He precluded that by joining the Jesuit province in Maryland after he had already become a priest.

Assigned to do parish work in the rural Chesapeake Bay area where his father had gone to college, LaFarge discovered anew "the sins of the fathers." Black Catholics still remembered how, in the 1830s, Jesuits had sold all the slaves they owned into the Deep South.[6] Father LaFarge worked to expiate that betrayal committed by his religious forebears. He opened a secondary school and vocational institute for blacks. He sought out and brought to Maryland teaching nuns, black and white. This remained the work nearest his heart to the end of his life: he was among those at Martin Luther King's side marching for civil rights.

LaFarge's work in the Catholic Interracial Council and the Catholic Rural Life Movement acquainted him with social issues in general, which led his superior to assign him to the Jesuit journal *America,* published in New York. LaFarge kept up his activism for black rights, and in 1937 published the pioneering book *Interracial Justice.* This was an incisive attack on the segregation laws of the South. It was temperately argued, almost scholastic in its methodical treatment of all conceivable defenses of the "separate but equal" mentality still prevalent in the North as well as the South.

LaFarge did not argue from natural law and Catholic theology only, but from anthropology and economics as well. He made the shrewd argument that segregation was the principal cause of the South's intellectual and economic stagnation—an argument strikingly confirmed when integration materially benefited the South four decades after LaFarge's book was published.

A sample of LaFarge's dry but devastating manner is his

response to the fear that integration would lead to "race-mixing." LaFarge recalled how Catholic bishops *opposed* laws against interracial marriage in Cuba because they led to illicit unions. Besides, racism had itself led to a race mixing obvious in the mestizo makeup of the black community of the South. There is in this passage a fine sardonic note, nicely muted, worthy of Henry Adams: "A racial status based upon a belief in essential inferiority, while it may be a deterrent to conscientious persons of the dominant group, is a temptation for the loose-living and unscrupulous to place the helpless and 'inferior' group at the service of the passions of those in power. This is a universal human phenomenon, against which the Prophet Jeremias protested in his prayers, which has accompanied every subjection of one race by another."[7]

LaFarge himself did not believe there can be "interracial" marriage, since "race" itself is a myth when considered as a science of essential qualities genetically determined. He substituted the nonjudgmental "population group" for the intrinsically biased term "race." "*Communis aestimatio* [folk hunch], rather than anything perfectly objective and tangible, is the real basis of much that is contained in 'being a Negro' in the United States. As this *communis aestimatio* changes, the make-up of the group itself alters."[8] Passages like this may well have impressed Pope Pius and led him to make the unexpected leap from blacks in Maryland to Jews in Germany—since Hitler's myth of Aryan purity was as much a social construct as the *aestimatio* of black impurity.

But can we really believe that an eighty-one-year-old pope, sick and grappling with world passions of staggering intensity, would read a book about the American South within a year of its publication? Odd as it may seem, we can. Achille Ratti had spent forty-five years of his life presiding over two great scholarly collections, in the Ambrosian Library in Milan and the Vatican Library in Rome. A linguist and polymath, he made it a point of librarian's pride that each book being accessioned should pass through his hands, and he held back any he felt he should be acquainted with, to read before it was catalogued.[9] This had taught him great confidence in his own judgment and knowledge of affairs—and, too, great confidence in the binding force of written documents (as his large collection of "concordats" with various dictators would demonstrate). After he became pope, aides in the Vatican never knew what book would pop up in the pope's conversation or go into his formulation of policy. All they knew was that books mattered deeply to him. In a rare personal session with Mussolini, the pope pulled his favorite author, Alessandro Manzoni, off the shelf and read the dictator's duties to him from an Italian classic.[10]

Ratti shared love of Manzoni with a fellow Lombard, Angelo Roncalli, who later became Pope John XXIII. They had other similarities. Living in the historic Milan diocese, both men admired and made scholarly studies of Milan's energetic church ruler, Cardinal Charles Borromeo. Each benefited from a long "backwater" period, when events were compromising more activist clerics. Ratti was secluded in his libraries while the fight over the pope's temporal power raged in the reigns of Pius X and Benedict XV. Roncalli weathered the rise of Mussolini and World War II in the comparative calm of Bulgaria.

Both men were sent late in life to diplomatic hot spots—Ratti to Poland as its borders were renegotiated after World War I, Roncalli to France after World War II (where he dealt with clerics who had collaborated with Hitler). Then each was given a cardinalatial see to die in—Milan for Ratti, Venice for Roncalli. Their lives seemed completed—until each was elected pope as a compromise candidate in a divided conclave.

Ratti, who became Pius XI in 1922, faced the problem of reengaging the modern world after Pius X's withdrawal from it. Pius IX, angered at the loss of his temporal domain, became "the prisoner of the Vatican," dramatizing his self-imposed seclusion. Since the Italian government had "stolen" his realm, he ordered Catholics not to participate in the Italian state's "illegitimate" politics. His order not to vote was called *non expedit* ("It does no good"). An attitude of contempt for liberal politics of the parliamentary sort, though mounted as a defiance of modern trends, obscurely fed the modern trend toward dictatorship. That, too, declared parliament illegitimate—undisciplined, relativistic, and dithery.

Both Pius IX's immediate successors eased off the *non expedit* policy, and a liberal Catholic party had arisen in Italy, under Don Luigi Bosco. But Pius XI did not want to trust to the bargaining even of politicians of this party, since they would inevitably compromise with the anti-clerical and altruistic politicians undermining the old claims of a state religion. Pius XI knew there was no returning to the established church in modern political regimes. He was content to guarantee enclaves of Catholic instruction, proselytization, and social life outside the sphere of electoral politics—what he called "Catholic Action." He sought concordats, rules of conduct, that would guarantee the independent life of these cultural bodies.

In the long run, Pius's stance can be seen as inching toward a Catholic acceptance of the separation of church and state (on the American model). The program can be seen in LaFarge's own document, which accepts a legitimate "territory" of politics which the church does not "encroach on" (paragraph number 3). But Pius's clumsy formulation of a separation between electoral politics and cultural activities ("Catholic Action") was naive and ill-timed. Because he despised parliamentary politics, he trusted the anti-democratic rulers who signed concordats to observe the terms of their agreement without any continuing political pressure. In fact, he was willing to give away the right of Catholics to engage in politics as the price for getting his enclaves of religious autonomy. This led him to undermine Catholic politicians throughout Europe—not only Don Luigi Sturzo in Italy but also Gil Rables in Spain and the Center party in Germany. In this sense, Pius's eighteen concordats eased the rise of dictators, since Catholic parties had made up the margin in coalitions opposed to Mussolini, Franco, and Hitler.

Mussolini knew the value of a concordat with the Vatican, and he went after it by shrewdly assessing Pius's priorities. The pope wanted paper guarantees for Catholic freedom to run schools, instruct families, and guard the nation's moral life *outside* of politics. So Mussolini became, in the early years of Pius's reign, as papal as the Vatican on "social issues." He outlawed divorce, contraception, and abortion. He increased the penalty for adultery, and made it a crime to swear, to have syphilis, or to dress immodestly.[11] He was making the pope a deal that looked better than parliamentary maneuver and the fickle commitments of political parties. The pope signed the Italian concordat in 1929.

Yet precisely because the pope trusted in his concordats, his sense of betrayal when they were not observed was highly personal. That made his diplomacy a tissue of legalisms torn across by pique. This remote and scholarly man became harshly punitive against individuals who would not keep their written word—not only Mussolini, and in time Hitler, but also Pilsudski in Poland and Lord Strickland in Malta (the latter he excommunicated, placing Catholic Malta under an interdict).[12] These highly personalized feuds threatened the calmer diplomacy of his experienced secretaries of state, Pietro Gasparri and (later) Eugenio Pacelli. As one papal emissary admitted to a British diplomat: "He has a way of bottling up things and not telling even his Secretary of State and [those in his] immediate surroundings of his intentions."[13]

At times this personal fury could serve a good purpose, as when, in response to Hitler's defiance of the concordat with

Germany, the pope intervened energetically, giving a secret commission to write an encyclical against the Third Reich's activities. As he would later do with LaFarge, the pope conferred with German bishops who were in Rome for another purpose, and asked Cardinal Faulhaber to draw up an encyclical (so secretly that the cardinal could not even use a stenographer). Then Pius used Pacelli's German contacts to have the encyclical shipped into Germany, to be read from pulpits and published by small local presses (circumventing the government's watch on the major Catholic publishing house).[14]

This 1937 encyclical—*Mit Brennender Sorge,* "With Burning Dismay"—is often called a denunciation of Nazism in general, but it is focused on one subject—Hitler's non-observance of his concordat with the Vatican, especially in the intimidation of those trying to conduct Catholic schools. This was a tactic adapted for both prudential and legal reasons. The pope's hope, if any, of moderating Hitler's totalitarian control of Germany was strongest on the points Hitler had himself agreed to. Besides, the pope had forsworn Catholic intervention into the "profane sphere" of politics, and Pius, ever the legalist, felt he could not hold Hitler to his word while breaking his own.[15]

Yet the encyclical's denunciation of Hitler's statism, which violated the cultural sphere of free religious activity, had obvious application to the violation of Protestant and Jewish freedom. This had become so obvious from Pius's nonofficial expressions of outrage that the Nazis resorted to their normal tactic, equating papal sympathy for Jews with a racial taint in Pius himself. The report was systematically put about that Ratti himself was half-Jewish—a report that Ratti referred to and denied in his dealings with the German ambassador to the Vatican.[16]

The accusation that he was a Jew made Pius's words all the more powerful when, in his famous 1938 address to Belgian pilgrims, he read Saint Paul's reference to *"our* patriarch Abra-

ham." The pope said that "we are the spiritual offspring of
Abraham.... We are spiritually Semites." Only in the context of
the time, at the very moment when Italy's anti-Jewish laws were
first being enforced and people were making panicky efforts to
distance themselves from all things Jewish, does this statement
acquire its full emotive meaning for Pius.

It has been objected that this was not an official document but
an address to a single group. True enough. But it was spoken
four months after the pope had commissioned the official document LaFarge had just completed. And it was supported by a
series of other attacks on the anti-Jewish laws, given to different
groups in the summer of 1938. It is known that Pius meant, in
the very week of his death in 1939, to denounce the anti-Jewish
laws in a public address on the tenth anniversary of the concordat
with Mussolini.

It offends some that the pope's criticism of the anti-Jewish laws
focused on the point where Catholic interests were most at stake,
especially the ban on intermarriage with converted Jews. But
Ratti, with his jurisprudential cast of mind, clearly thought that
the infringement of the concordat was the Achilles heel of the
anti-Jewish laws (no pun intended on Ratti's own first name). If
he could hope for anything, it was that this discrediting first step
would lead to the larger points he asked LaFarge to make. In the
event, he could not win even that minor first victory, despite
Mussolini's legal commitment—which suggests how little success
even larger protests would have met. Nonetheless, his speeches
of 1938 and his commission to LaFarge show that Pius was moving toward a violation of his own principles of political neutrality
where the Jews were concerned. By that time, he had seen his
neat little librarian's world of paper treaties come apart and was
addressing himself directly to human suffering, in the humane
spirit of Manzoni and of his other fellow Lombard, the later
John XXIII.

In retrospect, we all yearn for more dramatic actions, no matter how ineffectual. We see the Holocaust looming by 1938—a horror hard for many to recognize, even after it had arrived. But Pius deserves more honor than he is often given. Others, including Roosevelt and Churchill, proved even less outspoken. As Nicholas Cheetham wrote in 1982: "Guilty as Pius may have been of miscalculation in his handling of Mussolini and Hitler, his opposition to their acts and ideology was more vigorous and consistent than that displayed by any one state or combination of states."[17]

But when all this is said in Pius's favor, we must admit that there was an inherent flaw in whatever efforts he made. He was hobbled by his church's history of dealings with the Jews—a fact that comes out in the very document that he wanted to use in defense of Jewish rights. That document, drafted by LaFarge, repeats the theological nonsense about a historic curse on the Jews for their rejection of Christ. The conditions for transcending that traditional "teaching" had not yet arrived. It is painful to see that even such fine minds as those of John LaFarge and his two collaborators were still imprisoned by that ugly claim.

Though Pius wanted LaFarge's own insights into racism to be at the core of his encyclical, he ordered the American to work with two men who had prior experience of drawing up earlier encyclicals, Gustave Desbuquois of France and Gustav Gundlach of Germany (the two Guses of LaFarge's correspondence in 1938). LaFarge was happy to accept these men's help. They had records of enlightenment on economic issues, and he felt awed by the task of putting words into a pope's mouth ("All I can say is that the Rock of Peter has fallen on my head"). But the present book shows how flawed was the "liberal" Catholicism of the 1930s: Gundlach had written an encyclopedia article defending a "permissible anti-Semitism," the shadow of which would fall across the document he worked on with LaFarge.

The draft makes most of the arguments against racism contained in LaFarge's book on segregation, and actually strengthens them—a fact reflected in later editions of *Interracial Justice,* which include some material worked up for the draft. The pope is made to condemn any anti-Semitism based on racial inferiority or "alienness"—something not to be minimized given the fake scientific approach of Hitler and Mussolini to the claims of Jewish "animality." The document clearly indicts contemporary racial theory for being aimed solely at Jews (paragraph 131). It establishes very useful rules for any separatism—that it is valid only as it helps *promote* the general good, instead of setting itself in opposition to it (paragraph 98). It is eloquent on the ties of interdependence that weave the human community together over space and time (paragraph 76).

But the draft takes a fatal swerve from the subject of racial persecution of Jews to the subject of *religious* opposition to them. This latter is presented as "the authentic basis of the social separation of the Jews from the rest of humanity" (paragraph 133). The pope is even made to warn Catholics of "the spiritual dangers to which contact with Jews can expose souls" (paragraph 142).

We should not make too much of the latter warning. It reflected Catholic fears of the time about exposure to religious alternatives of *any* sort—Protestant and Orthodox as well as Jewish. There was a fear of marriage outside the faith, of education in secular schools, of attendance at Protestant church services that my contemporaries and I were hearing from our priests as late as the 1940s.[18] This aspect of the draft is not opposed to Jews as such but to all non-Catholics. LaFarge no doubt thought of *this* separation as serving the general good by keeping an orthodoxy available for others to embrace.

But there is also a specifically religious anti-Semitism in the draft, reflected in the claim—still part of Catholic seminary teaching at that time—that "the Jewish people put to death their

Savior and King" (paragraph 135). Even in the Gospels, it is not "the Jewish people" who put Jesus to death (or get the Romans to do it), but *some* Jews at a certain point in history. Other Jews were no doubt indifferent or uninvolved, and some of them were part of Christ's own all-Jewish following. But, more important, the Gospels are not a historical record. This latter point would have scandalized Catholics at a time when papal opposition to modern biblical scholarship was still strong. Most Catholics were still taught, at the time, that the Gospels were written by Christ's immediate followers shortly after his death, as literal reports of his words and acts.

Actually, only the letters of Saint Paul represent the immediate aftermath of Christ's death, and they treat the Jews' opposition to Christianity as a temporary phenomenon, to be rectified almost immediately (before the imminent end of the world).[19] The Gospels were written in the atmosphere of the Roman war with Judaea and its aftermath, when Christians were dissociating themselves from the Jewishness of the destroyed Temple (A.D. 70), detaching themselves from or being driven out of the synagogues that were their first home. The fictive trial of Jesus before the Sanhedrin was an emblematic presentation of Jesus's *current* suffering in his body of believers, instructing believers that they should stand nobly like Christ, not deny their part like Peter— who is, as Elaine Pagels put it, offered as "an example of how *not* to act when on trial."[20]

As theological documents, the Gospels offer timeless meaning to believers; but as historical evidence, they reflect conditions two generations after Christ's death. The fact that *some* Jews were opposing the Church then is no more binding on all later Jews than the fact that some Jews were the ones being persecuted. (It is important to see that the Church did not believe that its *own* medieval persecutions of Jews reflected a curse on all Catholics living today.)

The Church has been able to distinguish the Jews who became Christians from their successors: We are not told that Catholic priests must *all* be converted Jews, just because Christ's original disciples were. Then why must all later Jews be responsible for what some Jews did generations after Jesus was dead?

The tragic thing is that the theological materials for destroying religious anti-Semitism are present in the very draft La Farge prepared. Arguing for the essential unity of all mankind, the document notes that the very heart of the Christian teaching on redemption *requires* that unity. As all humans fell in Adam, incurring a general guilt ("original sin"), so Christ, the Second Adam, saved all humans who will accept this redemption when he died for the accumulated sins of the first Adam and his descendants (paragraphs 73–75). In that sense, *everyone* killed Jesus, and admission of that fact, of the sin needing forgiveness through his death, is the primary Christian responsibility. Theologically, it is unimportant what comparative role was played by Jews or Romans, by defecting Christian (Judas) or denying Christian (Peter), in the death of Jesus. Historically, whatever role Jews played was as accidental to the historic moment of Jesus' death as the fact that *only* Jews were present as disciples.

The teaching that Christ died because of all of us is older, broader, stronger, and better founded than the folk theology that blames Jews. It is the teaching of a puritan like Milton: "The curse to which we were subject [was] transferred to Him."[21] It is equally the teaching of a Catholic like John Henry Newman, who said that Jesus died "laden with every sin which has been committed since the fall, in all regions of the earth. . . . Of the living and of the dead and of the as yet unborn, of the last and of the saved, of thy people and of strangers, all sins are there."[22]

Yet the literal reading of the Gospels as history ignored this larger theological point about responsibility for Christ's death. And LaFarge was still shackled by that form of scriptural ignorance. His bungled effort at compassion, and the pope's own better instincts, were made feckless by this theological blindness. They would be the first, now that those blinders have been removed, to beg forgiveness of the Jews they wronged even as they tried to help them. They fought with such weapons as were given them, blindly but in motion toward the truth. We should all be able to say that of our lives.

Requiescant in pace.

The Hidden Encyclical
of Pius XI

The Search for the Documents

In December 1972 and January 1973 a series of articles in the *National Catholic Reporter* (Kansas City, Missouri) raised for the first time the issue of an "unpublished encyclical of Pius XI attacking anti-Semitism." Jim Castelli, the periodical's associate editor, had unearthed most of the information relating to this case through meticulous and prudent investigation.[1]

In June 1938, Castelli reported, Pope Pius XI had entrusted an American Jesuit at Fordham University, Father John LaFarge, S.J., with the drafting of preliminary documents for an encyclical condemning racism and anti-Semitism. Surprised, and a bit overwhelmed, LaFarge asked for assistance, and Gustav Gundlach, S.J., a German Jesuit, and Gustave Desbuquois, S.J., a French Jesuit nominated by the superior general of the Society of Jesus, Father Wladimir Ledochowski, S.J., were appointed as his collaborators. A second German Jesuit, Father Heinrich Bacht, S.J., joined them in order to translate their draft into Latin. The four men worked together in Paris throughout the summer, and toward the end of December, LaFarge went to Rome to give Ledochowski not one but *three* versions of the draft that had been asked for: three texts, then, written respectively in French, English, and German, one of which, at least, was titled *Humani Generis Unitas*, "The Unity of the Human Race."

And then . . . nothing. Pius XI died in February 1939, Cardinal Pacelli succeeded him in March under the name of Pius XII, and the Second World War began in September with the invasion of Poland—without the encyclical's having seen the light of day.

What happened? Jim Castelli offered no definitive answer to that question. But basing his views on the correspondence between LaFarge and Gundlach after LaFarge's return to the United States, he speculated that the superior general of the Jesuits must have deliberately delayed the transmission of the documents as too obviously contradicting his strategic choices, which were more anti-communist than anti-Nazi. When these documents reached Pius XI—if they ever did—the old pope Ratti was already too near his end to be able to transform them into an encyclical. As for Pius XII, who does seem to have been aware of the documents commissioned by his predecessor, he was said to have simply decided to bury them in the "silence of the archives."[2]

How did the *National Catholic Reporter* manage to break open such a delicate case? On what documentation were its revelations based? "Microfilmed copies of the encyclical and related documents," Castelli explained, had been given to his newspaper by a former Jesuit, Thomas Breslin, who as a seminarian had discovered them in 1967 while cataloguing the papers of John LaFarge. These papers, which had long been kept at the head offices of the Catholic weekly *America*,[3] had been passed to St. Ignatius of Loyola Seminary in Westchester County, New York, where Breslin was studying philosophy. The closure of the seminary in 1969 interrupted Breslin's work, and the LaFarge papers moved to Woodstock College in Manhattan, where cataloguing was not pursued further for lack of an archivist.[4]

In the course of his investigation, Castelli had taken care to confirm, by means of various independent witnesses, the existence of this documentation. According to the memoirs of Father

Walter Abbott, S.J., who had become friends with LaFarge in New York, LaFarge had never said a word about this project to any of his colleagues at Fordham. Shortly before his death in 1963, when persistently questioned on the subject by a former student of Father Gundlach's, he finally admitted, within community confidentiality, that he had taken part in this enterprise, but gave no further details. Abbott added that he had found the English and French copies of the encyclical among LaFarge's papers on the day of LaFarge's death. Another witness, Father Heinrich Bacht, S.J., the translator chosen to prepare a Latin version of the draft encyclical, and in 1972 the last surviving participant in the project, said that "Gundlach wrote the larger part of the draft, whereas LaFarge wrote most of the key sections on racism and anti-Semitism." Finally, the documentation was also attested to in an unqualified manner by Father Robert Graham, S.J., a co-worker with LaFarge at *America* for twenty years and, in 1972, the co-director of the section of the Vatican archives devoted to the Second World War.[5]

The *National Catholic Reporter* quoted in toto only paragraphs 126 to 130 of the draft encyclical itself, that is, solely the conclusions on racism in general. The paragraphs on anti-Semitism received only succinct mention.[6]

Castelli concluded his vast investigation by remarking, in an accompanying editorial, that "the story of this encyclical draft means that the question of the Vatican's failure to denounce anti-Semitism at the proper time in the prewar period involved not an oversight, but a conscious refusal to work with a document outlined by a pope himself," and that this inevitably raised "many questions about the internal workings of the Vatican during World War II." Moreover, "an earlier, hard-hitting statement on racism might have meant that we would have less racially motivated strife in the U.S. today."[7]

In a long scholarly article, Gordon Zahn, a specialist on the social encyclicals,[8] judged the rediscovered encyclical "perhaps the strongest Catholic statement on this moral evil" of anti-Semitism. As such, "it resurrects the 'Hochhuth problem'[9] in a new context, for now it is no longer a matter of Pius XII's *failure* to protest the systematic elimination of the Jews, but rather his apparent *refusal* to go along with the intention of his revered predecessor and sponsor. Add to this the fact that Pius XI would have protested early in the Nazi program while Pius XII maintained public silence long after it had escalated into the full horror of the Final Solution, and what once seemed a needless attack upon the memory of a beloved leader becomes a very real problem calling for serious study and reflection."

In addition, Zahn writes, "the newly 'discovered' encyclical adds a new dimension to the problem: It suggests that Pius XII, though no anti-Semite himself, did not share his predecessor's intensity of opposition to that moral evil and, as a consequence, did not place it as high in the order of priority in making his policy calculations as Piux XI probably would have. This, in turn, might reflect a personality difference between the two, Pius XII being less inclined to take a controversial stand and distancing himself from what he may have regarded as rash impulsiveness on the part of the other."[10]

The Vatican's Clarification

The information published by the *National Catholic Reporter* immediately attracted the attention of several leading periodicals,[11] but did not unleash a wave of polemics comparable to the one that had accompanied the production of Rolf Hochhuth's play *The Deputy* a dozen years earlier. Did this moderate response result from the celerity with which the Vatican reacted?

On 5 April 1973 the *Osservatore romano* published a clarification signed by one of the officials of the Vatican archives, Father

Burkhart Schneider. Seizing the opportunity afforded by the publication of a new volume in the vast corpus entitled *Acts and Documents of the Holy See Relative to the Second World War*,[12] Father Schneider explained, under the title "An Encyclical *Manqué*," that in this new volume, which also included documents belonging to the end of Pius XI's pontificate, "a document is lacking which has recently attracted the attention of the international press. The latter has repeatedly asserted that there has been discovered in the United States an unpublished encyclical of Pius XI on racism whose publication would have had immeasurable consequences at the time. In fact, during the summer of 1938, the Jesuit Fathers Desbuquois, Gundlach, and LaFarge began composing, in Paris, on the pope's orders, a document that would have set forth Christian doctrine on the unity of the human race (the title was to be *Unitas Humani Generis*), in opposition to all racist ideologies. The result was a work of more than 100 very dense pages written in a speculative, theoretical, and laborious style that more resembled Gundlach's manner of thinking than LaFarge's. Three versions exist (French, English, and German), which are not always coherent or identical with each other. These texts, transmitted to Pius XI by the then Superior General of the Society of Jesus, W. Ledochowski, at the end of 1938 or the beginning of 1939, cannot be considered a true pontifical document, but at most the draft, requiring many revisions and redevelopments, of a future encyclical. The concrete situation at the time, the health of the pontiff, who died a few weeks later, and his wish to commemorate the tenth anniversary of the Concordat (the *Conciliazione*), caused the texts prepared, along with many others on different themes, to end up in the silence of the archives. Part of their content can easily be discovered in Pius XII's documents, beginning with the encyclical *Summi Pontificatus*, and this is explained by the fact that Pius XII later made use of the services of Father Gundlach for documents, speeches and messages devoted to social and political problems. Since it is therefore a private work, even though it is preparatory to a possible document of the Holy See, it has not been taken into consideration for the present edition."[13]

Was this clarification judged sufficient? It seems, in any event, to have put a stop to this first effort to publicly exhume the documents in question. One thing had nevertheless been learned: the Vatican archives preserved many documentary traces of this case.

"Perhaps this is not the right moment"

One of the present authors, Georges Passelecq, a monk at the Benedictine abbey of Maredsous in Belgium, learned of the articles in the *National Catholic Reporter* shortly after they appeared, and decided to undertake his own investigation. As secretary since 1969 of the Belgian National Catholic Commission on Relations with the Jewish World, he had reason to believe that his hope of achieving his goal was not wholly chimerical. His first reaction was to write, on 11 October 1974, to Father Robert Graham, in Rome:

> Reverend Father,
>
> Some time ago Father Roger Braun, S.J.,[14] who edits the journal *Rencontre—Chrétiens et Juifs* in Paris, and myself were trying to collect some documentation concerning the encyclical on racism that was to be published by Pius XI, but which his rather sudden death caused to be placed among the papers of the Vatican. Recently Father Braun, who is not in good health, asked me again to pursue this matter, and he suggested I write to you, for he says that he learned from you yourself that you possess a certain number of interesting documents on this important question.
>
> Might I be permitted to appeal to you, and ask whether these documents could possibly be made available to us, with a view to

the eventual publication in *Rencontre* of an article on this subject?

If necessary, I would be willing to travel to Rome.

I know something about the question. Through American publications, I have already collected a good deal of information, particularly concerning Father LaFarge (whom I met personally in New York in 1950, if I remember correctly).

I would be extremely thankful for anything you could do to help us in this area, and I beg you to consider me, Reverend Father, your fraternally devoted and grateful, Georges Passelecq[15]

Here is Father Graham's reply, dated Rome, 21 October:

Dear Reverend Father,

I have received your letter of 11 October and I hasten to tell you that I do not have the text of the encyclical *Generis Humani Unitas*. Around 1959, I sent a photocopy to *Action populaire* in care of Father Bosc,[16] asking his advice concerning the possibility of publishing it. The reply was that as a provisional document, it was not of interest as a whole, although certain parts might be publishable. Then I heard nothing more. Nothing, that is, until Father Edward Stanton, a Jesuit in Boston, went to work. He had written a doctoral dissertation (1972) in Ottawa, Canada. To my shame, I cannot give you its title, or tell you whether the dissertation was brought out by a publishing house. In any case, I have not seen the final text.[. . .]

The documentation of which Father Braun speaks [. . .] consists of my own notes taken in New York after my conversations with him or others that I received from Father Abbott (who is in this house, but is gone on vacation). At a certain time I wrote up an account of these, but it remains unfinished. It is no more than an account, and not a discussion. I inform you that just before his death Father LaFarge—a great soul to whom I owe a great deal—had sent an article on racism to the *New Catholic Encyclopedia*. For that purpose he had dug the old "encyclical" out of his closet.

I wonder what value ought to be attached to the document, which was intended for the pope, to be sure, but which represents in itself only what Father LaFarge and Father Gundlach (and perhaps Father Desbuquois) thought at the time. The German Jesuits here believe they can discern Gundlach's hand everywhere in the document, a possibility I do not exclude, even though the pope's mandate was entrusted to Father LaFarge. In order to prepare a document for Pius XI they would have had to consult, of course, the many statements on racism made by the pope during the preceding months and years. —Why don't you write a study on *these* documents?

Could you let me know if I can help you in any other way? For I am eager that my master and benefactor "Uncle John" be duly recognized as a person who was early on sensitive to the needs of our time.

I am currently rereading some Catholic works on the Church and the Jews. I find it curious that no one mentions the audience Pius XII granted Jules Isaac, which nevertheless had one consequence about which Isaac said he was very happy. It had to do with non-genuflection during Holy Week. Today this amounts to little, no doubt. But then it was all the greater a gesture because it was the first.

May God bless you in your apostolic love!

I beg you, Reverend Father, to accept my respectful good wishes.[17]

Since Father Graham's reply seemed evasive, Passelecq asked Father Ambroise Watelet, O.S.B., also a Benedictine at Maredsous, who was then rector of the St. Anselm Pontifical College in Rome, to try again. It was no use. On 18 September 1976, Father Watelet wrote Passelecq from Rome:

My dear Father,

I have just had an hourlong interview with the charming Father Graham, S.J. I set forth your considerations. He immediately told

me that he feared you had arrived too late; in fact, a certain Father
Nota, a Dutch Jesuit, published at the beginning of the year a study
on this business of the draft encyclical. You will find this study in
the *Internationale Katholische Zeitschrift*, no. 2, 1976. Father Nota had
access to a German text of the draft encyclical, and gave an analytical
summary of it.

Father Graham has already indicated in his letter of 21 October
1974 that a photocopy of the French text must be at the offices of
Action populaire in Paris (Father Bosc); Graham himself no longer has
the text.

He emphasized two points:

1. This draft encyclical, which Pius XI personally entrusted to
Father LaFarge (to the surprise of Father General Ledochowski), was
no more than a *first draft* which does not necessarily represent Pius
XI's thought. The document reached the Vatican, but did Pius XI
see it?

2. The draft encyclical is not primarily concerned with the Jews,
but rather with the general problem of racism.

That said, there is a dossier on this matter in the Vatican archives,
but it is still in the secret part of the archives, and thus not accessible
through the ordinary avenues.

Father Graham added that the central ideas in the encyclical were
adopted by Pius XII, who published the document *Summi Pontificatus*
in October 1939.

Father LaFarge's ideas—as Father Graham wrote to you—were
expressed in his article on racism in the *New Catholic Encyclopedia*.

A final consideration: Father Graham thinks that so far as this draft
encyclical is concerned, the Vatican would probably not wish to draw
attention to the publications on the Jews at this moment of tension
in the Near East.

In conclusion, Father Graham advises you first to look into Father
Nota's recent article; you will see whether there is still anything new
and interesting to say. He himself does not think he can help you

very much; it might be worthwhile to contact Father Nota in Holland and Father Bosc in Paris.

He did not tell me that it would be impossible to gain access to the dossier in the Vatican archives, but perhaps this is not the right moment. I can inquire if you wish.

There you have, dear Father Georges, the information I have been able to collect for you. Let me know if you want to know more.[18]

Father Graham's "advice" was sufficiently imperative that Passelecq pursued the matter no further. He nevertheless resumed his research thirteen years later, after meeting Bernard Suchecky. In the course of their correspondence, avenues of approach to the problem appeared that circumvented the Vatican archives, which were apparently inaccessible: for example, the archives of the Jesuits at *Action populaire* in Paris; and the documentation that was probably in the possession of Father Nota, the author of the article mentioned by Father Watelet—and, of course, the microfilm that the *National Catholic Reporter* said it had acquired.

"God be praised that this draft remained only a draft!"

It was in July 1987, in a doubly polemical context—the dispute concerning the Carmelite convent at Auschwitz, and the beatification of Edith Stein in April 1987—that, looking through various files preserved at the library of the American Jewish Committee in New York, Bernard Suchecky learned about the article by Father Johannes Nota.

Titled "Edith Stein and the Draft for an Encyclical Opposing Racism and Anti-Semitism," this article had appeared in 1975 in the *Freiburger Rundbrief*, a German periodical on Judeo-Christian relations.[19] In it Father Nota, a Dutch Jesuit who devoted his life to studying and teaching the thought of Edith Stein, discussed the unsuccessful efforts made in 1933 by German philosophers to obtain an audience with Pius XI in order to persuade him to publish an encyclical condemning anti-Semitism. Edith Stein is quoted by Father Nota: "... my efforts in Rome led me to conclude that because of the large number of visitors (during the holy year 1933), I could not obtain a private audience. I could be given only a 'little audience' (that is, as part of a small group). This was useless to me. I therefore gave up my trip and transmitted my request in writing. I know that my letter was sealed when it was given to the Holy Father; some time later, I even received his blessing on me and those near me. But nothing more came of it. Is it impossible that he often thought of this letter afterward? My fears with regard to the future of German Catholics were gradually confirmed in the course of the following years."[20]

In trying to find this letter of Edith Stein's, Father Nota had learned for the first time of *Humani Generis Unitas*: "As early as 1968, Father Robert Graham, S.J., told me how, while he was doing research for the publication of documents in the Vatican archives, he had found a draft encyclical against racism and anti-Semitism."[21] Subsequently, the articles in the *National Catholic Reporter* complemented his information and strengthened his desire to learn more. But, Nota writes, "At first, it was extraordinarily difficult to obtain the whole text; the *National Catholic Reporter* had published only a few extracts from Father John LaFarge's draft. Letters sent to Rome, Paris, Germany, and North America generally elicited a few friendly words, but not the text. They did not have the text, my correspondents said, but they advised me to look in ... where the text was in fact, but it had to remain secret, etc. I nevertheless learned that four versions existed: in English, French, German, and Latin. Fathers Gundlach, LaFarge, and Desbuquois had apparently worked in concert.

"Finally, I received the English version from Father Edward Stanton, S.J., of Boston College—who had just completed a doctoral thesis, as yet unpublished, on Father LaFarge. [. . .] My efforts to find the other versions have unfortunately been unsuccessful, even though Dr. Johannes Schwarte—who was getting ready to publish his doctoral thesis on Father Gustav Gundlach —was also of enormous help to me. But his 'hands were tied' . . . He nonetheless gave me a precious bit of information: 'Up to the passages on racism and anti-Semitism, [the two versions] are on the whole identical.' "[22]

Having obtained the English version, Father Nota proceeded to analyze it. He found the part concerning the unity of the human race "very good," and the one on racism in general "excellent." But the sections on the Jews and anti-Semitism seemed to him so mediocre—the all-too-traditional theology used in them led to positions he described as "deplorable"—that he exclaimed: "If one puts these sentences back into the context of the racist legislation adopted in Germany at that period, one can say today: God be praised that this draft remained only a draft!"[23]

Upon learning of this article and, shortly afterward, of the *National Catholic Reporter*'s investigation, Suchecky began to question American specialists in Judeo-Catholic relations, both Jewish and Christian, academics and non-academics. At that time, he obtained two kinds of replies. Either a lapidary "Never heard of it!" or "It's like the Loch Ness monster. Every time the Church is embarrassed by the 'silence of Pius XII,' someone tries to play it down by resorting to this story about the encyclical. The 'good' Pius XI was going to speak out but he didn't have time; the 'unfortunate' Pius XII thought it preferable to do as much as he could to save Jews, but silently. However, no one has ever been able to produce these documents. . . . "[24]

Nevertheless, the Nota and *National Catholic Reporter* articles were sufficiently precise for Suchecky to find this story about an encyclical credible, and he in turn set out in search of *Humani Generis Unitas*. First he contacted the editors of *National Catholic Reporter*. They assured him that the paper's archives contained nothing on this subject, and that the microfilm Jim Castelli had acquired in 1972 "could not be located."[25] A similar approach to Georgetown University in Washington, D.C., which has held the LaFarge papers since the closure of Woodstock College in the 1970s, proved equally fruitless, as is shown by this letter from Nicholas B. Scheetz, manuscripts librarian at Georgetown University, dated 21 August 1987:

Dear Mr. Suchecky,

Thank you for your letter of 7 August concerning an unpublished encyclical of Pope Pius XI, *Unitas Humani Generis*, preserved in the papers of Reverend John LaFarge, S.J.

I have looked through the two catalogues of the LaFarge papers without finding the slightest reference to the encyclical. I have also checked the cartons that are supposed to contain these materials, unfortunately without success. Moreover, I have asked the person who catalogued the LaFarge collection whether he remembered having seen such materials while he was doing the cataloguing. Alas, he does not remember anything. He added that some time ago, in response to a request similar to yours, he had thoroughly searched this collection without positive results. It therefore seems to me that I can state that the materials you are looking for are not in the LaFarge papers stored at Georgetown.

The newspaper article that you sent me dates from 15 December 1972, well before the LaFarge papers were entrusted to us. It is possible that we did not receive everything; it is even possible that the documents relative to the encyclical were never put back in the archives after they were microfilmed for the *National Catholic Reporter*.

I think the best thing to do would be to write to Mr. Jim Castelli, the author of the article, to see if he still has the microfilm. If that is the case, or if you find the missing materials, could you inform me? I would very much like to put copies of these documents back into our LaFarge archives. In any case, I am truly sorry not to be able to provide you with the documents you desire.

With my best wishes for the success of your project . . .[26]

The next logical step was to locate Father Nota, since he had stated in his article that he possessed at least the English version of the encyclical draft. After some research, Suchecky learned that Father Nota was living in Thorold, Ontario, not far from Niagara Falls. Unannounced, Suchecky visited him on 29 October 1987. The old Dutch Jesuit told him that he could do no more than what had been done for him—that is, he could let Suchecky see a fragment of the English version of *Humani Generis Unitas* that he had earlier obtained from Father Edward Stanton. The fragment in question, about fifteen typed pages, contained paragraphs 131 to 152 of the document, which dealt specifically with the Jews and anti-Semitism. Suchecky thus had a first piece of the document.

On the occasion of Suchecky's visit, Father Nota gave him a few examples of the "extraordinary difficulties," as he had called them in his article, which he confronted when he tried to obtain the entire document. Following is one such example, and one not without importance for the research undertaken by the authors of the present work. It is a letter from Father Lamalle, S.J., dated Rome, 30 July 1973, asserting that nothing on this subject exists in the general archives of the Jesuits in Rome:

Dear Father Nota, Pax Christi.

Father Bumpel transmits to me with warm recommendation a twofold request from you: 1) the text of the encyclical planned but not published by Pius XI, *Humani Generis Unitas*, against racism, included in part in Pius XII's encyclical *Summi Pontificatus*; 2) the confirmation or disconfirmation of the claim that Father Ledochowski tried to delay publication in order to avoid further irritating the German government.

I greatly regret that I cannot directly satisfy you in this twofold request. First, because the text of this planned encyclical is certainly not in our archives. I believe I know them well enough to be able to say that. Second, as for the correspondence registered between Father Ledochowski and the Holy See, there is nothing on this subject.

This negative result is in my opinion completely normal. I knew Father Ledochowski well, and I worked for him on several occasions and with him during this period. I always noted his extreme concern not to leave behind writings that might be compromising in the event of persecution, perquisition, etc., especially when it was not a matter of things directly concerning the Society (in matters that concerned us directly, registration might become necessary). Of the little we had, the traces disappeared during the war, when the presence of hostile authorities in Italy and in Rome led us to fear that our papers would be seized. I remember having seen in recent years an article in which this "suppressed" encyclical of Pius XI was mentioned, in some journal, *La Civiltà cattolica* or another. But since it is a subject outside my professional specialty, I kept no notes. You would have a better chance of finding it by addressing yourself to one of the priests involved in publishing Pius XII's documents: Father Burkhart Schneider (Università Gregoriana, Piazza della Pilotta, 4, 00817 Roma), Father Angelo Martini, or Father Robert Graham (both at *La Civiltà cattolica*, Via di Porta Pinciana 1, 00187 Roma).

[. . .]sincerely yours *in X⁰*, Edmond Lamalle, S.J.

N.B.: The limit of accessibility of the documents in our archives, without very special authorization, is the year 1900. But this time, the question does not even arise: *deest materia.*[27]

Deest materia. In other words, these materials are not in the Roman archives of the Society of Jesus.

Two Doctoral Theses and a Microfilm

Toward the end of the summer of 1987, Georges Passelecq and Bernard Suchecky, who had met in Brussels a year earlier, decided to join forces in order to pursue their search for these documents. Between November 1987 and January 1988, they obtained without excessive difficulties the doctoral theses by Edward Stanton and Johannes Schwarte mentioned by Father Nota in his article.

Edward Stanton's 1972 dissertation,[28] "John LaFarge's Understanding of the Unifying Mission of the Church, Especially in the Area of Race Relations," is based almost exclusively on LaFarge's numerous publications. Only the section devoted to *Humani Generis Unitas* is based on archival documents.[29] But while Stanton mentions that he "was able to obtain from the LaFarge dossier a French version and two English texts" of the draft encyclical, he does not explain where these dossiers were stored or how he was able to gain access to them.[30]

According to Johannes Schwarte, who defended his dissertation on Gustav Gundlach at the University of Münster in late 1973,[31] and who bases his work on two different documentary sources, the papers of Gustav Gundlach and those of John LaFarge, the German Jesuit should be considered the true author of the draft ordered by Pius XI. But while Schwarte discusses at length the German version, which he regards as the main text, and reveals that it is titled *Societatis Unio*, "The Union of Society," rather than *Humani Generis Unitas*, he does not explain where he obtained it. He asserts that "all the documents on the basis of which the history of this composition and the later fate of the draft encyclical *Societatis Unio* were reconstructed are found in the archives of the Woodstock Jesuit seminary. All these materials were kindly made available to the author, on microfilm, by *Th. Breslin.*"[32]

This claim is confusing—we will see later that the microfilm mentioned in this note does not contain the German version—and perhaps intentionally so. Thus, in the bibliography published at the end of his dissertation, Schwarte inventories numerous unpublished manuscripts by Gundlach, mentioning in most cases the institution where they are preserved. This is not, however, the case for the draft encyclical:

—Gundlach, Gustav (with John LaFarge): draft of an encyclical, *Societatis Unio*, with an accompanying text by Gundlach on the contents of this encyclical. Summer–Fall 1938 (unpublished manuscript).[33]

Finally, in the parts concerned with the composition of the German version of the draft encyclical, Schwarte refers to information, memories, and comments by a certain "Prof. Dr. Anton Rauscher, S.J., Augsburg/Mönchengladbach," who is supposed to have personally known Gundlach and seemed to know everything about the document entitled *Societatis Unio*.[34] But he does not specify that this Dr. Rauscher was none other than the director, since its founding in 1963, of the Katholische Sozialwissenschaftliche Zentralstelle, where Gundlach's papers are stored, including the German version in question.[35]

In 1987, after further, concurrent research, Suchecky was able to locate Thomas Breslin. Breslin, then an associate professor at Florida International University in Miami, immediately sent him a copy of the microfilm which he had also sent to the *National Catholic Reporter* in 1972 and to Johannes Schwarte in 1973.[36]

According to Breslin, this microfilm reproduced all the documents relative to this case that he had found in the LaFarge papers in 1967: sixty-two different documents.[37]

"We will have to wait a few years"

Thus, thanks to Breslin, late in the fall of 1987 a significant portion of the necessary documentation came into Passelecq's and Suchecky's possession. But a portion only, for they still lacked in particular the German version of the draft encyclical and LaFarge's letters to Gundlach as well as to Father Ledochowski. On the basis of the various bits of information they had gleaned thus far, Passelecq and Suchecky decided that they had little to gain from the LaFarge papers, the Vatican archives, or the Roman archives of the Society of Jesus.

Two avenues remained to be explored, those constituted by Gustave Desbuquois and Gustav Gundlach. The first avenue, which passed through the review *Action populaire* in Paris, led nowhere. That was also the conclusion Father Paul Droulers, S.J., had reached in the late 1960s when he had attempted to find the draft encyclical in the papers of Father Desbuquois. In a voluminous study on the former editor of *Action populaire*, Droulers notes, in fact, that "Desbuquois's papers contain nothing on this subject. But if there had been anything there, he surely burned it in 1940, before leaving Vanves because of the [German] invasion."[38]

The avenue by way of Gundlach's papers led to the Katholische Sozialwissenschaftliche Zentralstelle. In November 1988, Suchecky wrote to the director of this institution, the same Father Anton Rauscher whom Schwarte had cited in his dissertation, in order to ask for authorization to consult Gundlach's papers. On 5 December, Father Rauscher replied that "... There is indeed a first draft of an encyclical of Pius XI [written] by Father Gundlach and an American Jesuit. This draft concentrates on society and, in this context, opposes racism and anti-Semitism. After Father Gundlach's death, the Provincial of the Jesuits told me that all the documents should be preserved. If you wish to obtain a copy of this first draft, you should write to Father Provincial Alfons Höfer, S.J., in Köln.[. . .]"[39]

Passelecq undertook to obtain the permission of the Jesuit provincial for northern Germany, who replied from Köln on 10 January 1989:

Dear Father Georges,

On the basis of the documents in our archives, it is apparently not possible to establish with precision whether the rights to the German version of the encyclical draft *Societatis Unio*, which was written by Father Gundlach, belong to the province of northern Germany. As far as I am concerned, I see no restriction on free access to the text. I therefore ask you to get in touch with Father Rauscher. If he still has doubts, from a legal point of view it is with him that you must arrive at an agreement.

I hope this information is of help to you in your work, and I remain[. . .][40]

That being the case, it took several efforts to obtain from Father Rauscher, on 7 July 1989, the following commitment:

Dear Dr. Suchecky,

Please excuse me for not replying earlier to your letter of 19 May 1989. Since I have taken advantage of the summer semester to carry on research projects that have often taken me abroad, I have not been able to reply more promptly.

In August, I shall copy and send to you the draft *Societatis Unio* which is among Father Gundlach's papers[. . .][41]

This commitment was nevertheless not fulfilled.

At this point, for various reasons (chiefly professional),

Passelecq and Suchecky suspended their research for some time. But in June 1994, Suchecky started over from the beginning. After numerous telephone conversations and a first visit to Mönchengladbach—which produced no results, since Father Rauscher "had had unexpectedly to be away"—Passelecq and Suchecky were finally authorized to examine on the premises, on 5 August 1994, the German version of the draft encyclical, but were not allowed to make a copy and take it with them. This document, Father Rauscher told them, belonged to the Vatican, and only the Vatican could authorize its reproduction and use. Consequently, Father Rauscher advised them to address themselves to the appropriate authority in Rome, and in particular at the Jesuit archives.

Passelecq thereupon wrote to Father J. De Cock, S.J., the adjunct archivist of the Society of Jesus's Roman archives, on 22 August 1994:

Dear Reverend Father,

Father J. M. Schiltz, the rector of the College of St. Paul de Godinne, recommends me to you, so that I am taking the liberty of appealing to your good will.

Our Commission has undertaken the publication of a study on the development of Christian (Protestant and Catholic) teaching regarding Judaism. An important document concerning the period between the two world wars has unfortunately never been published because of Pius XI's death on 10 February 1939. I refer to the draft of an encyclical on racism, entrusted to three Jesuit Fathers, of which there exist three versions, in English, French, and German. We have the first two (along with virtually all the related correspondence). The third version was written by Father Gundlach, and a copy is located at the Katholische Sozialwissenschaftliche Zentralstelle in Mönchengladbach.

Following a request I made to the Father Provincial of Westphalia–

Northern Germany, we have been given access to this document through the courtesy of Father Anton Rauscher. However, we have not been able to make a photocopy, "the document belonging," according to Father Rauscher, "to the Vatican."

Our interest resides in comparing the three versions, more than three quarters of which correspond word for word, with the goal, not of producing a "critical edition," but rather of determining with precision what doctrine was then intended to be submitted for the pope's signature.

It is because of this documentary lacuna, so to speak, that I am addressing myself to you in the hope that you might be in possession of another copy that does not belong to the Vatican, and which I could perhaps transcribe, if permission to do so were granted me.

On the other hand, we have already in our possession most of the correspondence exchanged among the respective drafters on this subject, and with Father General Ledochowski. We wonder whether possibly I might be allowed to see, under the same conditions, the letters that are missing from our documentation.

That is the purpose of the present request, which I trust is not indiscreet. If it meets with your approval, I shall come to see you during my visit to Rome next October and November.

I have addressed myself to you in all simplicity.

Please accept, Reverend Father, my anticipated gratitude and my fraternal devotion.

Georges Passelecq, O.S.B., Secretary

Here is Father De Cock's reply, dated Rome, 23 September 1994:

Dear Reverend Father,

I am finally responding to your letter of August 22. This delay is due to a prolonged absence on my part and not to research in our archives.

This research has in any case not been fruitful, at least so far as the German document written by Father Gundlach is concerned. As you yourself wrote, this document is in Germany. That is, moreover, the way things are done in the Society. On the other hand, I understand why Father Rauscher claims that this text belongs to the Vatican. In general, our archives, and in particular our Roman archives, follow the policies of the Vatican archives regarding access to documents. Currently documents are accessible only up to January 1922, the date of Pope Benedict XV's death.

You will thus understand that the correspondence between Father Ledochowski and Father Gundlach at that period is not yet open to research. I think we will have to wait a few years yet before studying this question in depth.

Regretting that I cannot be of more positive help to you, I beg you accept, very reverend Father, the expression of my fraternal devotion.

J. De Cock, S.J., archivist[42]

Incidentally, it should be pointed out that at the beginning of October 1994, during a trip to Austria, Suchecky happened to meet, altogether fortuitously, the director of the archives of the Gregorian University, Father Marcel Chappin, S.J. The latter, who was also interested in the history of *Humani Generis Unitas*, confirmed that the archives he directed for the *Gregoriana* contained nothing on this subject, all the documents that had belonged to Father Gundlach being preserved in Mönchengladbach . . .[43]

Having thus arrived at the end of their long investigation, which was partly unsuccessful, the authors of this work can only wonder about the motives that half a century later still lead various ecclesiastical officials to exercise such severe vigilance. Is it simply administrative inertia? Are still-current theological points at stake, even though it would be difficult to say what they might be thirty years after Vatican II? The answers to such questions may perhaps be found precisely in the parts of the file to which the authors were denied access.

The Commissioning of
Humani Generis Unitas

On 2 May 1938, the American Jesuit John LaFarge disembarked in England, at Plymouth, with eight hundred dollars
in his pocket. Three weeks earlier, in his request for funding,
he had written that that sum was "the minimum that seems
safe.... This includes $200 for return fare, $200 for travel fares,
and $300 for 100 days (maximum), at $3.00 per day. If we were
not so very short, I should take $1,000...."[1]

He had sailed aboard the Holland America Line ship *Volendam*,
and expected to spend three months in Europe before returning
to the United States around the third week of August.[2] Traveling
as a reporter, he had no idea that this trip was going to mark
"a great turning point in [his] life, especially as it was totally
unexpected."[3]

John LaFarge the Man

John LaFarge came from a good East Coast family,[4] and had taken
a B.A. in philosophy at Harvard, where he had shown an exceptional gift for languages.[5] He had continued his studies at the great
seminary in Innsbrück, Austria, and was ordained as a priest in
1905. The same year he had returned to the United States to

begin his novitiate with the Jesuits at Poughkeepsie, New York. After teaching at several colleges (1908–1909), and serving as a hospital and prison chaplain (1909–1910), he had gone to southern Maryland, where for fifteen years (1911–1926) he served as priest in various parishes that were predominantly African-American but also included immigrants from different parts of Czechoslovakia. This pastoral activity allowed him to make two decisive acquisitions: a thorough knowledge of Slavic languages and an exceptional experience of the struggle for "interracial justice."

During the summer of 1926, his provincial, Father Laurence J. Kelly, S.J., had given him a position on the great Jesuit weekly *America*, of which LaFarge was to be general editor from 1942 to 1948. Like other members of the editorial staff, LaFarge was responsible for covering a particular part of the world; his was France, Russia, and eastern Europe. In addition, he wrote a column headed "With Scrip and Staff," which he signed with the pseudonym "Pilgrim." In it he usually discussed rural life, interracial justice, liturgy, and liturgical art.[6]

A down-to-earth man, LaFarge referred less to the Scripture and to patristic literature than to Leo XIII's and Pius XI's social encyclicals, and especially to *Rerum Novarum* (Leo XIII, 1891), "the most significant milestone in Church doctrine and the key to all the problems of the time."[7] As a journalist who tried above all to address the ordinary reader, his style was popular, concrete, pastoral. "We need an image of the social Kingdom of Christ," he wrote in 1935 in a series of articles devoted to communism, "that is not merely sketched out in broad strokes but includes all its practical corollaries. [...] If we can express our doctrines in words comprehensible to children, in order to prepare them for their first communion, we ought to be able to express our doctrines in terms comprehensible to the multitude."[8]

His extensive journalistic activities had not, however, distracted him from the fight against racial discrimination. In 1934, in New York, he founded the Catholic Interracial Council, the center of a vast network of Catholic committees in which whites and blacks worked together for "interracial justice as a particular form of social justice in general."

LaFarge set forth the ideas of this movement in a book published in 1937, *Interracial Justice*, which firmly established his reputation as a Catholic leader in the struggle for interracial justice in the United States. Both a manifesto and a manual for the militant Catholic anti-segregationist, *Interracial Justice* is wholly organized around three main ideas, each of which is in conformity with the teaching of social Catholicism at the time: In its essence, the race question is a social question; the catholicity (universality) of the Church is the forerunner of a social and political order based on human rights and realizing the living unity of humanity; the means of achieving this are cooperation and collaboration among the groups constituting society, rather than class struggle.

"Many a conflict...which at first sight seems purely racial," LaFarge writes in his introduction, "when more closely analyzed is resolved into economic, educational, political, or other non-racial factors. The work of racial adjustment is simply a part of the great task of harmonizing the various cultures and civilizations of the world in such manner as to achieve cooperation and unity in essentials, without destroying human liberty and diversity of expression. Christianity, with its sublime doctrine of unity amid diversity in the universal bond of charity, points the way to the accomplishment of such a task."[9]

Drawing on modern anthropology and ethnology, LaFarge maintains that a "racial type is after all an artificial concept," that " 'Race,' as popularly understood, is a myth," and that therefore "this concept cannot serve as a practical basis for any type of human relation whatever."[10] "There is no Negro *race* in the United States," he concludes, "but rather a Negro *population group.*[...] The factors that mark off the Negro group from other ethnic groups in the United States are, *first*, a degree of identifiable African descent; and *second*, a *social experience* common to those who are known to be thus descended. [...] *Communis aestimatio*, rather than anything perfectly objective and tangible, is the real basis for much that is contained in 'being a Negro' in the United States. As this *communis aestimatio* changes, the make-up of the group itself alters. [...] The question is not the existence of differences but the *characterization* of these differences...."[11]

Having used the criteria of modern science as a guide for establishing the inanity of the concept "race," LaFarge then bases himself on Church doctrine in order to assert the unity of humanity: it is in the person of Christ, "the supreme representative of the human race itself," that all things are one.[12] Through Christ's sacrifice, offered for the redemption of all men, and "through the institution of His Church as a universal, perpetual, supra-national society, all mankind was offered participation in a unity infinitely higher than that which the mere fact of common creation and common anthropological origin afforded. This higher unity is symbolized in the figure of the Mystical Body of Christ. As members of the one Body of which Christ is the Head the children of God enter into a unique relationship not only with one another but with the whole of mankind as well."[13]

There follows an exposition of the traditional doctrine of natural law and human rights. These rights are "*natural,* they are something created with man and inherent in him; they are not something conferred on him as a privilege. [...] By the same token, human rights are not conferred or taken away by social custom or *mores,* [...] still less [...] by the civil state, by its constitutions or its laws. [...] Civil rights and civic duties alike spring, as from their ultimate source, not from any human instrument but from the citizen's relation to the Creator, as the

Author and supreme Ruler of human society. [... They] are equal, since all men are equally called to perfect their moral nature. It is, therefore, against human rights to impose *unequal opportunities* of moral perfection where rights are equal. [...] As the essential rights of *individuals*, according to Christian ethics, are equal, so are the rights of the various *groups* that make up society."[14]

The remainder of the work consists of the application to the case of American Negroes of the general teachings of the great social encyclicals of Leo XIII and Pius XI, in particular *Rerum Novarum* and *Quadragesimo Anno*, which LaFarge continually cites or invokes. Similarly for the social and political ideal that is to lead the fight: "Modern Catholic historians and sociologists, following the guidance of Pope Pius XI in his Encyclical, *Quadragesimo Anno*, see in the tendency of our times to subordinate all considerations of the dignity of the human person to the unbridled quest for material gain the primary source of interracial, as well as of economic, industrial, and international injustice.

"When the human personality is cheapened, when human life is set at naught, it makes little difference whether this is done in the field of finance, industry, war, or race relations. The root of the evil in each instance is the same. Cheap labor brings cheap lives. And from cheap lives follow customs and maxims sanctioning the cheapening of lives.

"To exploitations of the human personality in the unbridled pursuit of gain, Christianity opposes not class warfare, which merely aggravates the disease, but cooperation and collaboration for the sake of the common good.

"Such cooperation, in the Christian idea, applies to individual (producer and consumer, lender and borrower, labor and capital, etc.); to nations with one another; to the State itself; and to relations between the races.

"The type of social structure, therefore, which is the principle guarantor of relations between racial groups based upon human rights is the structure which will *embody* the principle of collaboration or cooperation in our society; not as a mere passing set of activities, but as a regeneration of our entire system of living.

"How shall the principle of collaboration or cooperation be embodied in modern society? The main lines thereof are laid down by Pope Pius in *Quadragesimo Anno,* in the vocational or occupational groups therein proposed. The establishment of such groups presupposes an organic or functional idea of society."[15]

LaFarge remained faithful to these ideas of collaboration and cooperation for the rest of his life, and for precisely that reason he was somewhat disturbed by the evolution of the American civil rights movement in the early 1960s. Nevertheless, on 28 August 1963, three months before his death, LaFarge, then eighty-three years old, walked at Martin Luther King, Jr.'s side during the great March on Washington.

LaFarge's European Trip

"In April 1938," LaFarge would write in his autobiography, "Father Francis Xavier Talbot, editor of *America,* decided to send me to the International Eucharistic Congress at Budapest." But his mission also involved looking into the situations in Hungary, Czechoslovakia, Hitler's Germany, Mussolini's Italy, and Spain in the midst of civil war. He was also to establish closer relations with European periodicals run, like *America,* by Jesuits: *The Month* (England), *Études* (Paris), *Action populaire* (Paris), *Stimmen der Zeit* (Munich), *La Civiltà cattolica* (Rome). He hoped also to take advantage of this trip to "become more closely acquainted with the Papal and Roman point of view on public issues, as treated for instance in the social encyclicals of Leo XIII and Pius XI."[16]

After arriving in England on 2 May, LaFarge did a little touring, met with the editorial teams of the Catholic periodicals *The Month* and *The Tablet*, and talked with various people, including Jan Masaryk, the Czechoslovakian minister posted in London. "Jan Masaryk invited me to lunch," he wrote to Talbot (from France) on 15 May, "which was an interesting experience. He started out at once telling his anxieties about Hitler; and I gather the situation is pretty critical. 'I have argued for hours and hours with Lord Halifax,' he exclaimed, 'saying to him that if only he would let me *know* where my country stands with Great Britain, I should then know how to act. If Great Britain is not going to support us, then I shall simply pack my valise, take a trip to Berlin, and lay all my cards upon the table before Hitler. The game will be up, and we shall simply take what Hitler chooses to leave us. On the other hand, if Great Britain intends to support us, we shall keep up the fight.' I gathered that the British, as usual, are playing their old canny game of helping no one except when they see it is to their own interest."[17]

On 13 May, LaFarge arrived in Paris, where the Jesuits at *Études* put him up for a week. There he made the acquaintance of the editor of *Action populaire*, Father Gustave Desbuquois (who will be discussed at length in the next chapter). In the May 15 letter to Talbot, he announces that he will soon leave for Germany and indicates that he may make a detour through Spain. "From what I am able to gather from various sources there is going to come sometime this summer more or less of a show-down between the two elements that are difficult to reconcile in Nationalist Spain: the Traditionalists and the Falangists. Fear is expressed that the Falangist element will harbor a good many ex-radicals, on the one hand; and German Nazis on the other; the result being an attempt to introduce strong-arm methods with regard to the Church in Spain, as is done in Germany.

"The traditionalists, on the other hand, who contain a number of Monarchists, aim at the Catholic corporative state. Their hope is to model the new Spain on the new Portugal; and to construct it on a federalist basis. While they would demand a uniform recognition of the Spanish language, the regional languages, such as Basque or Catalan, would be tolerated.

"From all indications it is going to be [a] pretty definite contest. Franco is said to be positively on the side of the Traditionalists, as opposed to totalitarianism, nazism, etc. It is likewise said that his model is Salazar, whom he intensely admires. Franco has with him the army, and it is through the sentiment of the army that he hopes to maintain the liberty of the Church in Spain."[18]

And LaFarge adds: "I cannot help thinking that things are drifting all over the Continent towards a bitter contest between two irreconcilable opposites: the subjugation of the Church [. . .] as an instrument of a fairly benevolent State—as in Italy—or its repression [. . .] and [. . .] a corporative society [with] corporate features in the State, and freedom for the Church. Coupled with this: a gradually growing rapprochement between Communists and Nazis.

"Curiously enough, Jan Masaryk, the Czech Minister in London, told me that he believed Hitler and Stalin would come to unite.

"Leonard Feeney[19] is right, when he says that it is the Church which is always the thing that matters. I think one may extend that a little bit, and include the Jews; and in the U.S., the colored people. But at present, the Church seems to be the center of everything in Europe. . . ."[20]

Into the same envelope, LaFarge slipped the following note:

If I send a card from Germany or Austria, following will be meaning of greetings at end:

Oremus pro invicem[21]—things are very bad, worse than you imagine.

Pray for me. About as we heard in the U.S.

Say a prayer for me on my travels. Not so bad, fair show of resistance, etc.

Greetings and prayers, Situation complex and difficult to analyze.[22]

This rudimentary code was soon put into use, since a week later, on leaving Koblenz, LaFarge sent Talbot the following postcard: "The famous old abbey is well worth seeing—enjoyed the grand view. *Oremus pro invicem.*"[23]

Let there be no mistake. LaFarge is not thinking about the general situation in Germany, but about the situation of the Church in Germany: Would it stand up against the blows struck against it by the Nazi government?

LaFarge left Paris for Koblenz, where he planned to "spend a few days with my old Innsbruck classmate Dr. Heinrich Chardon, pastor of the venerable Liebfrauenkirche."[24] On his arrival, the parishoners assailed him with questions, and when he informed them that he had left Paris that very morning, they exclaimed: "How fortunate to escape. We understand that in Paris the streets are running with blood; there is a terrible revolution and people are being murdered by the Jews and Bolsheviks." When LaFarge said this was not true, one man imprudently called out: "*Potztausend!* Look at the stuff they have been handing out to us here."[25]

After this edifying conversation, his impressions of Koblenz turned to this anguished observation:

In Coblenz you could not learn what was happening in Bonn or Cologne. You could not write. Obviously you could not telephone, and it was dangerous to send messages. As for the papers, they were devoid of information.

We sat until 2 A.M. in the presbytery talking about Hitler. I soon found the Hitler atmosphere was nothing imaginary, but thick enough to cut with a knife. In the parlor of the presbytery was an enormous oaken table about twelve feet long covered with innumerable documents. The unfortunate pastor and curates had to fill out these documents every day, every week, every month as the occasion might be. The movement of every person in the parish had to be accounted for. The curates took it philosophically. After all, they said, we are all going to Dachau sooner or later so what's the use of bothering.[26]

"Sure," said my companion, "we are still free to hold our beautiful pilgrimage and Corpus Christi processions. In fact, the government promotes them for propaganda use abroad so that people may see how much Hitler loves the Church. But woe to any government official or employee who is filmed in the procession. He gets a note a couple of days later saying he has lost his job. They don't use physical violence on you, but they use economic violence, especially if you have a home and children to support."[27]

LaFarge comments:

Here had flourished the center of a great organized campaign of intensive Catholic living, of charitable works, of religious instruction, of apostolic works for all classes, of social reform, of liturgical realization. Here the banner of Christ the King had been unfurled before vast multitudes in public squares. Here the clouds of godless Marxism had been rolled away, while Germany's great Catholic traditions were preserved or revived. Here non-Catholics and Catholics joined in fellowship for a new order and a peaceful and happy land. The inspiration for all this revival was the ineffably lovely old Rhenish statue of Our Lady.

When things are definitely past, they seem like dreams. The troubling thought drifted into my mind: will our Catholic churches in the United States some day seem like a dream? Will our thousands of parochial schools, our glorious college and university campuses, our hospitals and institutions and national organizations seem to us, even a few years distant, as remote as do today the Knights Templars of the Middle Ages? This could happen, if we relax an eternal vigilance for the Faith, or if we betray that Faith by lives that contradict its fundamental teachings. The Church of the future lies in the hands of the Church of the present. In England at the beginning of the sixteenth century, who would have dreamed that in a few decades the people of that most pious of Catholic countries would have been robbed of their faith? Nothing was more alien than Nazism to the spirit of Catholic Germany; yet that spirit did not succeed in resisting its outward conquests. The Church is never secure in a too complacent society.[28]

On 21 May, LaFarge was in Prague. He spent his first night in the little seminary, where, for lack of space, a bed has been put up for him in a room called the "Geographical Museum." "I slept amid maps, globes, and charts. Czechoslovakia was still upon the map that night [...]. The Republic remained upon the map that spring and summer, but fell from it like an autumn leaf when September blew its political gale. I am thankful that I saw Czechoslovakia at least once, before it passed from history as a free country."[29]

In Budapest, during the "few magic days of the Budapest Congress[,] a city and a nation and delegates from many lands poured out their hearts in solemn adoration to the Eucharistic King, with all the dignity and splendor they could muster."[30] On 31 May, LaFarge took the train to Zagreb, where he met, among others, Archbishop Aloïs Stepinac.[31] Then he went on to Rome via Ljubljana, Trieste, and Venice.[32]

Concerning Rome, where he arrived on 5 June,[33] LaFarge recalls first that "in the bookstores anti-Semitic material was appearing, translated from the German."[34] And then, while discovering in certain suburbs "greater squalor than I had ever seen even in the poorest Negro sections of the South," he does not fail to admire fascism's architectural, economic, and social achievements."[35]

On 7 June 1938, LaFarge met with the superior general of the Jesuits, Wladimir Ledochowski, and with his American assistant,

Zacheus Maher, S.J. "Indeed, I had to pinch myself a few times to realize that I actually was talking to the A.R.P.N. himself, the object of so many consultors' letters and generally for us such a mysterious figure."[36]

A Draft Encyclical

Shortly before departing Rome to return to Paris, following his original schedule—he was supposed to leave about 25 June—LaFarge was still planning a report on Spain.[37] But these plans were about to be upset most unexpectedly.

Just before he left, in fact, he took part in a general audience with Pius XI at Castelgandolfo, to which he had been invited by Father Vincent McCormick, rector of the Gregorian University. "A few days later a message from the Vatican was delivered to me in the well-known yellow and white envelope, saying that His Holiness would like to see me privately and appointing a time for the visit. I was mystified, wondering what it could be [...]."[38]

We do not know how the pope was informed of LaFarge's presence in the Italian capital, nor how the interview to be discussed below was decided upon. In any case, on 22 June LaFarge was once again in the pontifical antechamber in Castelgandolfo.[39] What took place there is recounted in various ways by LaFarge himself. Thus, in his 1954 autobiography, he writes:

> The Holy Father received me graciously. Apparently he had just returned from a walk and his white cane rested on a ledge behind him. I found he wished to talk to me on the question of racialism, which had now become a burning issue in Italy and in Germany. He said he was continually revolving the matter in his mind, and was deeply impressed by the fact that racialism and nationalism were

fundamentally the same. He had read my book *Interracial Justice* and liked the title of it. " 'Interracial Justice,' *c'est bon!*" he said, pronouncing the title as if it were French. He said he thought my book was the best thing written on the topic, comparing it with some European literature. Naturally, this was a big lift to me. Apparently what appealed to him in my little effort was the spiritual and moral treatment of the topic, and the fact that I did bring into synthesis the Catholic doctrine and the natural law and the pertinent facts, as well as some practical methods for dealing with the question.

He questioned me about my own work and was much interested to hear of the work of the Catholic Interracial Council and told me to keep going ahead and not be discouraged by obstacles. He also suggested to me that I should pursue the subject further from the standpoint of science and study, collect material on it and go into the whole question very thoroughly. If I were in Rome again, he said in conclusion, I should be sure to drop in to see him. He might like to talk to me again on the question and might have some further ideas.[40]

But in a memorandum sent from Paris to Father Joseph A. Murphy, dated 3 July 1938, LaFarge was more precise:

Confidential. Father Maher may have written to you what really did happen at the audience. What happened was that the Pope put me under secrecy, and enjoined upon me to write the text of an Encyclical for the universal Church, on the topic which he considered is most burning at the present time.

He told me that God had sent me to him, as he was looking for a man to write on this topic. He had considered another person— mentioning a *very* eminent scholar—but reflection had convinced him that Fr. LaFarge was more competent.

"*Say simply,*"[41] he told me, "*what you would say if you yourself were pope.*"[42]

It was the play *Monsignor* suddenly realized.

He then outlined the topic, its method of treatment, and discussed the underlying principles.

He told me he would write—which he did—to the V.R.Fr. General, asking him to give me every facility. "Properly," he said, "I should have first taken this up with Father Ledochowski before speaking to you; but I imagine it will be all right."—or some words to that effect. After all, a Pope is Pope.

Sunday after, Father General saw the Pope, who repeated in detail all he said to me, with equal emphasis. On Monday, June 27, day of my departure, I saw Fr. General at 4 p.m., and talked with him for one hour and a half. He said, of course, [that there was] nothing else to do, but to do my best. He named, at my request, two principal collaborators, one of whom is in Rome and one is here in Paris. I told Fr. General that I could not do anything if I remained in Rome, so he very kindly agreed I might return to Paris and work here. When the job is done, I shall probably take the MS down to Rome in person, & deliver it to whomever I am directed to do so.[43]

Fr. General gave me, of course, many advices and cautions, most of which are evident, since the matter is such that if it were known, every govt. in Europe would have people in 24 hours at the Vatican, urging the expression of their ideas.

Frankly, I am simply stunned, and all I can say is that the Rock of Peter has fallen on my head. Had I anticipated such a terrific development, nothing would have persuaded me even to go to Rome, much less see the Pope. As it is, nothing to do but to go through with the whole thing, as Fr. General says.

The General thinks one should work fast, though he agrees with my proposal that I get a bit of time to rest up and collect my thoughts and presence of mind after these adventures [. . .].

Persons in on this are, besides Fr. General himself: Fr. Maher; Fr. McCormick; Fr. Phillips; Fr. d'Ouince, the Superior here. I suppose Fr. Killeen, as substitute, will also know. Also the two men I have been asked to consult.[44]

The very day of the audience, I was all ready to engage passage back on the *Staatendam*, which should bring me to the States August 27. I shall make a desperate attempt to get back by Sept. 1; and will know in a week or so more definitely what I can do. I see no reason why not. Spain? Have not given it up, at least two or three days there.

Naturally, this will interfere with literary production, though will send in a thing or two to avoid suspicion and questions. Please pray for me, pray hard; for the task is superhuman, both as to nature and as to rapidity . . .

Some months ago I collected a few notes on the topic that the Pope assigned—with some references to Papal teachings. Leaving N.Y., I said, shall I take this with me or not? Well, I threw them in; and no[w] they are a partial life-saver. God's Providence is a queer thing [. . .].

Will you read all this to Rev. Fr. Provincial? This is irregular, but I am just too much upset and stunned to write anything more for a while. Later, I shall write him a nice orderly letter about the whole affair. I am sure he will understand and pardon my seeming negligence.

What is in the body of my letter of July 3rd to you is for general consumption of Ours, naturally with discretion. As the fact of my private audience was noted in the Osserv. Romano for June 26, one must have something to say about it; so those facts are not secret. But what is here written is a grave matter, and if known to the public, as I said, would create more than one can imagine. Besides, there is the direct command of the Pope, who said: "On dit que le secret du Pontife Romain est un secret de Polichinelle. Peut-être. Mail il ne doit être comme ça. Et c'est un *vrai* secret que Nous vous disons." ["People say that the Roman pontiff's secret is a fool's secret. Perhaps. But it need not be like that. And this is a true secret that We are telling you"].[45]

According to Father Bacht, LaFarge had begun this audience by offering Pius XI an "analysis of the racism problem in America, specifically the Negro problem. The pope was so impressed by his presentation that he spontaneously said, "We will issue an encyclical on these matters, one which you must prepare."[46]

The following document (written in French) found among LaFarge's papers is probably an outline for this "analysis of the racism problem in America":

1 —What we are trying to do is *to remove the main obstacle* to the conversion of the negroes (secondary Apostolate)—i.e., *the indifference* among whites regarding the spiritual and temporal needs of negroes.

2 —*Special mistrust* among negroes because of *indifference* to their temporal condition. We combat this indifference, showing that that the great *lessons of the social Encyclicals* offer a clear and adequate solution for all the problems or a temporal order that concern negroes, family, housing, salary, union organization, health, etc.

3 —Negroes and whites are *helped to work together* by studying and practicing the lessons of the Encyclicals:

lectures, study groups, retreats,

personal example, youth associations,

professional associations, etc.

4 —May the Very Holy Father deign to *encourage us* in this effort to promote the application of the Encyclicals to the temporal problems of the negroes[47] to awaken in whites an apostolic spirit for the conversion of negroes.[48]

On the afternoon of 27 June, LaFarge spoke again with Father Ledochowski. He left Rome for Geneva[49] that evening, and reached Paris a few days later.[50] It was in the French capital that the writers of the draft commissioned by Pius XI—LaFarge, Desbuquois, and Gundlach—were to work for almost three months. During the summer, Father Bacht came to join them in order to translate their final copy into Latin.

The Composition of
Humani Generis Unitas

And so at the beginning of July LaFarge returned to Paris, where, in the stifling heat of that summer of 1938,[1] he set to work on his new mission, together with Desbuquois and Gundlach.

Like LaFarge, Desbuquois and Gundlach were deeply involved in Catholic social activism, for which *Rerum Novarum* had laid the theological and practical foundations.[2] But unlike LaFarge, for several years they had been in close contact with Rome, which had already involved them in composing important documents. Both participated, albeit separately, in writing the encyclical *Quadragesimo Anno* (Pius XI, 1931), and Desbuquois worked on *Divini Redemptoris* (Pius XI, 19 March 1937). Thus, although their work on the new encyclical was not a necessary consequence of their earlier activities, neither was it merely accidental.

In 1938, the name of Gustave Desbuquois[3] had long been synonymous with *Action populaire*, the journal which he had helped to found in 1903, and of which he had been director since 1905. Under this banner a team of a dozen Jesuits worked in Vanves, a suburb of Paris, and constituted one of the main centers from which social Catholicism reached out all over France. Publishing articles, giving lectures, leading seminars, and annually organizing, along with a similar team in Lyons directed by Joseph Folliet, the *Semaines sociales en France*, the *Action populaire* group had acquired considerable influence on labor unions and Catholic employers, on youth movements, on the cooperative movement, and so on.

Some twenty years younger than Desbuquois, Gustav Gundlach[4] had followed a very different path, which early on led him toward some of the most progressive Catholic intellectual circles in the Weimar Republic. While he began by studying philosophy at the University of Freiburg im Breisgau, he later turned to economics, at the express request of the Society of Jesus, which wanted to him explore Heinrich Pesch's notion of "Christian solidarity."[5] For this purpose he went to Berlin at the beginning of the summer of 1924, where, on the advice of Pesch himself, he immediately took a course on national economics given by Werner Sombart, with whom he worked for several years. It was also at this time that he began his very long collaboration with the current apostolic nuncio in Germany, Eugenio Pacelli, to whom he had been introduced by a mutual friend, Father Robert Leiber, S.J.[6]

By the end of the 1920s, Gundlach had participated intensely in the political life of the Weimar Republic. Confronted by the ambiguous attitude of many Catholics with regard to the republic, and by the rise of anti-republican forces,[7] he had concentrated his activities on social and economic problems. Thus, he took part in the Volksverein für das katholische Deutschland, frequented the Königswinterer Kreis,[8] taught social ethics and sociology at the Hochschule für Philosophie und Theologie St. Georg in Frankfurt, and published numerous articles in the Jesuit periodical *Stimmen der Zeit*. His articles on "Class," "Class struggle," and "Class State," which appeared in the *Staatslexikon der Görres-Gesellschaft* (5th ed., 1929), caused a sensation in Catholic circles, which generally associated the idea of class with Marxism. In these articles Gundlach defined class as a "large group within the state,

seeking—by struggling against another group—a certain organization of the common good," and noted that "in this reality ever
more distant from the Ideal, the division of society into classes
can be, under certain conditions, an appropriate and even necessary means of realizing the State interest." The class struggle
thus had a meaning if it was understood as a "process of organic
healing of society." It followed that "the true goal of the class
struggle is a creative unity which serves a superior third term,
namely the totality [constituted by] the people and the state."[9]
Such ideas did not fail to exercise an influence on the writing
of the encyclical *Quadragesimo Anno*. And that was where
Gundlach's and Desbuquois's paths first crossed.

As the fortieth anniversary of *Rerum Novarum* approached,
Pius XI decided to bring the latter up to date, taking into account
the intervening economic and political transformations, within
the framework of a major new social encyclical. Ledochowski,
whom the pope entrusted with having the encyclical confiden-
tially drafted, went to Father Oswald von Nell-Breuning in the
fall of 1930. The latter had written a preliminary text drawing on
the contributions of his friends in the Königswinterer Kreis, without, however, informing them about what he was doing. "Everything that was discussed in this group was useful for my work on
the encyclical," Nell-Breuning later said, and he offered the
following description of Gundlach's role in this elaboration:
"Gundlach, who was the deep thinker in the group, defined its
position not only on the fundamental questions of social philosophy, but also on politics in general [to the point that one could
consider the encyclical] a large-scale plagiarism of Gundlach [. . .].
His analysis of class society, set forth in his celebrated articles in
the *Staatslexikon*, constituted its keystone."[10] According to Nell-
Breuning, Gundlach's contribution to *Quadragesimo Anno* was
particularly evident in the discussion of the "structural problems
of society" and in the formulation of the principle of "subsidiarity."

In his preparatory text, Nell-Breuning recommended substituting for capitalist "class" society, as well as for the "classless" society urged by various forms of socialism, a democratic society in which there would be collaboration between private organizations. He also dealt with property, capital, and "income without labor," with the salaried class and its transcendence, and with the state's role in general harmonization and supplementation ("subsidiarity") in the interest of the common good, etc.[11] However, this draft seemed to Ledochowski too theoretical and "solidaristic," and he asked a Jesuit from Antwerp, Father Albert Muller, S.J., to rework it with Nell-Breuning. Moreover, in October the superior general had asked Father Desbuquois to prepare an analogous draft. Meeting with Muller several times, Desbuquois and his collaborator, Father Danset, drew up a more concrete text, showing on the one hand that free-market capitalism had been supplanted by a dictatorship of a few powerful leaders, managers of enterprises and capital, having control over the life of nations, above and beyond the state and without concern for the overall good of society, and, on the other hand, that socialism had been transformed into violent communism or into a "moderate" socialism whose postulates were closer to those of the Christian tradition concerning respect for the human person. The remedy they proposed was a "rationalization" inspired by the Christian spirit of concord and charity, with a view to progress in the condition of human life. Muller having become the leading voice in the group, Desbuquois and Danset joined him in Rome for the final revisions. On the whole, nonetheless, these multiple collaborators were in substantial agreement.[12]

Desbuquois's and Gundlach's paths had almost crossed again on the occasion of an initiative of considerable interest (although its goal was never attained). Toward Easter 1933, in Frankfurt, the very first international meeting of Jesuits concerned with social action was to take place. Organized by Fathers Desbuquois and Nell-Breuning, this meeting was to bring together fifty-four participants from fifteen different European and Latin American nations, to debate in particular the following questions: "Is it not the case that events, the progress in material and cultural solidarity, call for a new order, which already seems about to be realized as a result of an immense social upheaval, or can we expect and hope for social peace based on legislation and social work in a capitalist regime? In the meantime, what must we do, teach, preach—we who cannot be the active agents of a revolution?" As an introduction, Gundlach was to have discussed "society and social systems." But this meeting was countermanded at the last minute by Father Ledochowski, because of the situation in Germany.[13]

Toward the end of 1936, at a historical juncture marked by the war in Spain, the Popular Front, the repression of the Church in differing ways in Mexico, the USSR, and in Germany, "atheistic propaganda" on every continent, and Nazi racism's rise to power, Pius XI set to work on two new encyclicals: *Mit Brennender Sorge* ("With Burning Dismay"), 13 March 1937, (to which we shall return in chapter 5) and *Divini Redemptoris*, 19 March 1937, "on atheistic communism" and the necessity of working toward the transformation of society through professional organizations. To prepare the latter, Ledochowski, once again entrusted with setting up the project, gathered Jesuits from five or six different nations, notably Fathers Hermann Muckermann, Ledit, and Coffey, who each took charge of certain aspects of the writing. Desbuquois, who had been asked to contribute to the enterprise, had sent in several pieces, written by himself or by members of *Action populaire*. Urgently called to Rome at the beginning of February, Desbuquois took part in the meetings and revised the whole text in order to ensure that it was not limited to a simple condemnation of communism. Considered as a complement to *Quadragesimo Anno* on social doctrine and social action, subjects that occupied two-thirds of the document, *Divini Redemptoris* "reminds us of the Church's constant rejection of communism, shows that Marxism-Leninism is an aggressive and repressive, atheistic and inhuman form of statism, disguised as a crusade for human progress. Then Catholic thought on the subjects of justice and social progress based on respect for the human person and its freedom is restated, with a more precise definition than before of 'social justice' and an appeal for the construction of a 'healthy corporatism,' under the surveillance of the state, for an 'organic collaboration.' The fourth part, the one on which Desbuquois probably collaborated most, 'is the most vigorous,' and develops 'the remedies and means' by which Christian doctrine is to be put into practice—fundamentally, a renewal of personal spiritual life; 'justice can be observed by everyone only if all agree to practice it together through institutions,' 'professional and inter-professional [institutions],' which are here described, in nuanced expression, as 'what is called the Corporation,' and with a par-ticular appeal, whose tonality we recognize, 'to you, Christian employers and industrialists, whose task is often so difficult be-cause you bear the heavy legacy of the faults of an unjust eco-nomic system.' The end insists on the necessity 'of studying social problems in the light of Church doctrine and gradually making them better known,' on the duty of every individual and of as-sociations for professional and religious action. These are indeed developments continuous with what had been taught six years earlier."[14]

Gundlach's contribution to *Quadragesimo Anno*[15] did not go un-noticed by Father Ledochowski, who soon called him to Rome. Like many others in the Vatican, Ledochowski thought that National Socialism would not long remain in power in Germany; his chief concern was bolshevism ("the principal enemy is still Moscow ... a compromise with Berlin is still possible"). The bet-ter to combat it, the general of the Jesuits wanted to create a Center for Jesuit Action in Rome, and he considered entrusting its scholarly direction to Gundlach. The latter nonetheless declined this offer, arguing from the fact that "such an enterprise could act as a moral support for the Axis forces, lead to confusion among Catholics in these countries, and diminish the moral influence of the Church elsewhere." Ledochowski then offered him a post as professor of social ethics at the Gregorian University. From that point on, with the exception of the year 1937, when Gundlach was seriously ill, he divided his time until 1938 between Rome, Frankfurt, and Berlin.[16]

Here it is worth examining two of Gundlach's activities that are not without importance for gauging his contribution to the writing of *Humani Generis Unitas.*

In 1930, he had signed the article "Anti-Semitism" in the *Lexikon für Theologie und Kirche,* which we give here in translation:

Anti-Semitism: a modern movement seeking to combat Judaism politically and economically. Two types of anti-Semitism can be distinguished, one national and politico-racial, the other politico-governmental. The former combats Judaism simply because of its racial and national foreignness, the latter because of the excessive and deleterious influence of the Jewish segment of the population of a given people. The second type corresponds to the first to the extent to which it connects this harmful and exaggerated influence to the racial and national particularity of Jews.

According to A. Wagner *(Grundlegung der polit. Ökonomie,* 1892–1893, 817), Jews belong precisely to the elements of the population "which have positions, education, [and] tend to adapt their economic dealings as much as possible to the conditions of this struggle (competition in a private economy)." Thus they succeed the best where this animal capacity for adaptation is the most necessary: in commerce. "The legal order of the system of competition in modern private economies has Judaism's fingerprints (or rather, the mark of its spirit and its character) all over it, as if it had been cut to its measure." That is why professions in which there is economic progress, the development of luxury, improvement of the opportunities for educating future generations, as well as the "liberal professions, especially those that gravitate around economic life oriented toward profit (attorneys, medical professions, journalism) are flooded with Jews—without counting those who have been baptized: such a development (especially within only two generations!) gives one pause," in particular in the interest of national harmony,[17] of the "community of the people[18] as a moral and cultural community. The influence of Judaism has in the meantime greatly increased. Only anti-Semitism linked to the rise of moral decadence (the decline in births) represents an internal anti-Semitism.

The first type of anti-Semitism is not Christian, because it is contrary to brotherly love to oppose men solely because of the difference in their nationality, rather than because of their actions. This type necessarily also turns against Christianity, on account of its internal link with the religion of the Jewish people formerly chosen by God (the search for an "aryo-germanic" religion). The second type of anti-Semitism is permissible when it combats, by moral and legal means, a truly harmful influence of the Jewish segment of the population in the areas of economy, politics, theater, cinema, the press, science, and art [liberal-libertine tendencies]. Here we must reject exceptional laws directed against Jewish citizens *qua* Jews, and do so from the point of view of the modern legal state. The positive means are: impregnating social life with the Christian spirit, fighting against not only Semitic but also "Aryan" vermin, reinforcing positive, moral and religious factors within Judaism against the liberal, "assimilated" Jews who, being for the most part given to moral nihilism and without any national or religious ties, operate within the camp of world plutocracy as well as within that of international Bolshevism, thus unleashing the darker traits of the soul of the Jewish people expelled from its fatherland.

The anti-Semitism of Adolf Stoecker's party in Berlin, and of the Christian Socialists in Vienna (together with Schönerer's anti-Semitism), belongs to the second type. After the war, anti-Semitism of the first type developed very strongly, along with racial hatred, within the popular movement (particularly among the Nazis) and even in the German National Party, for it was believed that Jews helped bring about the war and the defeat, and profited from them. In other countries as well, political tensions have easily provoked anti-Semitism.

The Church has always protected Jews against anti-Semitic practices proceeding from false jealousy, false Christian zeal, or from economic necessity. On the other hand, it has inspired and supported measures opposing the unjust and harmful influence of economic and intellectual Judaism (such as the Christian impregnation of the labor movement, the Catholic press). The Church must reject modern systems of anti-Semitism that are based on false theories of man and of the course of history, by constantly stressing the preponderant role that has been assigned to Judaism as a chosen people within the divine and Christian economy of salvation (see the Holy Office's decree on the Friends of Israel, 21 March 1928[19])—G. Gundlach.[20]

Let us note that the author of this text adopts the point of view of the modern legal state, which is already remarkable in itself, that he firmly opposes politico-racial anti-Semitism, and that he rejects the passage of any exceptional law against Jewish citizens qua Jews. But without examining assertions that are at the very least debatable, such as "the Church has always protected Jews against anti-Semitic practices," let us stress this text's ambiguity. For how is it possible to fight with "legal" means "a truly harmful influence on the part of the Jewish segment of the population" in various domains without these legal means being exceptional, from the moment that they are aimed restrictively at Jews qua Jews? And how can legal arrangements be restricted to Jews, or solely to Jews, without identifying Jews according to criteria that are based precisely on their "racial or national [or even their religious] foreignness"? Let us observe, finally, that by closely associating the misdeeds of a modernity impugned by the Church—"an animal capacity for adaptation" to competition, an orientation toward profit, Jews "flooding" the liberal professions, the "harmful influence" and "moral nihilism" of "assimilated" Jews operating "within the camp of world plutocracy as well as within that of international Bolshevism" to destroy society— Gundlach's remarks fully participate in the dominant ecclesiastical way of imagining Jews, which ever since the middle of the nineteenth century had produced a caricaturally anti-Semitic representation of Jews.

On the other hand, on 1 April 1938, on German-language Vatican Radio, Gundlach had condemned the Austrian episcopacy's endorsement of the Anschluss, the incorporation of Austria into the Third Reich, in terms that did not go unnoticed.[21] First, let us recall the context.

On 12 March 1938, German troops crossed the Austrian border. The next day, Austria was proclaimed a province of the Reich. On 14 March, Hitler made his triumphal entry into Vienna; on 18 March, he announced that Germans and Austrians would be asked, on 10 April, to vote in a plebiscite on the Anschluss and, at the same time, to elect new deputies to the Reichstag. A powerful propaganda campaign began, in which the Nazis reserved a choice role for the Church.

On 15 March, after visiting Hitler, the archbishop of Vienna, Cardinal Theodor Innitzer, addressed the following directives "to the Catholic clergy and to faithful Catholics in the archdiocese of Vienna and Burgenland":

> 1. Those who are entrusted with souls and the faithful will unconditionally support the great German State and the Führer, because the historical struggle against the criminal illusion of Bolshevism and

for the security of German life, for work and bread, for the power and honor of the Reich and for the unity of the German nation, is obviously accompanied by the blessing of Providence.

2. The exclusive mission of priests is to care for souls [... they] must remain at a distance from politics and await with trust the development of events.

3. Faith and the intimate union of souls gives Christians the conviction that the natural community of the nation is called upon to realize a divine idea, and it follows that a truly religious life presupposes the practice of national virtues.

4. I urge the heads of youth organizations to promote membership in the German Reich's youth organizations.

"The Church will not regret its fidelity to the great German state." This statement by the Führer is a guarantee that the true mission of the Church can be fulfilled.

And so Catholics in their totality serve in the best way the good of the Reich, the nation, and the fatherland.[22]

On 27 March, a collective declaration by the Austrian episcopacy, dated 18 March, was read "in all the Churches on Austrian territory":

[...] We joyfully acknowledge that the National Socialist movement has done and is still doing eminent work in the domain of national and economic construction as well as in the domain of social policy, for the Reich and the German nation, and notably for the poorest strata of the population. We are also convinced that the activity of the National-Socialist movement has averted the danger of an all-destroying atheistic Bolshevism.

For the future, the bishops confer their heartiest blessing on this activity, and they will instruct the faithful to this effect.

On the day of the plebiscite, it goes without saying that it is for us a national duty, as Germans, to vote for the German Reich, and we also expect all believing Christians to demonstrate that they know what they owe to their nation.[23]

On 1 April, Cardinal Theodore Innitzer expressed to Cardinal Adolf Bertram, the president of the Fulda conference,[24] his hope that German bishops would rally to the Austrian episcopacy's declaration regarding the plebiscite. He added that this declaration must not be "weighed down with restrictive clauses." At the end of this message, the signature of the Austrian primate is preceded by a scandalous, handwritten "Und Heil Hitler!"[25]

On 2 April, the *Osservatore romano* explains simply that "we are authorized to report" that the Austrian episcopacy's declaration "was written and subscribed without any previous understanding with or later approbation by the Holy See, and on the sole responsibility of the same episcopacy."[26] But at 8 P.M. the preceding day, Vatican Radio had broadcast a "talk in German by an anonymous Jesuit" on the subject "What is political Catholicism?" This much more severely criticized the Austrian episcopacy and Cardinal Innitzer, whom it is not difficult to recognize in the description of the partisans of a "false political Catholicism" (see point 3 below).

The "anonymous Jesuit" was none other than Gustav Gundlach. Here is a transcript of his famous "talk," as reported in the *Osservatore romano*:

The *Schwarze Korps*[27] for 17 March 1938, on the subject of the first declaration of the Cardinal Archbishop of Vienna concerning the new situation in Austria, writes notably that: "Political Catholicism, the most infamous of all political systems, has just incurred a terrible, definitive defeat on Austrian territory and in the hearts of all Germans. From now on, we must condemn as criminal any effort to go on practicing politics."

To this claim on the part of the *Schwarze Korps*, one must, in principle, reply as follows:

1. In the opinion of the Church's adversaries, political Catholicism signifies that the pope or the bishops or the faithful simply use moral principles as a pretext for acting on the State and society, but actually aim at obtaining or retaining terrestrial advantages or positions of power.

This way of understanding political Catholicism already existed among bourgeois liberals and Marxists, so that the National Socialism that today insistently describes itself as anti-liberal and anti-Marxist, on this point speaks in the same way as the liberals and the Marxists, and adopts here as on all other topics the same cultural attitude.

2. In its true and genuine sense, political Catholicism—if we want to use this inelegant expression which occasions all sorts of misunderstandings—signifies that the pope or the bishops or the faithful must do what they can to realize the principles of the Creator and the Savior of the world in the domain of the State and society, as in all other domains of creation.

This political Catholicism is thus, in its profoundest sense, a religious and Christian matter.

To call it "criminal" would be to combat the very nature of Christianity by abusing the power of the state. And in the service of this "political Catholicism," the authority of the Church and its current pope, especially in his teachings and in his solemn encyclicals, have endorsed the moral principles of political and social life. And in this same service, the faithful, equally conscious of the obligations contracted through baptism and confirmation, have united, in the most diverse countries and in the most diverse ways, to obtain the realization of the aforementioned principles.

In the same way Catholic Action, which has been promoted by the Holy Father, if it wants to remain faithful to its founder's intention, cannot give up the attempt to put the principles of moral life to work in all domains of terrestrial life without exception. To give this up on principle and to confine, on principle, Catholic practice to the so-called purely religious domain, as people like to say ambiguously these days, would be equivalent to heresy, an error in faith.

3. No doubt there also exists a false political Catholicism. But the latter is not the illusion indicated at the beginning, and created by National Socialism in imitation of liberals and Marxists.

This false political Catholicism consists, rather, in the behavior of Catholics, whether simple faithful believers or official dignitaries, when it is dictated solely by excessive tactics and prudence, by a weak-willed adaptation to actual or anticipated facts.

There is no doubt that in the course of history this false political Catholicism has caused the most serious harm to man and to esteem for the Church, and by the same token, to the minister of souls, especially in a time when the adversaries of Christianity boast of their own intransigent principles and accuse Christians of spiritual feebleness. The harm was and is still greatest when this spirit of false political Catholicism seizes the highest places in the divine order and keeps them hypnotized by power and temporary success.

Then it can happen that such pastors' eyes no longer recognize, contrary to their duty, the wolf in sheep's clothing, and that they believe the promises of certain men against whom they should have already been forewarned by the sad experience of others, and even by the words of the supreme Pastor.

The outcome of this behavior, then, will always be that such protectors of the Church's interests will want to impose, in a deplorable manner, their moral and religious authority in the exclusively political domain. For example, they employ their moral and religious authority to convince the faithful of the truth of certain assertions of a purely practical order, even when these assertions and the facts on which they are based are judged otherwise by many serious and competent men. For example, it is not appropriate for ecclesiastical doctrinal authority as such to make declarations that measure and evaluate the purely economic, social, and national-political results of a government.

No believer should feel obliged by conscience to obey these declarations as if they were judgments of ecclesiastical doctrinal authority, and to conform to them in making use of his political rights.

Still more harmful would be the all too comprehensible adaptation of this false political Catholicism, when ordinary believers at all social levels have to pay for their courageous adherence to the foundations of the divine order and especially of natural law, and pastors simply go along with whatever is currently successful.

All righteous and well-intentioned people, of whom there are many outside the Church, can only consider this behavior on the part of pastors as lacking in dignity and fidelity. It is true that good personal intentions may exist; but in this case it is not according to intentions that we must judge.

The Church's adversaries may then triumph, because the necessary, personal links within the Church are breaking, in particular the boundless confidence between pastor and flock. This sort of political Catholicism would doubtless be an achievement foreign to Catholic Action and to its essential goal, which is collaboration between lay people and the hierarchical apostolate. For it would mean that practically all the hardships and the burden of this Action would weigh exclusively on the lay person.

And that is why this false political Catholicism is everywhere and always to be condemned and stigmatized. It is true that National Socialism would not condemn this political Catholicism as false, any more than the *Schwarze Korps* would consider it "criminal"; on the contrary, they would employ it as a way of leading Catholics away from the true faith. But this false political Catholicism cannot stand before Christ's tribunal.

Neither can it stand before the tribunal of the Bride of Christ, the Holy Church, which—whatever happens—as the spotless, stainless Bride, remains, in the eyes of all faithful Catholics, elevated far above this human cowardice.

Down with the false, then, and long live the true and genuine political Catholicism![28]

The *Osservatore romano* for 4 and 5 April asserts that the radio "talk" in question "was a theoretical study proceeding from a private source; it was therefore neither official nor officious, nor inspired, and—as is the case for all others of a similar kind—the Holy See does not assume responsibility for it."[29] According to Gundlach, however, "Cardinal Secretary of State Pacelli, who had corrected and approved this talk, had the complete endorsement of Pius XI."[30]

Urgently called to the Vatican, to which he flew on 5 April, Cardinal Innitzer was first received at length by Cardinal Pacelli, and then by the pope. A new statement resulted, made in his own name and "in the name of all the Austrian bishops," and unanimously seen as a retraction:

1. The solemn declaration of the Austrian bishops on 18 March of this year was clearly not intended to be an approval of something that was not and is not compatible with God's law, and with the freedom and rights of the Catholic Church. Moreover, the State and the party are not authorized to interpret this declaration and to use it in their propaganda as imposing a duty on the conscience of the faithful.

2. With regard to the future, the Austrian bishops demand that:

a) no modification of matters relating to the Austrian Concordat be made without previous agreement with the Holy See;

b) in particular, all educational organizations and all upbringing of the young be maintained in such a way that the natural rights of parents and of the moral and religious education of Catholic youth in accord with the principles of the Catholic faith is guaranteed; propaganda hostile to religion and to the Church be stopped; the right of Catholics to proclaim, defend, and practice the Catholic faith and Christian principles in all domains of human life by all means available to contemporary civilization be guaranteed.[31]

For his part, Gundlach, denounced in Berlin by an informer operating within Vatican circles, was warned,[32] at the end of May 1938, that he would be arrested by the Reich's police if he returned to Germany. He did not go back to Germany until the end of the Second World War.

As for the rigged plebiscite on 10 April,[33] it was rewarded with a massive "*Ja.*" The Anschluss was ratified by 99.08 percent of the voters in greater Germany and 99.75 percent in Austria. The Austrian question was settled. On 21 April, Hitler asked General Wilhelm Keitel, head of the high command of the Reich's armed forces, to draw up, with a view to promptly carrying it out, the "Green plan"—that is, the plan for a blitzkrieg attack on Czechoslovakia.

The Writing of Humani Generis Unitas

So now the drafters of the encyclical were ready "to work hard, in the heat of the Parisian suburbs," as Gundlach writes in his autobiography, remaining very circumspect regarding the work accomplished.[34] The conditions under which the three Jesuits began their work were not the most favorable. According to Heinrich Bacht, "The whole time we worked on this 'secret project,' we were gripped by the fear that the Gestapo would try something, [because] it had been keeping an eye on Gundlach ever since his famous radio broadcast; in any case people said at the time that there was a quasi-official Gestapo office in Paris. Thus, when one day Stefan Andres, accompanied by a Jewish journalist, came to the offices of *Études* to ask for help, and the porter asked me to handle this business with him, Gundlach and LaFarge were terrified, [fearing] that he was an *agent provocateur* from the Gestapo. I was myself obsessed by the fear of speaking about this undertaking. It was moreover not in my interest to take with me, when I returned to Germany, any paper that might seem suspect if examined by the authorities."[35]

However, LaFarge talked too much. Perhaps he felt the need to talk to someone; the importance and scope of his mission made him diffident. In order to reassure him, and to inform him that he would soon be permitted to make the four vows that would make him a Jesuit of the first order, his direct superior, Father Talbot, writing from New York on 13 July, showered the following encouragements on him:

STRICTLY CONFIDENTIAL.[36]

Dear Father John,

Before speaking about your news, I am going to act most irregularly, and I trust there is a sufficient reason in the circumstances. You need courage and confidence, and the news I am quite certain you will soon be receiving should prepare you for your tremendous task, laid on you by obedience, the highest on earth. Simply, all the preliminary processes have been completed—favorably, I am assured—for you to take the four vows of the Profession. Fr. Blakely and I talked it over toward the end of last year. The request was made about the New Year. The answer should soon be officially returned. All of this is absolutely confidential; I would not feel justified in breathing a word of it in advance to anyone—except to one who finds himself forced to summon every power at his disposal to carry through a task such as yours. The Society recognizes you and gives you the highest commendation possible: therefore, the Society has the supreme confidence that you can worthily perform what the Holy Father requires. We put our trust and faith in you. Have faith in yourself. We have no fears about you; have none about yourself.

The Holy Father said your coming was providential. It seems to be such. We may take his word for it, and say it was providential and Divinely ordered. It was, naturally, amazing, and even uncanny.

That he should leap on you, a chance pilgrim, when he had the pick of Rome, that he should have thought about you merely from your writings and what he had heard and should have decided on that basis that you were *the one*—sounds like stark madness or inspired wisdom. I am convinced it was a flash from the other side of our surface world. The Holy Father, let us say, judged inspiredly. I judge without inspiration of any sort: you are *the one* best equipped to do this work. You have been preparing for this topic throughout years; you have probably read more on it, thought more on it, analyzed it more, solved it best. You have the supra-national mind. You have worked out already the broad principles, either explicitly or implicitly, in your writings and in your thoughts. You are most familiar with the upheavals of the modern nations, with their ideologies, with their acts, with their aims, and you know the history of the fallen nations. What is your greatest asset is this: you have the Faith burning within you and you have the spiritual insight. Speak yourself, and you will be speaking in the voice of the Holy Father himself, and He will not be speaking alone through you, for He will be speaking in the voice of the Holy Spirit. You will succeed or you will fail— what of it. If you succeed: well; if you fail: well also, someone else will do it. But you will succeed. And I am getting the nuns to join us in prayer for you. God bless you and your work. . . .[37]

Moreover, on 18 July Father Joseph A. Murphy, S.J., assistant to the provincial of New York, wrote to Talbot:

Dear Reverend Father,

Pax Christi. It is interesting to note that the very day on which the attached memo from John LaFarge reached us, we also received the documents authorizing John LaFarge to make the four solemn vows of the Profession. I return the letter with the assurance that there is no need for excuses. This procedure was regular in every way. I thank you for [illegible]. I have an inkling of the subject, but I have not heard anything else said.

The date for the event has not yet been chosen. When the Father returns, if you inform me we shall choose the first Feast of Mary afterward—Greetings to all [. . .] in Jesus Christ, Joseph A. Murphy.[38]

On 17 July, writing from Naples, Ledochowski informed LaFarge that his work might take longer than anticipated, and urged him to be more circumspect. This letter is handwritten in French, like all those the general of the Jesuits subsequently sent to LaFarge:

My Reverend and very dear Father,

Father Assistant Maher told me yesterday that you were thinking of returning to America on 20 August. It seems to me that will not be possible. It is true that you were not to write a long scholarly work, but nevertheless the subject is so delicate that every position taken must be examined closely by various competent people. In addition, the whole must be given *the desired form*, which is not so easy: *experto crede!* . . . The turns of phrase and the whole must correspond to the signer's point of view.

All these things cannot be achieved within a month, and anyway it is not appropriate for you to leave before the work is finished. — A second thing I wanted to tell you is to be very rigorous about observing secrecy. You see, I have spoken about it only with the [illegible]. I have often wondered whether I could speak about it to the American Father Assistant, and it seemed to me I should do so before his departure, and I was very surprised to learn that you had already spoken to him about it and also to Father Phillips. We have always followed this rule, making privy to the secret only those who were necessary to us in order to carry out the work; no one else. And you must also follow this rule now and also after the work, with God's help, is finished, otherwise we might have serious problems.

You have probably seen that in his address to the Ladies of the Cenacle (*Osservatore romano* 17.VII) the Holy Father already alluded to the matter,[39] but that does not prevent us from continuing to be very reserved about it. In unity with you [. . .], W. Ledochowski.[40]

On 21 July, LaFarge cabled Talbot: "Severe warning received on padlock—cannot inform even Murphy—if you informed him urge him not to intimate same—if Maher mentions it, it is his responsibility—Pilgrim."[41] The next day, Talbot sent this cable to Murphy:

Reverend and dear Father Provincial,

I am enclosing a copy of the cable that I received this morning. Father LaFarge has evidently been talking to Father Assistant. This cable, it seems to me, puts us in an embarrassing situation, as regards Father Maher. I do not see how we can conceal the knowledge of the fact from him. Apparently Father LaFarge did not fully comprehend the extent of the secrecy.[42]

The necessity of observing the "most absolute secrecy" is mentioned again in a letter sent to LaFarge by Ledochowski from Naples on 26 July:

Reverend Father,

Thank you for your good letter of 22 July. I fully approve of your work plan and I have no doubt that Father D[esbuquois] will be of great help to you.

You are entirely right that being too reserved could be harmful. You can say truthfully that the General assigned you to do some work, but concerning the work you are doing now you cannot speak to anyone except in cases of genuine necessity and with the most absolute secrecy.

Let me know when you expect to return to Rome.

In unity, Your devoted,

W. Ledochowski.[43]

From August on, the correspondence available to us shows above all that the task the three drafters had set themselves was progressing more slowly than LaFarge had expected. He longed more and more to return to the United States. For example, "They are wonderful to me here," he wrote to Talbot on 5 August, and "do everything in their power to make things agreeable, in the house. But if I ever was a patriotic American, it is now." The same letter offers a good example of LaFarge's sense of humor, which he apparently never lost. Thus, during a dinner organized within the framework of the *Semaine sociale* in France, for which he had allowed himself a day off, LaFarge found himself "sandwiched between the Nuncio and the archbishop of Rouen, and I had the president of the *Semaine* and bishop of Evreux across from me. The dinner was grand, course after course; it had nothing in common with what is usually served at conventions. However, the entrée was pig's knuckle. I'd never eaten pig's knuckle before, although it is the standard dish in the countryside. I resisted pig's knuckle in Maryland, I resisted pig's knuckle in Woodstock, I resisted pig's knuckle in New York, I've resisted pig's knuckle all my life. I have never surrendered to pig's knuckle. But sandwiched between a Nuncio and an archbishop, I had to give in. To my great surprise, I found it good..."[44]

On 11 August, he wrote to Talbot:

Dear Frank,

By a miracle, things are coming through. Someone must have been praying. Will contain, if the draft is allowed to pass, a stiff blow toward the end in favor of Catholic higher education. Rapidly taking shape.

Will probably go to Rome on the 30th, & stay there till they liberate me. Will move Heaven and earth to get back before Sept. 30.

Immense relief that heat is over here. Not so much that I suffered, but everyone else was groaning about it. If I were to have to stay over here, I should pass away—any part of Europe. Wonderful for a short visit, but I could never accommodate myself to their ideas and their regimes. One can go through a tour de force,[45] upheld by God knows what; but to live and work here![46]

LaFarge to Talbot, 23 August:

[...] 1. Expect to leave here for Rome Aug. 30 or thereabout. Have engaged passage on *Volendam*, from Boulogne. Sept. 24, arriving N.Y. Oct. 3rd. *If* they let me out of jail earlier, will endeavor to get an earlier boat, but fear this is the best I can do. [...]

6. The work is progressing—as if by a miracle. [...] What I wrote that is positive about conditions in Germany is accurate,[47] for example, the good things I saw—The state of mind is admirable. Naturally, I said nothing about the other aspect, in particular because the article was sent from Italy (I was afraid it would be lost in the Italian mails). In Rome, I formed a more complete picture of the situation—I read all the secret correspondence between Pacelli and the Nazis—It was a revelation—Things are much worse.[48]

On 31 August, from Frascati, Ledochowski wrote to LaFarge:

[...] I hope you will be able, perhaps more quickly than you think, to return to America. Do not come to Rome before having received another letter from me.[49]

The next day, Ledochowski wrote to him again:

Good news! I am authorized to inform you that you may, after finishing your work, leave immediately for America. Please be so good as to deliver your work to Father Desbuquois and ask him to send it to me by a secure route. Later, on the basis of the comments we receive, we will make the necessary revisions.[50]

On 2 September, LaFarge sent a postcard to Talbot:

Things going along quietly. Looks as if they would carry me well into October.[51]

Finally, on 18 September, LaFarge wrote a letter to Talbot, in which the end of the second paragraph appears, with hindsight, to be a premonition:

[...] Tuesday, 20 September, I expect to leave for Rome, taking with me the completed work. Unfortunately, it still has to be retyped before being fit for presentation, but I trust they will let me have someone to do this job. Then comes the scrutiny, the results of which I have no idea of. However, it has been subjected to some very searching criticism here, and has stood the test.

Fr. General was willing to let me return to the U.S. from Paris, having me send it down to Rome by someone. But I wrote him I felt I could not accept his offer, tempting as it was (for I dread the trip). I am convinced one must be on the spot to explain the why's and wherefore's; and have learned the need of that from various sources. [...] Let us *hope* they let me go by October 15. [...]

I am somewhat worried about finances. Strictly speaking, I think I can squeeze through with what I have left, which is about $390 after buying my fare to Rome and back. But it makes me nervous, and if you can send me another $200 it will put my mind at rest. I have considerable expenses with regard to this affair, amounting in all to about $200: some $100 for typing, and $100 for other aid; and all this has been by strict economy. [...][52]

Nothing in the documentation we possess indicates the precise date on which LaFarge finally returned to Rome to deliver the result of these difficult months of work. But in his autobiography, he indicates that he was at the general curia of the Jesuits on "that fateful September evening" when Hitler gave his speech in the Berlin Sportspalast.[53] LaFarge is almost certainly referring to Hitler's speech of 26 September 1938, in which he informed the world that the fate of Czechoslovakia was already sealed.[54] LaFarge left us a description of the evening that demonstrates his journalistic talents. "The circumstances were dramatic. Father Ledochowski invited all the Fathers to attend toward the close of the recreation period which customarily follows the evening meal in Jesuit houses. Father General seated himself in his usual alert fashion close to the instrument, while the others were grouped around. The transmission was perfect, as if we were seated in the vast hall itself. The speech was a rhythm of passion. Starting in a quiet, reasoning voice as if he were taking the great audience into his confidence, Hitler rose rapidly to frantic screaming of fanaticism, followed by the terrific rumbling roar from the audience: 'Sieg Heil! Sieg Heil! Sieg Heil!' My own bones quaked at each of these recurrent episodes. Over and over the voice died down and rose again, but Father General's attentive face and eager form remained impassive. Beneš was the main object of all this oratory.[55] Beneš the aggressor. Beneš the tyrant. Beneš the betrayer of civilization. Beneš the enemy of the German People. Beneš in whom Hitler had put his childlike trust only to be betrayed. Beneš the tool of foreign perfidy.

"The shouting in the Sportspalast was the voice of impending war; it was furthermore the voice of a blind, dark passion which might erupt anywhere in the world. Echoes of it even appeared in the United States; the voice of the mob, of hate, of hysteria. Trotsky and Lenin had shouted in that voice yet those who opposed them could be stirred up to the same degree of insanity. Curiously enough with all his denunciations Hitler still had a kind word to say of the French and the British. They might understand him or sympathize with him.

"The oratory went on. The bell rang for the evening's spiritual exercises at the close of recreation, but Father General remained at the radio. Again the bell rang fifteen minutes later for the examination of conscience, customary at the close of a Jesuit's day, but he still remained. I could not avoid wondering what would have passed in Hitler's mind if he had realized that on that night he was upsetting the inflexible time-order of Jesuit headquarters in Rome and making us all stay up and listen to the radio when we should have been quietly saying our prayers. Finally with a last effort the Fuehrer screeched to a finish. Father General rose abruptly, darted to the door, then turning back, simply said: 'Don't worry, there will be no war.' And sure enough there wasn't—not then."[56]

From Rome, LaFarge went back to Paris, where he telegraphed the *America Press* in New York on 29 September before going on to Boulogne: "Sailing October 1 *Staatendam*. LaFarge."[57]

October 1 was the very date on which, two days after the English and French abdication in Munich,[58] German troops invaded Czechoslovakia and occupied the Sudetenland.

What Happened to the Draft?

OCTOBER 1938 TO MAY 1940

What happened to the documents John LaFarge deposited in Rome at the end of September 1938?

To answer that question, we have scarcely more than six letters sent by Gustav Gundlach to LaFarge between 16 October 1938 and 30 May 1940,[1] and five others sent to LaFarge by Fathers John Killeen, Zacheus Maher, and Vincent McCormick. The second set of letters generally corroborates the information in the first set. But is that enough to lend more credibility to Gundlach's interpretation of what happened?

Incomplete and one-sided though it is, Gundlach's correspondence is worth quoting in full. For apart from its informative value with respect to the subsequent fate of the draft encyclical, it constantly refers to a threefold backdrop, which the German Jesuit describes at length to his American correspondent: (1) the conflicts and intrigues played out at the Vatican during the final months of Pius XI's pontificate and the first months of Pius XII's; (2) the deterioration of relations between the Fascist government and the Vatican, which increasingly undermined the peace concordat signed in 1929, and the rise of the racist movement's power, which led to anti-Semitic legislation in Italy in the fall of 1938; (3) the aggravation of tensions in Europe, which led to the occupation of the whole of Czechoslovakia (March 1939), the invasion of Poland (1 September 1939), and the beginning of the Second World War (3 September 1939).

Gundlach returned to Rome on 1 October 1938, expecting to meet LaFarge, who sailed for the United States on the same day. Nine days later, a letter from Father John Killeen, the American representative of the Jesuits' superior general, informed Gundlach that on 8 October Father Ledochowski had transmitted the "abridged version" of the draft encyclical to an editor at *La Civiltà cattolica*, Father Enrico Rosa, S.J., for his expert opinion. On his own initiative, Killeen added to it "all [the] other documents in order to ensure in this way that no modification would be made that did not correspond to the intentions of the authors." Noting with irritation that precious time had thus been lost, and already suspecting Ledochowski of yielding to a temptation "to sabotage, through dilatory action, for tactical and diplomatic reasons," Gundlach urged LaFarge, on 16 October, to write directly to the pope:

Very dear Reverend Father LaFarge,

Pax Christi! This Sunday is the third I am spending once again in Rome after my long journey. As agreed, I was here on 1 October, although my convalescence in Switzerland was as necessary as it was pleasant. How can I describe my surprise on finding, on my first visit to the Reverend Father Rector,[2] that E[uere] H[ochwürdigkeit][3] had left. I thought I might be able to find out something at the Borgo,[4] and so I called the German Assistant. Curiously, he came immediately to my lodgings, with the intention, as I realized, of finding out whether I had met this or that interesting person in P[aris]. I had to reply in the negative, for you know well what a secluded life I led there. He knew nothing *about our business*, and assured me only that E. H. had left; moreover, his—and our—Boss[5] had never spoken to him about this business. As usual, he could not and would not give me any idea about what might happen to our business now.

Monday (October 3), I had in my hands your E.H's letter of September 28, which showed me first that you were still alive, and secondly, made things a little clearer. I then spent a day thinking about this business, and then I decided to write the Am[erican] Repr[esentative], pointing out the very natural interest that led me to inquire at least about what had happened to our documents. Sunday (October 9), the Am[erican] Repr[esentative] came to visit me, but I was not in. On October 10, I received a letter from him, in which he told me that our Boss had submitted your abridged version of the text for the approval of Mr. Rosa, of the well-known review. The Repr[esentative] added that this had been done three days earlier, that is, on October 8, and that he had himself added all our other documents in order to ensure in this way that no modification would be made that did not correspond to the authors' intentions. Finally, he promised to keep me informed of any new developments that came to his attention. It goes without saying that the friendly explanations of the Am[erican] Repr[esentative] must be treated with the utmost confidentiality.

That is the situation; I have heard nothing since. Dear Father LaFarge! You see that your intention not to let the document pass through other hands has not been realized. Your loyalty to the Boss, for which I had already shown my understanding in Paris, even though it seems to me rather excessive, has not been rewarded. Indeed, you might be subject to the reproach that your loyalty toward Mr. Fischer[6] has suffered from your loyalty to the Boss. If one considers, in addition, that it took the Boss two weeks to submit the business to the person mentioned, and that he has since remained completely silent, one begins to have strange ideas. A person unconnected with the affair might see in all this an attempt to sabotage, through dilatory action, and for tactical and diplomatic reasons, the mission with which you were directly entrusted by Mr. Fischer.

The fact that the Boss did not find it necessary to ask my view about this business is already remarkable in itself; under the present circumstances, this is first of all simply painful to me. But I can bear it, and I shall bear it. What I find unbearable, on the other hand, is that what ought to happen in the interest of the good cause, and which ought necessarily to happen very soon, is not happening right away.

Under the circumstances, my opinion is that E. H. should think about the obligation to write to Mr. Fischer, for it is *you*—and no one else—who were directly entrusted with the mission. In order not to make this a futile gesture, I suggest that you write the following: You transmitted the text to our Boss for subsequent delivery, because you were forced to leave for personal reasons. Now that you have returned to the United States, you have reconsidered the matter, and you are convinced that the texts and the method proposed in fact reflect real and urgent needs. You want to reconfirm all this in writing. In my opinion, this letter can be sent by way of the A[postolic] D[elegate] in W[ashington].

I am very sorry to have to tell E. H. this. But I am obliged to do so, because it is completely impossible for me to do anything at all concerning this matter, and because of the necessity of [acting] for the good cause. I pray that the Holy Spirit may enlighten you.

In the hope that Country, People, and Nation over there are strengthening your health, I am ever your grateful Gust. Gundlach, S.J.[7]

Several of these points are confirmed by a letter Father Killeen sent to LaFarge on 27 October:

Dear Father LaFarge,

Although I have not much information to give you, I thought it time to write and let you know as much as I do about what has happened since you left. For a week or more no move was made in any direction. Then one day Father General told me to send one of the French copies you left with me to Father Rosa at the Civiltà. Father General sent an accompanying note but did not advise me of its contents. In view of what he had told you just before you left, it seemed most probable to me that Fr. General was just submitting the document to Fr. Rosa in order to play the prudent part and get the judgment of one more man about it. But of this I am not sure, so in order to safeguard your wishes in the matter, in case Fr. Rosa did think of proposing any changes, I also enclosed a set of your notes and explanations, together with a copy of the final sheet you left with me in which you asked that, no matter what was to be done to certain passages, others might be left intact, especially the famous 126–130. Since the document went to Fr. Rosa, I have heard nothing further, and that is where things stand at present. If I hear of any more developments, you may be sure you will hear from me promptly. Fr. Gundlach was also anxious to know what had happened and I have informed him of the above [...].[8]

Enrico Rosa, S.J.

We now pause a moment to discuss Enrico Rosa, S.J., to whom the Jesuits' superior general went to get an expert opinion—or, according to Gundlach, to delay the transmission of the documents to the pope. Invited in 1905 to join the editorial board of *La Civiltà cattolica*, the principal Jesuit review in Italy, Father Rosa had become its editor in 1915. Though he had given up that post in 1931, he nonetheless remained a member of the editorial board and henceforth devoted himself solely to the review. After his death, on 26 November 1938, the obituary notice published in *La Civiltà cattolica* describes him as "[...] an intrepid interpreter and defender of the Holy See's directives, [...] the man who set the tone in practically all the battles waged in the defense of truth." His name "remains principally associated with his articles against the many errors of liberalism, with the extremely hard-fought campaign against the Sphinx of modernism, [...] with the refutation of old and new calumnies directed against the Society of Jesus throughout the world [...] and more generally against the history of the Church, with the thankless task of dealing with the problem of the *Action française*, [with the condemnation of] the bloody persecution in Mexico, [of] the anti-Christian attacks by German Nazism, [with the defense of] the legitimacy of Franco's action in Spain [...]."⁹ Father Rosa's peers thus considered him an anti-modernist "opinion leader."¹⁰

We shall return in chapter 5 to the articles on the "Jewish question" Father Rosa wrote during the 1930s. More levelheaded than some of his brother Jesuits, he nevertheless defended a seg-regationist solution in line with what *La Civiltà cattolica* had been calling for since the end of the nineteenth century—in short, a position close to the one Gustav Gundlach had characterized in his 1930 article on anti-Semitism as being that of a "permissible anti-Semitism."

That said, no document in our possession tells us the result of Father Rosa's expert examination, supposing that he had the time to study *Humani Generis Unitas* carefully. When he died on 26 November, a month and a half after having received the various copies of the draft, he had been gravely ill for several months.

"Aren't we going to put 'peace' in danger with our project?"

On 18 November, Gundlach told his American correspondent about his growing concern. Since the health of Pius XI was rapidly deteriorating,¹¹ he was closely guarded, "in such a way that he gets only what others want him to get..." Moreover, since tension between the Vatican and the Italian government was mounting because of the racist laws promulgated by Mussolini,¹² it seemed that attention to the encyclical project could well be further postponed: "Aren't we going to put 'peace' in danger with our project?" Be that as it may, Gundlach is resigned to "waiting patiently":

Very dear Reverend Father LaFarge,

Your letter of 5 November reached me 16 November, at noon. I was very happy to receive a reply from you; these days bizarre things often happen to mail. You indicate that you have received only one letter from me; however, I had slipped into the same envelope another letter concerning the search for a position for Dr. Friedmann-Friters. I hope you have received it, and that you will be able to do something for him. I understand very well what great difficulties you may encounter over there. But you must also put yourself in our place: every day we receive visits from people who are truly very unfortunate. It is doubly distressing when, as in this case, a very serious convert is involved.

Let us return to our own business. I am very happy that you have written the letter I suggested to you. Father L...r,[13] to whom I spoke about this matter, also believes that you have taken the right path. I am curious to see what will happen now. Unfortunately, according to concordant reports obtained recently, the physical health of the man in question has become very precarious, so that even in his immediate entourage he is no longer thought to have much time left. Things seem to be proceeding in such a way that he gets only what others want him to get; he is supposed still to be in good psychological condition, to be sure, but not able to do very much on his own.

Another difficulty could arise from current relations with the present strongman.[14] The two parties are clearly avoiding a confrontation regarding the well-known legislation.[15] Whereas one party protests and uncompromisingly maintains its point of view, in practice the other intends to resolve future cases within the framework of exceptions to the legal conditions of the concordat. Such is the widely accepted opinion here. Aren't we going to put "peace" in danger with our project?

In the meantime, I join with all my heart in your prayer, and share your hope that the late Mr. Cabr[ini] will intercede. The new developments of the situation in Germany will tarnish the image of the Church as the guarantor of order if it [the Church] continues to remain silent.[16]

According to certain informants, the Great Personage there whom you mention is supposed *not* to have the intention you attribute to him. On the other hand, there are also people here who, like the Am. bish.,[17] consider such projects with a great deal of skepticism.

In closing, I send you again my cordial sympathy on the occasion of the death of your brother, whom I have remembered in my prayers. At present, I am completely convinced that you left at the right time.

We shall therefore entrust all our hopes entirely to Providence, and we shall wait patiently.

I remain, with cordial greetings, your devoted brother in Jesus Christ,—G.[18]

"We cannot look for immediate publication"

At the beginning of January 1939, everything was still "in suspense," according to Father Zacheus J. Maher, the American assistant to the general of the Jesuits:

Dear Father LaFarge,

I have just said goodbye to Father Killeen who left this morning, though he will not arrive in New York until Feb. 3, on the *Aquitania*. Last evening in conversation with Father General he learned that the matter in which you are so interested is for the moment "in suspense," and so we can not look for immediate publication.

Personally I have not had the opportunity of speaking about it to His Paternity, though I did have the pleasure of meeting Father Gundlach, who was relieved to know that the German, the French, and the English version are in my care. He intimated that he was going to suggest to you, or had suggested, that you write to the one who first spoke to you of the matter, to say that you had finished the work and had given to Fr. G. for transmission. May I say that I do not think it would be well under present circumstances, to so write. You may rest fully at ease in what you have done so far and be sure that all will be properly cared for. All you have done is greatly and gratefully appreciated [...].[19]

Time was passing. And in vain, according to Gundlach, who was feeling more and more isolated at the Vatican, and expressed his bitterness and "desolation" to LaFarge on 28 January 1939:

Very dear Reverend Father LaFarge,

It has been a long time since I have written to you, and you seem for your part also to prefer silence. This situation is more bearable for you, since you are involved in public activity and have many relationships on the soil of your homeland. But the wretched man that I am sits here in the middle of four walls, in foreign surroundings, dependent on the good will of high personages, on their desire to speak to him or not and to answer his questions or not. In short, it is a child's existence for a man nearing the end of his forties! After the return of the American assistant, I went personally to see him in order to discuss our business. He was in possession of the writings, with the exception of the French text, which had been given at a certain time to Father R[osa]. He told me that he would speak to the Admodum[20] about this matter "the next day"—this was at the end of December—and that afterward he would tell me what happened. I am still waiting for a response. In the first week of January, Father D[esbuquois] from Vanves spent a week here; he was making a sort of retreat among the French Ursuline nuns; apparently he hid out and did not even visit me. You see: this can't go on like this. If the Admodum really wants to prevent the business, they could at least give me back what I worked out. As you know, I have no copy of the German text, no more than the table of contents. I have only the unabridged French version of the first and second parts of the text. So please write to the Father Assistant and ask him to return to me what I mentioned above. What we have sweated and labored over so long is perhaps worth making into a book. After all, it is not right that other people are able to publish on this subject, while we cannot because we are under supervision.

There is a second question concerning which I must unfortunately bother you—the matter of my converted Jew, Dr. Friedmann-Friters, which is, alas, still not resolved. In the interim, the fateful day—14 March—is rapidly approaching, the date on which all foreign Jews must have left the country.[21]

I thank you very much for the greetings you have sent me through Dr. Herz. We continue to give our courses at the school, but everyone fears that we will soon find ourselves in the same situation as in September. In addition, many people predict that the Church here will follow the same course as the Church in Germany. In His always benevolent but obscure foresight, God leads us altogether away from our own projects and thoughts.

In my desolation, I commend myself strongly to your prayers,

Your devoted brother in Jesus Christ, Gust. G.[22]

"A bit premature"

Struck by another heart attack, Pius XI died on the night of 9 February 1939. Cardinal Pacelli succeeded him on 3 March, under the name Pius XII. For Gundlach, who wrote to LaFarge on 15 March, this death and this succession might be more than an unfortunate complication; while he hopes that "the right line will be followed as in the past," he already fears "seeing diplomatic influences accorded more importance than is right":

Very dear Reverend Father,

I did not want to reply to your lines of 16 February before the good Dr. Fr[iedmann-Friters] had sailed to cross the Great Waters. Today, it is done, for his boat, the *Excambion* (Export Line) is leaving Genoa this very day. He is very grateful for your invitation, which the American consul was all the more inclined to regard as sufficient reason to issue a tourist visa because he knew personally one of the people mentioned in your letter. However, the consul still wanted, for his personal assurance, a declaration made by a qualified person, preferably American, stating that Mr. Fr[iedmann-Friters] *could*, after having achieved the goal of his visit, leave the United States. This was no more than a formality; however, we did not want to send a telegram, so I saw our current Rector, who was so kind as to write the statement required by the consul. I told him that it was only a formality, that he was running practically no personal risk. Dr. Fr[iedmann-Friters] thus obtained a visa at little cost, which is here, be it said in passing, very rare in such cases. Once again, thanks very much! In the meantime, we have received a second invitation from over there, which was no longer of any use to us. Next, the negotiation with the American Express travel agency was very difficult. Here, our patient had to bleed himself dry. He had to buy a "one-way" ticket ($175), a "return" ticket ($160), and in addition deposit a guarantee of $500 in case possible difficulties led to the maritime company's being fined. You see: nothing is done to make things easier for this category of poor people. To be sure, he will not lose the money for the return and the guarantee; he will get it back some day. But it was difficult for him to get together the required sum; he more or less emptied his London account. I was able to find another 2,000 lire to lend him, so as to deal with other necessary costs of the trip. Unfortunately, we are still far from the point where

the social service set up in the Vatican would be capable of intervening financially, if necessary. In addition, there are the difficulties
having to do with the situation of Italian currency. Then we had to
wait about another two weeks, while the various offices granted at
least three exit permits. Yesterday, fortunately, everything was in
order; Friedmann-Friters will therefore arrive in New York on
29 March. I am writing at the same time to Dr. Herz, so that
Friedmann-Friters will be met at the dock and can avoid further
difficulties. Perhaps you might also remind her [Dr. Herz] once
again.

Let us now move on to our other "great business." I received
today a letter sent by the Am[erican] Ass[istant] on March 14. He
writes that "last evening the first opportunity to speak to the
A.R.P.N.[23] about this matter presented itself. The A.R.P.N. considered speaking to Mr. Fischer[24] about it, to find out what he intended
to do. As I know (?), the documents were given to M. Fischer
senior[25] and no doubt are still in his study." First of all, I did not
know whether the documents were in fact transmitted, and this is
now certain; secondly, the good Assistant took two months to mention the matter. If you had not written to him, the *timor reverentialis*[26]
would still not have been overcome. Moreover: on the new Fischer's
second day, a good acquaintance here in the house—you also know
him—talked with the new man and reminded him, citing names—
yours and mine—of the projects already in progress. The great personage knew nothing about anything(!) and told him that he would
ask the A.R.P.N. what this meant and how matters stood. Therefore,
something is going to happen, and fortunately I have now a good
relationship there. The matter came up for discussion when Mr.
Fischer jun[ior][27] offered the idea, which the other side apparently
suggested to him, of letting the Vatican deal with our problems. His
interlocutor—my informant—stressed the technical difficulties and
the rough going that would result for anyone taking on such an
enormous task, and suggested that he follow "our" line instead. That

was the reason for the thing. Yesterday I had occasion to speak with
the Episc. Berolinensis,[28] who is a good friend of Fi[scher] jun[ior]'s.
In the meantime, I am waiting and making nothing public concerning the subject of the documents.

The attitude of the A.R.P.N. with regard to the diverse "isms"
is vacillating. Let him receive information about all the anti-Christian
and socially destructive things that are happening to popular morality
in Germany, especially in the domain of religious instruction and the
morals of the youth, and he proclaims to anyone who will listen that
National Socialism is at least as dangerous as communism. People
appear from Germany with information on some (apparent!) concession or other that National Socialism is supposed to have made
in the religious domain, and he is all optimism. Let next similar
reports about communism come in from America, and now communism is once again the sole true enemy! What is lacking is precisely a position based on fundamental principles and especially on
natural law; and in addition, unfortunately, there is a great misunderstanding of the causes and the facts. Moreover, the A.R.P.N.
unfortunately is strongly influenced by the privileged and property-
owning groups in almost all countries. Any legislation that incon-
veniences in a greater or lesser degree the property-owners in the
so-called "economy" is simply presented as leading toward communism, as an influence of communism, and is denounced as such.
Moreover, the bourgeois and industrialists in many countries are so
blind that in order to oppose the so-called pressure of labor unions
and workers' organizations, they support forms of government in the
German style; for over there, they say, the workers are completely
docile and no longer have any power. Let's do the same thing here
politically, they say, and the economy will do well. They don't consider the fact that this German system is pure State socialism, or that
the middle class is ultimately the one that truly suffers, and soon
"Capital" will suffer as well. These people are blind, and my opinion
is and remains: fight communism, whether it is red or another color.

Fight communism in a positive way, by representing, in matters of social and economic life, the line of natural law and the gospels, which is taught by the Church. But it is erroneous to want, out of fear of red communism, to spare the bourgeoisie, and especially the Catholic bourgeoisie, all real sacrifices, by presenting anti-communism as a *simple* reform in mentality and by giving the "good" bourgeoisie gooseflesh by holding up frightful images of communists attacking religion and the Church. It is clear that the A.R.P.N. is not very satisfied with those who see *his* anti-communism in this way. But the Church will not be able to exist honorably and successfully unless it clearly supports the challenge of the gospels and of natural law, *everywhere* and with regard to *everything*. Please look up, in the most recent great biography of Montalembert,[29] what this great patriot and Catholic was saying, and writing, at the time of Bonapartist absolutism, when so many prelates were resigning themselves to the system. Because the churches remained open, these prelates thought they could overlook all the arrests contrary to natural and administrative law, the violation of postal secrecy, etc. Today, at the same time that the newspapers are describing the fall of the rest of Czechoslovakia and Prague, we have to see clearly that this crazy business of race could become no less a danger to the world than red communism. May the Lord preserve other countries from having to be cured of their blindness by going through similar practical experiences.

Here we hope that the right line will be followed as in the past. We are nonetheless concerned to see diplomatic influences accorded more importance than is right. But it is certain that the new Man does not spare himself and never goes astray. His decisions and his proclamations may be less exuberant, perhaps, but they are more carefully weighed.

And now very dear Reverend F., I thank you once again for your great help in the case of Dr. Fr[iedmann-Friters]. I shall say a mass for your enterprise. If I learn anything new regarding our great business, or if I have something important on the docket, or if something strikes me in reading the A [?], I shall let you know. Write me only in English for I must necessarily forego recourse to my beloved German.

Your ever-devoted brother in Jesus Christ,—G.[30]

Gundlach was convinced that the new pope knew nothing about the encyclical project on which he and LaFarge had worked all summer. On 16 March 1939, Father Maher informed LaFarge, in fact, that the preparatory documents had indeed been transmitted to Pius XI before his death, but that the new pope had not yet had time to become acquainted with them:

Dear Father LaFarge P.C.

[. . .] I submitted your request RE the documents to His Paternity who begged me to state as follows: since the documents pertinent to the subject matter had been given to the one therein interested, who had but recently passed away, and since his successor doubtless has not as yet had time to go over sundry papers left on his desk, it was felt that just now it was a bit premature to ask what his good pleasure might be in the case, but that just as soon as a favorable opportunity would present itself he would bring up the matter and learn his good pleasure therein.

Of this he took a special note so that I am sure he will be mindful of it: meantime I have notified Fr. G. of all this so that he too is informed [. . .][31]

Is this a sign that the "subject matter" was already buried? On Easter Monday 1939, Maher informed LaFarge that the "French and English versions" would be returned to him shortly, and that Ledochowski had authorized him to make use of them in a future publication:

Dear Father LaFarge,

His Paternity has instructed me to inform Your Reverence that if you wish, you may now profit by your recent work and proceed to its publication, subject of course to the usual censorship of the Society.

Father General however is particularly insistent that there shall not be the least allusion to the work as having in any way had any connection with anything requested of you by His late Holiness.

I am informing Fr. Gundlach of this instruction and am also returning to him the German manuscript. The French and the English I shall forward you by the earliest carrier, perhaps by one of the Maryland scholastics[32] now here en route from Innsbruck to Woodstock.

The Lord will surely bless you for all the effort and anguish this work caused you even though it will not have the outlet at first anticipated [. . .].[33]

In fact, LaFarge did make use of the work he had completed with his two companions during the summer of 1938. In 1943, for example, a second edition of his *Interracial Justice* appeared, this time entitled *The Race Question and the Negro*, and augmented with several new chapters in which can be found sometimes the letter, sometimes the spirit, of his 1938 writings.[34] Moreover, in his posthumously published article on "Racism" in the *New Catholic Encyclopedia*, he mentions Pius XI's "Ineditum" and transcribes virtually verbatim paragraphs 111 to 128 of the English version of *Humani Generis Unitas*.[35]

On 10 May 1939, Gundlach, who had just received the "German manuscript," once again expresses to his New York correspondent his conviction that "nothing was transmitted" to Pius XII, and, as a result, "our project has gone the way of all earthly things, which, from the outset, better corresponded to the ideas and objectives" of the general of the Jesuits:

Very dear Reverend Father,

Pax Christi! Your last letter arrived about two weeks after the Am[erican] Ass[istant] returned the German manuscript to me; attached was a copy of a summary that had been written. Nothing prevents us from publishing our work elsewhere, so long as the censorship rules are observed and no mention is made of the high mission [that was entrusted to us] at the time. You can well imagine that I was very shocked, less by the content of the response—I was no longer expecting anything else—than by the peculiar fashion in which this enterprise and we ourselves were treated. I am trying to determine *sine ira et studio* the truth of following propositions: 1.— After having remained for a rather long time among the papers Rosa left at his death, the project was not submitted to Fisch[er] sen[ior] at all, or else at a time when—contrary to the end of summer or the beginning of fall 1938—he was no longer capable, because of the state of his physical health, to deal with this matter. 2.—Nothing was transmitted to F[ischer] jun[ior]; this matter must have been buried casually during a discussion between the most highly placed Man and Pat.[36] Reasons: things too delicate to be taken on by the new Man right after he came in; during the first weeks, he wanted to feel out the other side, to see if it might be open to some concessions. I add that this effort apparently met with no success, and that now people here have realized it as well. In the meantime, in any case, our project has gone the way of all earthly things; from the outset, this better corresponded to Pat.'s[37] ideas and objectives.

It only remains for me to thank you once gain for having afforded me an opportunity to reflect on this problem, in depth and in this context. And although in this circumstance I was not able to get to know the beautiful city on the S[eine], I was at least able to see it. Now, so far as the eventual use of the work is concerned, I am in general agreement with you, and believe that we must *not* make use of it for the moment. The hope that you express, that people in high places will return to it at the right moment, is currently minimal, but it is there and is not wholly without foundation. In the interim, we shall therefore abstain from any kind of publication whatever. Fiat.

Affairs in general seem to be following, so far as Fischer is concerned, a diplomatic course. That was to be expected. It remains to be seen whether the result will be up to the mark. In our times, when the *Status propagandisticus* seems to have become the norm, discreet diplomatic work occupies a less prominent place than the manipulation of public opinion. This seems to me to be also the decisive value of the step taken recently by your high-placed man over there;[38] independently of the immediate practical result, it is still important to continue to be concerned about public opinion and not surrender it to the two well-known "strongmen." At a time when the country of the Weichsel[39] is threatened and when many people perceive the specter of a B[erlin]-Mosc[ow] alliance, naturally our current direct superior's whole sky is falling. For because of the friendship between the Spree[40] and the Weichsel up to this point, B[er]l[i]n's anti-Bolshevism was taken seriously and it was thought that the fight against the Church and Christianity was no more than an "episode" that could more or less be allowed to pass by with tacit awareness. Moreover, as a result of [our] own anti-communism, it was already secretly hoped that we could present ourselves as allies and companions, in one way or another, of the Authoritarians and the Totalitarians. If to informed observers all these opinions and hopes seemed false in themselves, it is natural that now, following the concrete developments, this so-called "purely religious" anti-communism, whose tendency is nevertheless fundamentally political, is collapsing under its own weight. In addition, because of the secondary social and economic effects in the authoritarian and totalitarian states, the communist danger, far from diminishing, is spreading among the dispossessed masses who have been deprived of all rights.

There is no "purely religious" anti-communism. Without a program oriented toward socio-political goals, based on the principles of natural law and revelation, a program which can obviously not be the same in all countries, anti-communism on our part is without influence. Anyone who rejects such a program, because it is "political," is either not a Catholic, and clearly an idealist and spiritualist with Protestant tendencies, or even a "politician" who is hiding his cards, for he refuses to require of certain groups a Christianity of sacrifices or wants to please the dominant systems. Worse yet, these "purely religious" people are helping the radical Catholics such as the well-known radio preacher over there, because "purely religious people" have nothing positive to oppose to this Catholic radicalism.

That is why we have to have a social program with at least some goals, founded on the principles of natural law and revealed law and taking local relationships into account. Without wanting in the least to claim to know what these relationships are, in my opinion the principal point of view ought to be: the security and promotion of what is called *the middle class*, which means: guaranteeing and promoting above all *property acquired through personal labor* and which supports *the economic unity of the family*. Contrary to some European industrial countries, it seems to me Christian social reform *over there* must still aim less at guaranteeing the existence of the salaried worker *qua* salaried worker than that of the middle class. Hence: maintenance of property acquired through personal labor as the basis for the unity of family economics. From a negative point of view, this implies that one must approve the state's intervention in social and economic questions, not only in theory, but also in practice, and that one must not oppose measures of this kind [under the pretext that they would amount to] socialism. Frankly, a social and popular policy carried out by the State would necessarily affect the federal structure of the United States through its economic impact, which might turn out to be negative primarily in child-raising and in schools, as we conceive them. But I don't see how one can avoid this risk, which is far more moderate; the use of another possible means of social reform seems to me currently impossible over there. This would be to make social reform the responsibility of autonomous trade associations, which would propose the appropriate legislation; to do that, however, it seems to me that the preliminary sociological conditions have not yet been met in the United States, insofar as both the people and the state of things are concerned. It would be in other respects negative to refuse to allow our anti-communist movement over there to derive inspiration, by giving them a Christian interpretation, from the slogans and formulas of the communists; for example, in place of "the world revolution of the proletariat," "the world revolution for Christ." But as a method, that is a bit rudimentary. Moreover, that would disturb other groups of collaborators and would unfortunately serve only to cover up a personal lack of positive social ideas.

Why all this in relation to our unfortunate activity of last summer? Because the gap still remains, but now it has to be filled in other countries. And there appears to be a great danger of seeing a choice between communism and national totalitarianism imposed on South American minds, far more than on those in the United States. That must be avoided at any cost. In order to do so, we need a true and adequate social program. For neither the "purely religious" nor the radical Catholics will be able to provide the Church with a solid point of view in the difficult conflicts to come. Both will act on behalf of Capital, which, in order to protect itself against a socialism of the masses, is rushing toward an American national totalitarianism on the model already seen in Europe. When that happens, there will no longer be anything to do but to pray for the Church there, because it will appear as a foreign body to be combated, still more than it has been under German totalitarianism. Or else then there will be communist-revolutionary explosions that will ravage from within the unity of the faithful in this country. At that moment, the "purely religious," for lack of a coherent social program, will have nothing to say to the belligerents. As for the radicals in the clergy, they will be on the right or on the left, and thus they too will fan the flames. And the Church there will demonstrate that it has no clear orientation.

These social dangers will certainly increase, because they are there already. Simply having a social program will not get the Church out of such a tense situation. But it will be a beacon and a support for the believer. Clearly, the social program must live within souls through an elevated spiritual culture, and above all, through the merciful forces of Faith and Hope. It seems to me that, in the end, history has allotted wretched Europe a far better place. Because its spiritual substance remains Christian in spite of everything. Actual religious wars were waged in the past, heretics were burned with the utmost solemnity, but the *absolute* of Christianity was experienced in Europe, and it continues to operate. But there, you arrived too early at objective tolerance and recognition of schisms, which are considered the same, just as in other areas the existence of diverse kinds of "merchandise" is recognized. It therefore seems to me that this is the growing difficulty of the Catholic position, which is particular and historical, in which Christianity is not in the same way—it would seem, at bottom, the cultural substance. We must reckon with this situation, which naturally has its good aspects. In an approaching planetary crisis, which will in fact be a total cultural crisis, the particular historical evolution of these regions might manifest itself in its most negative aspects.

And now, dear Reverend Father, I finish my thoughts, which remind me of our exchanges of opinion last summer, which were so fruitful. I thank you again for the promised prayers; I shall not fail to say some myself.

With warmest greetings, your devoted brother in Jesus Christ, G.[41]

The events which Gundlach anticipated in this letter with such intense concern—the specter of a Berlin-Moscow alliance"; the threats hanging over the "country of the Weichsel"—became realities at the end of the summer. Following the signing of the German-Soviet pact on 23 August, German troops invaded

Poland on 1 September.[42] On 3 September, France and England declared war on Germany. The Second World War had begun.

On 20 October 1939 *Summi Pontificatus* appeared, the first of Pius XII's encyclicals. A week later, the *New York Times* reported that "according to high-placed sources in the Vatican, the theme of the encyclical, especially concerning totalitarian governments, was taken from an unpublished address which Pius XI, the predecessor of the current pontiff, is supposed to have written just before his death."[43] Similarly, the rector of the Gregorian University, Father Vincent McCormick, wrote to LaFarge on 31 October that "the world-letter had been almost finished when I arrived. You have read it, and have recognized some parts, no doubt."[44] In any event, McCormick informed LaFarge, the project had been definitively shelved:

Dear Father LaFarge,

Your document came through without difficulty and is resting in our archives. The world-letter had been almost finished when I arrived. You have read it, and have recognized some parts, no doubt. It seems to have been well received abroad. Another letter should be published shortly after you receive this, and I hope that it will be a consolation to you and a help in your apostolate outside the editorial room. Not a great deal can be said on such occasions; but make the most of the little and you will be in conformity with His will.

Sunday was consecrated the first real, negro Bishop [. . .].[45]

Finally, on 30 May 1940, Gundlach informed LaFarge that he had put his manuscript in a secure place, but that he might use it again to draft an encyclical that Pius XII had commissioned from him to celebrate the fiftieth anniversary of *Rerum Novarum*:

Very dear Reverend Father,

I have taken the opportune occasion of our librarian's trip to send you my cordial greetings, after such a long time. It has already been two years since you were here and almost two years since we worked together in Paris. I have recently put my manuscript in a secure place; people here are afraid that if the Man down here goes to war in the near future, the Man in the north's police might be granted more or less extended powers in the Eternal City. In my opinion, these fears are exaggerated, for the Germans living here are in any case not much liked by the people, and not the least reason for this is their strong influence in the ministries, the press, and the police. The Man down here ought to be very prudent, then, especially if he wants to make the people bear the whole unpopular weight of fighting alongside the Man in the north. Moreover, entering the war depends on two conditions, which are determined by the situation in this country: 1) the partner with whom one allies oneself must be certain to win; 2) the war adventure must not last too long. The Man down here might in fact be forced to come into the war in the event that the Soviets, whose resentment toward Germany is continually growing, take the lead in the fight and in the Slavs' resistance against Germany. In that situation, not only the Czechs and the Poles, but also the whole of the population of the Balkans would start to move, which could not leave the Man down here indifferent. In any case, we have not yet seen the end of all the possible developments, and my opinion would be that the supremacy of the Man in the north would be all the more in peril, so far as the Western powers are concerned, the closer it seems to being realized.

In the West, the situation is in fact very grave. The Blitzkrieg conducted by G[ermany] at the price of enormous human and material sacrifices could, in my opinion, be compromised if the French resisted for several weeks and were able to slow it down or even immobilize it. Then the weakness of the Man in the north might become evident: in fact, he was pushed into war—a quick and victorious war—when confronted by growing internal opposition and problems with finance and with supplies of raw materials in his country. But perhaps it is already too late. The Western powers have not taken this dictator seriously enough. First, they cleared the way for a nationalist dictator in G[ermany] after the world war through an intransigent and unconciliatory policy; then, after 1933, they strengthened his position by making it easy for him to have a series of foreign policy successes through their attitude of indulgence and concessions. This lack of principles, this obvious indifference, with regard to the dictator's frequently repeated distortions of natural and divine law, has been paid for in the most dreadful manner by the Western powers. The dictator recognizes no limits based on legality or religious morality. His adversaries, who do not know this, or prefer not to know it, are not making proper preparations: they are not putting fully in place the necessary means for their defense; on the political as well as on the military level, they are still content with half-measures and will someday end up being overthrown by the dictator. It happened that way in *domestic* policy, and now it is happening in foreign policy, and all that in spite of the bitter experiences of the last few years. People have been too polite with this unscrupulous dictator, instead of treating him as he ought to have been treated; if they had been *sufficiently* reasonable to get rid of him entirely and at the right moment, that would have been decisive. As I said, the same thing is now happening in G[ermany's] foreign policy that happened earlier in its domestic policy. This is all the more inexcusable because everyone could have gradually understood the goals the dictator was pursuing and the methods he was employing. In short, now we find ourselves in the situation described in the exercise manuals: the old *vexilla Luciferi*[46] has been run up the flagpole. In addition, ours is the defeat of those who, confronting such a banner, resort to half-measures. I remember that in Paris, concerning the document, you said that we should also strongly stress the role of the devil. Time has only accentuated the sound basis for your words. Perhaps that is the true misfortune of statesmen who have become indifferent or blind to attacks on the divine moral order, or at least on natural law in everyday life, to the point of no longer perceiving in time, no longer recognizing, the power of God's adversary, the devil, and as a result being incapable of correctly evaluating what a warrior possessed by the devil is capable of undertaking with modern technology and organization. In fact, what he achieves is astonishing, almost inhuman. My sole consolation is the thought that the fall of Lucifer into the abyss is ineluctable, if it pleases God to deliver the people of Europe from this deserved punishment.

The Holy Father thus finds himself in a difficult situation. His three telegrams are well-known; they were good and beneficent. But now the sempiternal opportunists and idolaters of success are back, and they are exhorting him to remain silent. Here come those who, never learning anything, say: the dictator, after having imposed a victorious peace, will reign with good will and wisdom, and will come to terms with the Church. These eternal stupidities have already done so much damage and caused so much confusion among Catholics in all countries! Everything we know concretely about the dictator's intentions points to the contrary: *he wants to destroy Christianity and the Church, or at least to let them die out!* All the same, the Holy Father has to reckon with the possibility that the dictator will win, for millions and millions of Catholics live in this future empire, in G[ermany] itself, in Czech territory, in Poland, in Austria, in Switzerland [?], in Belgium, in Holland, and also in Denmark and Norway, not to mention the flourishing missions in the Congo.

One more thing: in April, Mr. Fischer had me informed that I could prepare a document on and against Collectivism, on the occasion of the fiftieth anniversary of *Rerum Novarum*. This is confidential! Our work in Paris might thus regain its honor!

I commend myself to your prayers so that the spirit of Divine

Providence might sustain me and keep me from ever falling into the terrible adoration of success.

In this spirit, I remain your always grateful brother, G.[47]

With this letter, we end the publication of the original documents put at our disposition, in microfilm, by Thomas Breslin— with the exception, of course, of the complete text of *Humani Generis Unitas*, which will be found at the end of this book.

At this point, we must step back and inquire into the imprecisions and gaps in this documentation, and on the meaning of the narrative that it has allowed us to construct.

A Few Supplementary Documents Concerning *Humani Generis Unitas*

The documents published in the preceding chapters raise numerous questions relating not only to the commissioning, drafting, content, and ultimate fate of *Humani Generis Unitas*, but also to the context—the context of the 1930s, certainly, but perhaps also, more broadly, the context of the "modernist crisis" in the Catholic Church, which began toward the end of the nineteenth century.

Thus, if we go back to the procedure followed in the writing of *Quadragesimo Anno* and of *Divini Redemptoris*, which was discussed at the beginning of chapter 3, or in the writing of *Mit Brennender Sorge*, which will be discussed a little farther on, it appears that in the case of *Humani Generis Unitas*, Pius XI took many liberties with Roman customs. Not only because he entrusted such a project to LaFarge, a "simple pilgrim passing through," who moreover lacked the required legitimacy, but also because by acting impulsively, as if in the grip of a feeling of urgency, he short-circuited the Jesuit hierarchy—Ledochowski was informed only after the fact. What were the pope's reasons for acting in this way?

Moreover, what precisely did he commission? "The pope," LaFarge wrote, "enjoined upon me to write the text of an

encyclical for the universal Church, on the topic which he considered is most burning at the present time. [. . .]" According to
LaFarge, Pius XI told him in French, "Say simply what you
would say if you yourself were pope [. . .]." "He then outlined
the topic, its method of treatment, and discussed the underlying
principles." This doesn't tell us very much.

In addition, did the preparatory documents that were transmitted to the pope meet his expectations? Was it solely because
he quickly fell ill and died that Pius XI did not publish this encyclical? Isn't it possible to imagine that he found the project that
was submitted to him inadequate or inappropriate?

Let us return to the superior general of the Jesuits. In his letters
to LaFarge, quoted in chapter 4, Gundlach casts grave suspicions
of "sabotage" on Ledochowski and suggests the following scenario: Obsessed by the communist danger and hoping, against
all the evidence, that the Church and the German government
would ultimately find a modus vivendi, Ledochowski could not
look with favor upon an encyclical that would have been more
severe with regard to Nazism than *Mit Brennender Sorge* had been
(discussed later in this chapter). Pius XI, who was aware of the
opinions of the general of the Jesuits, would thus have been seeking some writer who did not share Ledochowski's views—didn't
he describe LaFarge's presence in Rome as "providential"? Since
Pius XI's decision to act alone deprived him of all control over
the choice of writers and thus over the content of the document
to be prepared, Ledochowski then gradually deterred the progress
of the project, drawing it out, especially by asking Father Rosa
to offer an expert judgment on the preparatory documents. Finally, ordered to transmit these documents to the pope after
LaFarge, acting on Gundlach's advice, had written directly to the
pontiff, Ledochowski had to obey. But he had gained enough
time, and death, by striking down Pius XI, put the final, victorious seal on his tactic of bureaucratic delay. This scenario, which

has the merit of offering a coherent explanation, presupposes a genuine autonomy of the Jesuit hierarchy within the institution of the Vatican, and the existence of deep political differences between Pius XI and Ledochowski. In this respect, it is worth noting that Gundlach's letters stress Ledochowski's anti-communist obsession, his concern above all to preserve the concordat peace agreement, and his tactical opportunism, lacking any line of conduct "based on fundamental principles and especially on natural law," but make only brief allusions to the "Jewish question" and the attitude to be adopted with respect to state anti-Semitism in Italy as well as in Germany. In any case, if this scenario is coherent, is it also in agreement with reality?

Finally, is it plausible that Cardinal Pacelli was completely ignorant of this project, as Gundlach also claims? If we answer that question in the negative, why, when he became Pius XII, didn't he carry through to completion the project so close to his predecessor's heart?

If we now turn our attention from the circumstances to the content of *Humani Generis Unitas*, how can we evaluate it without comparing it to many other documents: encyclicals published by Pius XI and Pius XII; doctrinal teachings of the Church and numerous positions taken within the Catholic world of that time, regarding questions such as the Catholic critique of the modern world, of secularism, of statism, of nationalism, of liberalism, of socialism; Leo XIII's, Benedict XV's, and Pius XI's social doctrines; Catholic Action movements, and so on?

A vast field of investigation thus opens up before us, which we cannot hope to explore in its entirety. And that would remain true even if we were to limit ourselves to the subject that from the outset has been the central focus of our interest: the attitude of the Catholic world with regard to Jews and anti-Semitism on the eve of the Second World War.

In this last chapter, nevertheless, we will attempt to understand the evolution of Pius XI's thought and attitude with regard to racism and anti-Semitism over the last two years of his life. We will do this by examining various statements published in the press at the time, which are generally known to specialists, and which we will relate on one hand to the events that probably elicited them, and on the other, to the content of *Humani Generis Unitas*. Since this examination can be no more than a necessarily limited determination of the main points, we will undertake an exhaustive and systematic study of the same questions.

We shall begin with two documents that are frequently mentioned and indeed quoted in part, but usually in a vague manner, or even in a way that misrepresents them: first, the Holy Office's decree of 25 March 1928, ordering the suppression of Opus sacerdotale Amici Israel; second, the encyclical *Mit Brennender Sorge* of 14 March 1937.

The Suppression of the Friends of Israel

On 25 March 1928, after having obtained the approval of Pius XI, the Holy Office decreed the suppression of Opus sacerdotale Amici Israel, the sacerdotale association of the Friends of Israel. Since then, many authors have cited this decree, which asserts that the Church has always condemned "in the highest degree hatred against the people formerly chosen by God, the hatred that is commonly designated today under the name of 'anti-Semitism.' " This is the case, moreover, in Gustav Gundlach's 1930 article entitled "Antisemitismus," and in paragraph 144 of the draft of *Humani Generis Unitas*. This way of using the text nevertheless does not explain why the Friends of Israel Association, alone among those devoted to the conversion of the Jews,[1] found no favor in the eyes of the Holy Office and the pope. Let us therefore briefly return to this question.

The Friends of Israel Association appeared in 1925 and was

definitively founded on 24 February 1926.[2] Its principal founder, Father Anton Van Asseldonck, had received the support of Cardinal Van Rossum, the prefect of the Holy Congregation for Propaganda. The association, whose program was set forth in various pamphlets written in Latin,[3] was addressed to priests and, without requiring any financial contribution, asked them to affiliate themselves in writing, to offer a daily prayer for the conversion of the Jews, to enlighten Catholics about Israel through their sermons and writings, with a view to combating hostile prejudices, and to show good will to Jews as well as a sincere apostolic zeal. By the end of 1927, nineteen cardinals, 278 archbishops or bishops, and 3,000 priests were cited as having joined the association. Such a demonstration of sympathy was supposed to be a peremptory argument for showing Jews how much the true Catholic spirit was opposed to anti-Semitism. Nonetheless, on 25 March 1928, the Holy Office decreed the suppression of the association:

The nature and goal of the association called "Friends of Israel" having been submitted to the judgment of the Congregation of the Holy Office, together with a pamphlet entitled *Pax super Israel*, published not long ago by the directors and widely distributed the better to make its characteristics and methods understood, the Most Eminent Fathers responsible for protecting faith and morals first of all recognized the praiseworthy aspect of this association, which is to exhort the faithful to pray to God and to work for the conversion of the Israelites to the kingdom of Christ. It is not surprising that since this association had at first only this single goal in view, not only many of the faithful and priests, but also a significant number of bishops joined it.

The Catholic Church, in fact, has always been accustomed to pray for the Jewish people, which was the depository of divine promises up until Jesus Christ, in spite of the continual blindness of this people, and indeed precisely because of this blindness. With what charity the Apostolic See has protected this people against unjust persecutions!

Because it disapproves of all hatreds and animosities among peoples, it condemns in the highest degree hatred against the people formerly chosen by God, the hatred that is commonly designated today under the name of "anti-Semitism."

Nonetheless, noting and considering that this association of the "Friends of Israel" has subsequently adopted a manner of acting and thinking that is contrary to the sense and spirit of the Church, to the thought of the Holy Fathers and the liturgy, the Most Eminent Fathers, after having received the votes of the Consultants of the Plenary Assembly of 21 March 1926, have decided that the association of the "Friends of Israel" should be suppressed.

They have declared it abolished *de facto*, and have prescribed that no one, in the future, may be permitted to write or publish books or pamphlets that in any way promote such erroneous initiatives.

The following Thursday, the 22nd of the same month and the same year, in an audience accorded the Assessor of the Holy Office, the Very Holy Father Pius XI, pope by Divine Providence, approved the decision of the Very Eminent Fathers and ordered its publication.

Issued in Rome, in the palace of the Holy Office, 25 March 1928.[4]

What had happened? Although it informs the reader that "the association [. . .] subsequently adopted a manner of acting and thinking that is contrary to the sense and spirit of the Church, to the thought of the Holy Fathers and the liturgy," this decree nevertheless does not explain this accusation in detail. We are therefore obliged to resort to the commentaries published soon afterward in serious and well-informed periodicals. For example, one in the *Nouvelle Revue théologique*, signed by Father Jean Levie, S.J., began by mentioning the "essential part" of the association's program, explaining that the latter was "clearly praiseworthy" and "included nothing that was not in absolute conformity with the Catholic ideal":

"One should, according to the [association's] program, avoid speaking 1) about the *deicidal* people; 2) about the *deicidal* city; 3) about the *conversion of the Jews;* one should rather say: *return,* or *passage;* 4) about the *inconvertibility* of the Jews; 5) about the incredible things said of Jews, and especially 'ritual crime'; 6) avoid speaking disrespectfully of their ceremonies; 7) in a way that exaggerates or generalizes a particular case; 8) in anti-Semitic terms.

"Rather, on the basis of the Scriptures, one should stress: 1) a prerogative of Divine Love toward the people of Israel; 2) the sublime sign of this love constituted by the incarnation of Christ and His mission; 3) the permanence of this love; and even its increase because of the fact of Christ's death; and 4) the testimony to, the proof of this love, in the conduct of the Apostles."

But next the commentator challenged the "manner of speaking" adopted by the promoters of the association: "Although it is praiseworthy to recommend truth and justice toward the Jews (5 to 8), never to doubt God's grace (4), is it legitimate to conceal the role played by Israel with regard to Christ (1, 2)? No one wants to make 'deicide' a sort of 'original sin' borne by every Jew today, but one cannot remain silent about Israel's unfaithfulness to its mission, [...] its participation in Christ's death [...]. It would be still more regrettable, when speaking of Jews, systematically to omit the word 'conversion,' if we think of the Divine punishments of the destruction of Jerusalem, during the long centuries of disbelief."

Father Levie also attacked another paragraph in the Friends of Israel pamphlet that was probably a target of the decree: "There followed, on the basis of the Fathers' books and discussions 'opposing the Jews,' a certain mutual hardening and distancing of hearts. It would be of no use to anyone to dilate on this story." Father Levie thought that "Such a sentence seems to assume a general denunciation of the Fathers' attitude toward the Jews."

Finally, Father Levie stressed what seemed to him to be an "error in method" in the "tactics" proposed by the Friends of Israel: "Isn't it as excessive as well as inexact to praise Judaism so much that one seems to attribute to the *Jewish race* today a place of honor within contemporary Christianity, a place reserved for it and remaining vacant until its arrival? [. . . That is] an error in method. Certainly we must show the Jews that their race is not the object of any kind of scorn, any kind of prejudice on our part, but to make conversions easier is it necessary to magnify the race as such, and to create in that way in the future, among converts, a sort of sullen and proud 'separatism,' which would be a possible source of disappointment and perhaps of backsliding? In order to enter with one's whole heart into the 'Catholicism' of the Church, one has to have a breadth of spirit that is scarcely promoted by voluntary exclusivisms of race or religious confession. If one wants to foster conversions, one should not strengthen among Jews, who are already so fiercely nationalistic, an anti-Catholic mentality whose omissions and deficiencies were admirably pointed out by St. Paul" [e.g., Romans 9–10].

All this suggests that the Friends of Israel Association was really suppressed because it was accused of challenging, within the Church itself, an interpretation of tradition, a manner of speaking and prejudices that could only add to the scorn and hatred for Jews professed among groups that were not always associated with Christianity.

Nonetheless, in 1928 the Holy Office had indeed expressed "one of the most explicit condemnations of anti-Semitism that Rome has pronounced up to this time."[5] This was not to be the case with the encyclical *Mit Brennender Sorge* in 1937.

Rereading Mit Brennender Sorge[6]

In 1937 Pius XI promulgated two encyclicals in quick succession, *Mit Brennender Sorge* on 14 March and *Divini Redemptoris* on 19 March. These encyclicals condemned in the same breath Nazi neo-paganism and atheistic communism. We have already discussed *Divini Redemptoris* in chapter 3. As for *Mit Brennender Sorge*, which is commonly presented as Pius XI's solemn protest against Nazism—but sometimes it is also said to be a protest against anti-Semitism—we will limit our aim here to outlining its actual scope and giving the reader the basis for making a comparison with the draft of *Humani Generis Unitas*.

Mit Brennender Sorge came after four years of retreats, tactical concessions, and strategic compromises in relation to Nazi power, made by both the Church in Germany and the Vatican itself.[7] In an always measured tone, the encyclical indirectly addresses to the "other contracting party," namely, the German government, in the 1933 concordat complaints regarding the alarming situation of Catholicism in Germany. Consider for a moment what these involved: wholesale sackings and arrests of Catholic officials, the liquidation of the Catholic schools, the dissolution of social organizations and youth movements, the arrest of priests, an assault on religious orders made by ordering prosecution for alleged trafficking in currency or for sexual perversions, the setting up of a German national church, the invasion of a neo-pagan and racist ideology, etc. But the list could have been much longer had Rome also taken an interest in other categories of victims: for example, the dissolution of all political parties, among them the great Catholic Center Party,[8] the opening of the concentration camps; anti-Semitic propaganda and legislation,[9] etc. In the course of the preceding years, the Holy See had not failed to send the German authorities numerous protest notes. Nevertheless, Cardinal Pacelli's moderating influence had up to that point kept the pope from expressing himself publicly.

It was, however, under the personal direction of Cardinal Pacelli that the text of this new encyclical was prepared.[10] Brought secretly into Germany, secretly printed and within a few days distributed by messengers to the clergy of the whole country, it was read in the pulpit on 21 March, Palm Sunday, in all the Catholic churches of the Reich.[11]

"It is with ardent concern[12] and growing amazement," Pius XI began, addressing his "Venerable Brothers" of the German episcopacy, "that We are following with Our eyes the painful travails of the Church and the increasingly grave persecutions suffered by the men and women whose hearts and conduct remain faithful to her[13]...." But the expression of the initial concern quickly gave way to another concern, explicitly formulated as early as the second paragraph:

> The frankness that is required by our Apostolic office, which is so full of responsibilities, and the decision to lay reality in all its gravity before your eyes and the eyes of the whole Christian universe oblige Us to add: Nothing causes Our Pastoral heart greater sorrow or more bitter pain than learning that many people are abandoning the path of truth.[14]

These are in fact the two principal axes on which *Mit Brennender Sorge* turns: on one hand, protest against "a position that seeks through the overt or covert use of force to stifle the right guaranteed by the treaties"[15] protecting against "plots which from the outset sought only a war of extermination [waged] by every means against Christ and his Church";[16] on the other hand, a warning to all those who "are going astray along the paths of error and unfaithfulness," particularly by "adapting themselves to the mentality of their new surroundings, [having] for the paternal home they have abandoned and for the Father himself only defiant, ungrateful, and even insulting words [. . .]."[17]

In the first part of the encyclical, the pope reaffirms, in a tone that often approaches admonishment, the importance of the articles of faith with which Nazi ideology was competing in the conscience of the faithful. Faith in God, first of all, which is irreconcilable with the deification of the values of the human community:

> Take care above all, Venerable Brothers, that faith in God, the first and irreplaceable foundation of religion, is preserved in Germany, pure and without falsification. No one truly believes in God who [. . .] identifies, through a pantheistic confusion, God with the universe [. . . who,] in accord with a so-called conception of the ancient Germans who lived before Christ, puts a somber and impersonal destiny in the place of the personal God, [. . . who] takes race, or the people, or the State, or the form of the State, or those holding power, or any other fundamental value of the human community [. . .] and deifies it through idolatrous worship [. . .].
>
> Take care, Venerable Brothers [. . .] Act on your faithful, so that they may be vigilant in responding to such an aberration with the rejection it deserves, [. . . see to it] that pernicious errors of this sort, which are usually followed by still more pernicious practices, do not gain a foothold among the faithful, [. . .] so that God's commandments may be considered and observed, as being the obligatory foundation of all morally ordered private and public life [. . .].[18]

Second, faith in Christ, which is irreconcilable with the deification of a leader:

> [. . .] No other name has ever been given by men to the one by whom they may be saved than the name of Jesus. No man, even if all the knowledge, power, and external strength of the world were

incarnate in him, can lay any foundation other than the one that has already been laid: Christ. Anyone who, in a sacrilegious misunderstanding of the essential differences between God and creature, between the Man-God and the children of men, dares to raise up a mortal, even were he the greatest of all time, alongside Christ, or even over or against Him, would deserve to be told that he is a prophet of nothingness, to whom apply the dreadful words of the Scripture: He who resides in heaven cares nothing for them.[19]

Third, faith in the Church one and indivisible:

The Church founded by the Redeemer is one, the same for all peoples and all nations. Under its cupola, which, like the firmament, covers the whole earth, there is a homeland for all peoples and all languages, there is room for the development of all the particular qualities, of all the advantages, of all the tasks and vocations granted by the creating and saving God to both individuals and ethnic communities. [. . .] Anyone who disrupts this unity and this indivisibility steals from the Bride of Christ one of the diadems with which God himself has crowned Her. He subjects its divine structure, which rests on eternal foundations, to the criticism and modifications of architects whom the Heavenly Father has not authorized to build.[20]

Finally, faith in the primacy of the Bishop of Rome, which is irreconcilable, in particular, with the goal of building a German national church:

[. . .] In the Church and the Church alone, authority has received the promise that it would be guided by the Holy Spirit and enjoy his invincible assistance. If men who are not even united by their faith in Christ come to present to you the seductive image of a German national church, know that this is nothing other than a renunciation of the one true Church of Christ, a clear betrayal of the mission of universal evangelizing for which only a worldwide Church can suffice and adapt itself.[21]

A long discussion of the foundations of positive law then opens the second part of the encyclical. We quote it in its entirety because it seems to us important for the assessment of other statements we will quote later:

> It is in accord with the commandments of natural law that all positive law, no matter what legislator it proceeds from, can be assessed with regard to its moral content, and for that very reason, with regard to the authority that it has over conscience. Human laws that are insolubly contradictory to natural law are marked by an original vice that no constraint, no external display of power can cure. It is in the light of this principle that we must judge the axiom: "Law is what is useful to the people." One may, to be sure, give this axiom a correct meaning, if one makes it say that what is morally forbidden can never serve the true interests of the people. However, ancient paganism already recognized that this axiom, in order to be fully correct, had in reality to be turned around and put this way: "It is impossible for anything to be useful if it is not at the same time morally good. And it is not because it is useful that it is morally good, but rather it is because it is morally good that it is useful." Freed from this moral rule, this principle would mean, in international life, a permanent state of war among the different nations.
>
> In national life, it misunderstands, by amalgamating the considerations of law and utility, the fundamental fact that man, as a person, possesses rights that he holds from God and which must remain, with regard to the collectivity, beyond the reach of anything that would tend to deny them, to abolish them, or to neglect them. To disregard this truth is to forget that the true general good is determined and recognized, in the final analysis, by the nature of man, which harmoniously balances personal rights and social obligations, and by the

goal of society, which is also determined by this same human nature
[. . .]. The believer has an inalienable right to profess his faith and
to live it as it is intended to be lived. Laws that stifle or make difficult
the profession and practice of this faith are in contradiction with
natural law. Conscientious parents, who are aware of their duties as
educators, have a primordial right to direct the upbringing of the
children God has given them in the spirit of their faith, in accord
with its principles and prescriptions [. . .]. The Church, whose mission makes it responsible for preserving and explaining natural law,
which is divine in its origin, cannot avoid declaring the most recent
enrollments in the schools, which were made in the notorious absence of all freedom, to be a result of force, which totally lacks the
characteristics of law.[22]

Let us recall that at practically the same moment, in the United
States, John LaFarge was writing in *Interracial Justice* very similar
paragraphs on the relation between natural law and positive law.
This conception, which is deeply anchored in Christian tradition
since St. Augustine—and beyond that, in the whole of Western
legal thought—is obviously found in *Humani Generis Unitas*
as well.

In two other passages in *Mit Brennender Sorge*, the pope once
again stresses the rights of Catholic teaching and youth movements, major preoccupations all during his pontificate. The rights
of the youth, first:

If the State founds a national youth movement, this obligatory organization must be open to all, and then—without abridging the
rights of religious associations—it is for the young people themselves,
and for the parents responsible for them to God, an incontestable
and inalienable right to require that this State organization be purged
of all manifestations of a spirit opposed to Christianity and the
Church, manifestations which, very recently and still today, confront

the consciences of Christian parents with an insoluble dilemma, since they cannot give to the State what it demands except by taking away from God what belongs to God. [...] What We are protesting, and what We must protest, is the voluntarily and systematically provoked antagonism between the concerns of national education and those of religious duty [...]. Anyone who sings the hymn of fidelity to the earthly fatherland must not, through infidelity to his God, to his Church, become a deserter and a traitor to his celestial fatherland.[23]

Then the rights and duties of Catholic parents:

The rights and duties as educators conferred by God [on Catholic parents] are precisely at the present time at stake in a struggle such that one could hardly imagine another with more serious consequences. The Church cannot wait until altars have been overthrown and sacrilegious hands have destroyed the temples before beginning to cry out and protest. If someone tries, through an education opposed to Christ, to profane the tabernacle that is the soul of the child consecrated by baptism [...] then it is the duty of anyone who believes in Christ to clearly disengage his responsibility from that of the adverse camp, to free his conscience from all guilty cooperation with such machination and corruption [...].

The merely formal preservation of religious teaching—a teaching moreover controlled and hobbled by men with no mandate—within the framework of a school which, in other domains of education, works systematically and maliciously against that religion, is not enough to provide a faithful believer in Christ with a legitimate excuse for lending his complacent support to such a school intent on destroying religion [...].[24]

This exhortation to resist pressures is broadened to all believers, and in particular to "certain classes of Catholic officials":

In your countries, Venerable Brothers, voices are resounding whose chorus grows increasingly louder, encouraging people to leave the Church [... and] seeking to create the impression that leaving the Church and the infidelity that it involves toward Christ the King constitute a particularly convincing and meritorious proof of fidelity to the current government. Through hidden or apparent measures of constraint, through intimidation, through the prospect of economic, professional, civic, and other disadvantages, the attachment of Catholics to their faith, and in particular the fidelity of certain classes of Catholic officials, is subjected to a pressure that is as contrary to law as it is to human dignity. All Our paternal indulgence and Our deepest compassion go out to those who must pay so dearly for their fidelity to Christ and to the Church; but from the moment when the most supreme and elevated interests are at stake, when it is a question of saving oneself or being lost, the believer has before him only one path to salvation, that of heroic courage [...] even at the price of the greatest earthly sacrifices [...].[25]

Finally, from priests and monks, Pius XI expects an "intelligent and sympathetic charity toward those who have gone astray, even toward those who insult you." But that cannot mean "any sort of renunciation of speaking out, of protesting, of courageously defending the truth and its straightforward application to the reality that surrounds you. The first gift of love made by the priest to those around him, the one that is most obviously required, is the one that consists in serving the truth, the whole truth, in uncovering and refuting error in any form, no matter how it is masked or disguised. A failure on this point would not only be a betrayal of God and of your holy vocation, but also a crime against the true interest of your people and your country."[26]

In short, *Mit Brennender Sorge* was neither a condemnation of Nazism as a whole nor the expression of solidarity with all of its victims; according to Guenter Lewy, this encyclical "only emphasized the outrageous points in Nazi doctrine in order to condemn them in a manner that did not entail the condemnation of political and social totalitarianism."[27] Neither was it a protest against anti-Semitism and the persecution of the Jews in Germany, which the text does not mention at all. But in this regard we must quote, in order to be comprehensive, the passage that denounces those who wish to ban "Biblical history and the wisdom of the teachings of the Old Testament from the Church and from the schools" in order to attack Christianity and its religious foundations:

In Jesus Christ, the Son of God made man, appeared the fullness of divine Revelation. In many ways and on many occasions God spoke to our forefathers through the prophets. When that time was completed, he spoke to us through his Son. The sacred books of the Old Testament are entirely the Word of God and form a substantial part of His Revelation. In harmony with the gradual development of Revelation, a still-veiled light plays over them, the light of the times that prepared for the full splendor of the Redemption. As it could not have been otherwise in the historical and didactic books, they reflect, in more than one detail, human imperfection, weakness, and sin. Along with countless marks of grandeur and nobility, they also describe the chosen people, the bearer of the Revelation and the Promise, as constantly straying far away from its God in order to turn toward the world. For eyes that are not blinded by prejudice or by passion, there nevertheless shines forth all the more luminously, in this human corruption, as it is recounted in Biblical history, the divine light of the plan of salvation that finally triumphs over all faults and all sins. It is precisely against this often obscure background that the most striking perspectives of the Eternal's pedagogy of salvation emerge, alternately warning, admonishing, smiting, raising up and beatifying His elect. Only blindness and pride can close our eyes to the treasures of saving teaching that the Old Testament contains.

Anyone who wants to see Biblical history and the wisdom of the teachings of the Old Testament banished from the Church and the schools blasphemes against the Almighty's plan of salvation, raises up a narrow and limited human thought and judges Divine designs on the history of the world. He renounces faith in the true Christ, as he appeared in the flesh, in the Christ who received his human nature from a people who were to crucify him. He remains without understanding anything before the universal drama of the Son of God, who opposed to the sacrilege of his tormentors the divine sacerdotal action of his redeeming death, thus giving in the new covenant, the accomplishment, end, and crown of the old one.[28]

Far from explicitly condemning anti-Semitism, or even offering an expression of compassion toward the Jews persecuted in Germany, almost two years after the adoption of the Nuremberg racial laws, this passage refers, on the contrary, to the infidelity of the "chosen people [...] constantly straying far away from their God," and "who were to crucify" Christ. From this point of view, we have to conclude that *Mit Brennender Sorge* represents a step backward with respect to the decree issued in 1928 by the Holy Office. And this occurred in a context that made such a condemnation more urgent than it was in 1928.

One year after the promulgation of this encyclical, Nazi racism was about to gain ground in Italy and to challenge the pope at the very portals of the Vatican. Would Pius XI then make up for the deficiencies of *Mit Brennender Sorge*?

Confronting Racism (Summer 1938)

On 2 May 1938, the very day on which John LaFarge disembarked at Plymouth, Hitler was beginning a weeklong official visit to the Italian capital. In Italy, this visit was to mark a decisive turn toward making racism officially part of state ideology, and toward the promulgation, in the course of the following fall and winter, of anti-Semitic legislation. This context strongly affected the writing of *Humani Generis Unitas*; the text reflects it in more than one passage and the correspondence we have cited in the preceding chapters refers to it repeatedly. But this element of the context takes on its full meaning only if it is combined with a fact of at least equal importance for our subject, namely the Holy See's exasperation with regard to the repeated violations of the concordat with Italy, which went back to 1929.

An article by Father Yves de La Brière, S.J., which appeared in *Études* on the occasion of the tenth anniversary of this concordat,[29] characterizes this period of Vatican-Italian relations as follows: On 11 February 1929, in the Apostolic Lateran Palace, the Italian government and the Vatican had signed a diplomatic treaty and a politico-religious concordat. The former led to the birth of a small, independent pontifical State, the Vatican City; the second settled the public legal status of Catholic institutions in Italy "in a manner fully consonant with the canon law of the Church."[30] After a half-century of tense confrontation between religious and secular power in Italy, the time for *conciliazione* seemed to have come. Father de La Brière draws up a lukewarm balance sheet of the Italian concordat's achievements ten years later. On the plus side, he lists respect for the international status of the Vatican City and "the observance of the whole administrative part of the Italian Concordat: the legal status of the dioceses, parishes, communities, educational establishments, ecclesiastical and congregational patrimony." On the minus side, he lists an increasing contentiousness in a domain "whose practical importance was considerable: that of Catholic Action and youth organizations. The *totalitarian* tendency of the regime made it difficult for it to accept the free existence of a whole set of institutions that exercised over their own members a significant moral and psychological influence in a zone of activity where the regime wanted to increase its sovereign grip on the people, on the elite, on the youth, on the national soul."

To counter this tendency, on 29 June 1931 Pius XI had promulgated the encyclical *Non Abbiamo Bisogno*, "against the *totalitarian* conception of law and the role of the State. A conception propagated by fascism, but which it did not itself invent, and which it shares not only with Nazism [which had not yet seized power in Germany], but also with Bolshevism, Jacobinism, and all other *statolatrous* ideologies."

There followed, on 3 September 1931, an "amicable arrangement with the Holy See to interpret article 43 of the Lateran Concordat and to clarify the legal status of the Italian organs of Catholic Action."

But in 1938 a new complication arose:

The policy of the Rome–Berlin Axis had caused German racist propaganda to move south of the Brenner pass, and it had led to the adoption in Italy, as an official doctrine, of a somewhat mitigated interpretation of the racial ideology of Hitler's Germany.

One can guess how the attitude to be taken toward the new State doctrine raised anew the problem of Catholic Action and the role of Catholic youth organizations. What a novel pretext for Garibaldian anticlerical zealots to arouse scurrilous disputes, accusations of anti-patriotism, crude demonstrations on the part of the populace [...].

The racial question is moreover complicated by the question of anti-Semitism and by the unprecedented penetration of *Aryan* [or anti-Judaic] requirements in the fascist legislation of the current kingdom of Italy [...].[31]

Let us remember that in 1931 Pius XI had already devoted an encyclical to criticizing "statolatrous ideologies"—one of the major themes of the first part of *Humani Generis Unitas*. We note, with Yves de La Brière, that the establishment of a form of state racism in Italy interfered with the concordat arrangements of 1929, and thus constituted a situation with regard to which the Vatican could not remain indifferent. In order to examine this new legal issue more closely, we again take up the thread of events starting with Hitler's official visit to Rome between 2 May and 9 May 1938.

"While the Führer was making his entrance into Rome, which the pope had just left,"[32] one reads in *La Croix* for 6 May, it was learned that an important document of the Holy See against racism was going to be published."[33] In fact, on 3 May there appeared on the first page of the *Osservatore romano* a letter sent by the Sacred Congregation of Seminaries and Universities, whose prefect was Pius XI himself. Dated 13 April, this letter was addressed to the rectors of all Catholic universities throughout the world. Here is the text in its entirety:

> Your Eminence, last year, on eve of the nativity of Our Lord, the august Pontiff, felicitously reigning, in his address to the eminent cardinals and the prelates of the Roman Curia, spoke with sadness about the grave persecution that is raging, as everyone knows, against the Catholic Church in Germany.
>
> But the Holy Father's principal source of distress is the fact that, in order to carry out such a great injustice, the most impudent calumnies have been invoked, and the most pernicious doctrines have been spread all about, falsely presented as scientific, with the goal of perverting minds and drawing them away from true religion.
>
> Confronted by this situation, the Sacred Congregation of Studies urges other universities and Catholic faculties to make use of biology, history, philosophy, apologetics, legal and moral studies as weapons for refuting firmly and competently the following untenable assertions:
>
> 1. Human races, by their natural and immutable characters, are so

different that the humblest among them is farther from the most elevated than from the highest animal species.

2. It is necessary, by all means, to preserve and cultivate the vigor of the race and the purity of the blood; anything that leads to this result is, by that very fact, proper and permissible.

3. It is from the blood, the seat of the race's character, that all man's intellectual and moral qualities derive, as from their principal source.

4. The essential goal of education is to develop the characteristics of the race and to ignite in minds an ardent love for their own race as the supreme good.

5. Religion is subject to the law of race and must be adapted to it.

6. The primary source and supreme rule of all legal order is racial instinct.

7. There exists only the Cosmos, or the Universe, which is a living being; all things, including man, are only diverse forms of the universal living being, growing through the course of the ages.

8. Each man exists only through the State and for the State. Everything he possesses by right proceeds solely from a concession by the State.

One might, moreover, easily add others to these detestable propositions.

The Most Holy Father, the prefect of our Holy Congregation, is certain, your Eminence, that you will spare no pains in order to bring to their full realization the prescriptions contained in this letter.

In acquitting myself of my duty to inform you of this, I express to you my very respectful sentiments, humbly kissing the sacred purple.

From your most reverend Eminence's very devoted servant in Christ, Ernest Ruffini, secretary.[34]

This letter, in which the French Catholic press immediately saw a "*Syllabus* against racism,"[35] still denounced racism only as an instrument of the "grave persecution [raging] against the Church in Germany," and only insofar as it was competing in people's minds with the "true religion" and participated in a totalitarian conception of the state. The numerous reactions it provoked in the course of the following months, on the part of both Catholic university professors and major ecclesiastical figures, remained generally within the same limits, emphasizing the incompatibility of racism and modern science, morals, natural law, and denouncing its "religious" and political attacks directed principally against Christianity, but without making anti-Semitism the subject of any specific commentary.[36]

Three weeks after Hitler's visit to Rome, an office of the Nazi party's racial police was discreetly set up in Milan to help the Italian fascists write the racial laws that would be promulgated the following fall.[37] This was probably one of the reasons the adoption of legislation under the general rubric "for the defense of the Italian race" was preceded, as in Germany three years earlier, by an intense propaganda campaign. The latter achieved an early peak on 14 July 1938, when Fascist university professors made public, under the auspices of the minister of popular culture, a long *Dichiarazione della Razza*. This text, which is supposed to have been vetted by Mussolini himself, summarizes in ten points Italian Fascism's new position with regard to racial questions. Here are some extracts:

1. Races exist.

    [This is] a phenomenal, material reality perceptible through our senses [. . .].

2. There are great races and small races.

    [Along with] the major systemic groups, which are commonly called races, and which are individualized by only a few characteristics, we must also acknowledge the existence of minor systemic groups (for example, the Nordics, Mediterraneans,

Dinarics, etc.), which are individualized by a larger number of common characteristics. From the biological point of view, these groups constitute the true races, whose existence is an obvious truth.

3. The concept of race is a purely biological concept.

Consequently, it is based on considerations different from the concepts of people and nation, which are founded essentially on historical, linguistic, and religious considerations. Nonetheless, racial differences are found at the bases of the differences between peoples and nations. If Italians are different from Frenchmen, Germans, Turks, Greeks, etc., that is not solely because they have a different language and a different history, but also because the racial constitution of these peoples is different [. . .].

4. The population of contemporary Italy is of Aryan origin and its civilization is Aryan.

This population, which has an Aryan civilization, has inhabited our peninsula for several millennia [. . .]. The origin of contemporary Italians begins essentially from elements of the same races that constitute and have constituted the eternal living tissue of Europe.

5. The notion that there has been a significant influx of people in historical times is a myth.

Since the Lombard invasion, there has not been any further significant movement into Italy of peoples capable of influencing the racial physiognomy of the nation [. . .].

Today's 44 million Italians are descended, in their absolute majority, from families that have inhabited Italy for at least a millennium.

6. Thus there now exists a pure "Italian race."

This assertion [is based] on the very pure heritage of blood uniting contemporary Italians with the generations that have populated Italy for thousands of years [. . .].

7. It is time the Italians openly proclaimed that they are racists.

Everything the Regime has achieved up to now in Italy is ultimately racism [. . .].

The question of racism in Italy must be discussed from a purely
biological point of view, without philosophical or religious
intentions.

The conception of racism in Italy must be essentially Italian, and
its orientation must be Aryano-Nordic. That does not mean,
however, that we should introduce into Italy German theories
of racism just as they are, or claim that Italians and Scandinavians
are the same. We only want to show Italians a physical, and
especially a psychological, model of the human race which,
through its purely European characteristics, distinguishes itself
completely from all European races [. . .].

8. It is necessary to make a sharp distinction between the Medi-
   terraneans of Europe (Occidentals), on the one hand, and the
   Orientals and Africans on the other.

   Hence, there is reason to consider as dangerous the theories that
   argue for the African origin of certain European peoples, and
   that include the Semitic or Hamitic populations within a common Mediterranean race, thus establishing absolutely inadmissible relations and ideological sympathies.

9. Jews do not belong to the Italian race.

   Of the Semites who over the centuries have come onto the
   holy soil of our fatherland, in general nothing has remained.
   Similarly, the Arabic occupation of Sicily left nothing beyond
   the memory of a few names; and in any case the process of
   assimilation was always very rapid in Italy.

   Jews represent the only population that has never been assimilated in Italy, because it is constituted by non-European racial
   elements which differ absolutely from the elements from which
   Italians descend.

10. The purely European physical and psychological characteristics
    of Italians must not be altered in any way.

    Union is admissible only within the circle of European races, in which case one must not speak of true hybridism, properly speaking, in view of the fact that these races belong to a common source and that they differ only in a few characteristics, whereas they are the same in many others.

The purely European character of Italians is altered by crossing with any extra-European race that bears a civilization different from the ancient civilization of the Aryans.[38]

Reproduced by all the Italian dailies on the first page of their editions for 15 July,[39] this *Race Declaration* caused a sensation and unleashed immediate public reactions on the part of the ecclesiastical institution, in Italy as well as abroad. We shall see later that these reactions were, however, not all equally vigorous, and that for the most part they continued to discuss racism in general, even though Jews are explicit targets of the Italian racist *Declaration*.

The pope responded as early as 15 July, during an audience accorded to the general chapter of the Sisters of Our Lady of the Cenacle, in the presence of Cardinal Pacelli and Mgr. Beaussart, the auxiliary bishop of Paris. Let us recall in passing that it was concerning this speech that Father Ledochowski wrote to LaFarge on 17 July: "You have probably noted that in his address to the Ladies of the Cenacle (*Osservatore romano* 17.VII) the Holy Father already alluded to the matter."[40] We quote from the *Osservatore romano*'s account of this address:

The Holy Father wished to make a third remark that might be called a preview of an "unpublished document" [. . .]. It concerns the great question that is currently being debated throughout the world under the name of nationalism exaggerated in every way, nationalism misunderstood, which the Sovereign Pontiff had already had the painful duty of denouncing as erroneous and dangerous [. . .]. This exaggerated nationalism, which presents an obstacle to the saving of souls, which puts up barriers between peoples, which is contrary not only

to the law of God but also to faith itself, to the Credo itself [...].
The words of the Credo are the first words that issued from the
Apostolic College, the first formulas of evangelistic teaching, promulgated by Jesus's words: *Docete omnes gentes.*[41] And these words say:
Credo sanctam catholicam Ecclesiam.[42] But "catholic" means "universal."
There is no other possible translation [...]. Now, the contrast between exaggerated nationalism and Catholic doctrine is evident: the
spirit of this nationalism is contrary to the Credo, it is contrary to
the faith.

The Sovereign Pontiff added that he had never thought about
these things with so much precision, with, one might almost say,
with such absolutism, formulated with such intransigence.

Next the pope mentioned the racist *Declaration* published that
very morning, and added that "this same day, precisely, he had
learned of something very serious: it is henceforth a matter of a
genuine form of apostasy. This is no longer merely one or another
false idea, it is the whole spirit of the doctrine that is contrary to
the faith of Christ.

" 'Credo sanctam catholicam Ecclesiam,' means everything that
signifies the redemption and sanctification of the world, whereas
this other doctrine signifies exactly the opposite."[43]

On 21 July, Pius XI returned to the same themes in an address
delivered to 150 ecclesiastical assistants to the Italian youth movement and Catholic Action. He told them in particular:

[...] Catholic means universal, not racist, nationalist, separatist; no,
catholic. And it is thus that Catholic Action must be, it must be
inspired by this spirit, because there is something one might say is
more and better even than faith: the spirit of the faith; in the same
way, alas, there is something much worse than one or another formula of racism and nationalism: the spirit that dictates them. We
have to say, in fact, that there is something particularly detestable,

and that is this spirit of separatism, of exaggerated nationalism, which, precisely because it is not Christian, because it is not religious, is ultimately not even human [. . .].[44]

On still another occasion, at considerable length, on 28 July, in a speech to two hundred seminarians from the Urban Pontifical College of Propaganda received at Castelgandolfo:

[. . .] The pope has already said and repeated it [. . .]: catholic means universal, not racist, not nationalist, in the separatist sense of these two attributes [. . .]. Catholic Action must be inspired by these two principles: that is indisputable, because Catholic Action means catholic life, and it is precisely for that reason that Catholic Action is like the pupil of the Sovereign Pontiff's eye. [. . .] Catholic Action, like the Catholic Church, is catholic [. . .] that is, universal. [. . .] The world is in a bad way, because too many individuals know nothing about universals.

People forget that the human species, the whole human species, is a single, great, universal human race [. . .]. One must say that men are above all a great and single species, a great and single family of living beings, engendered and engendering. Thus the human species is a single race, universal, "catholic" [. . .]. Within the human species, there exists a single great human race, universal, catholic, a single great and universal human family, with diverse internal variations.

One may therefore wonder how it happens that, unfortunately, Italy needed to imitate Germany. [. . .] Anyone who strikes a blow against Catholic Action strikes a blow against the Church, because he is striking a blow against catholic life. The comparison is consequently easy to make: anyone who strikes Catholic Action strikes the pope. And the pope says then: Be very careful; I advise you not to strike Catholic Action; I urge you not to do it, I beg you not to do it for your own good, because anyone who strikes Catholic

Action strikes the pope, and anyone who strikes the pope dies. *Qui mange du Pape en meurt*.[45] That is true, and history has demonstrated its truth [. . .].

What is the pope doing at the Propaganda college, that is, at the place where there are students from thirty-seven nations? It is very clear: they are all sons of the same mother, of the same family; all cherished and raised at the common table of the same truth and identical goods. Propaganda is the true, just, and healthy practice of a racism that corresponds to human dignity and human reality; for human reality is to be men and not wild beasts, not just any sort of existence; human dignity is to be a single great family, the human species, the human race [. . .]. This is for the Church the true racism, racism properly speaking, healthy racism that is worthy of all men in their great collectivity. All men being in the same way the object of the same maternal affection, all men are called to the same light of truth, of good, of Christian charity; all are called to be in their own country, in the nationality peculiar to each of them, in their particular race, the propagators of this great idea which is magnificently maternal and human even before it is Christian [. . .][46]

Delivered at the very time that Fathers LaFarge, Gundlach, and Desbuquois were working on the encyclical in Paris, these addresses express, in a redundant manner that makes clear their importance to the pope, a theme that will be among the central ideas of *Humani Generis Unitas*: that the universality of Christianity abolishes in both spirit and fact the barriers set between peoples, nations, and races; "Within the human species, there exists a single great human race, universal, catholic . . . with diverse internal variations." But there is still no reference to Jews or anti-Semitism.

These reactions on Pius XI's part were published in the *Osservatore romano*. They also appeared in *La Civiltà cattolica*, which also reproduced on 29 July the complete racial *Declaration* of 14 July, and offered its readers the following commentary:

Anyone aware of German racism's theses, which we have mentioned,[47] will immediately note the remarkable divergence that exists between the latter and the theses that are proposed by the Italian "group of fascist scholars." This further confirms that Italian Fascism does not wish to be confused with Nazism or German racism, which is intrinsically and explicitly materialist and anti-Christian. There is an important point which we cannot and must not minimize or conceal, the one where the "scholars" say that "the question of racism in Italy must be discussed [...] without philosophical or religious intentions," and without "introducing into Italy German theories of racism." But while this is an important point, it is nonetheless negative and does not suffice by itself to eliminate the dangers of the conclusions or acts that too superficial or audacious partisans might deduce from these principles, as commonly happens.

These are theses which, because they hew closely to a known line of thought, conceal the danger that would be involved in following them. That is why they have aroused such legitimate fears on the part of right-thinking people concerned about the future, even though at present these theses do not profess, and even exclude, the error of German racism, with its historical, philosophical, and especially religious aberrations. The terrain is so slippery that this shows through in the document we have published in its entirety. And although it affirms the desire to discuss racism "from a purely biological point of view," it nevertheless speaks of a "physical and especially psychological model of the human race," and disapproves of the "crossing with any extra-European race that bears a civilization different from the ancient civilization of the Aryans." Now, the "psychological" element and the "civilization" that is as it were derived from it move beyond the "purely biological" domain and enter into "philosophical and religious" regions in which the lack of conceptual precision and rigorous terminology gives rise to interpretations and applications which could, ultimately, correspond to German racism, which the authors of the document claim they do not to wish to introduce into Italy. We therefore understand all the seriousness of the words of warning uttered by the Holy Father, which we have cited above.[48]

On one hand, the restrained tone of this commentary contrasts with the passionate tone of Pius XI's remarks to which the commentator refers at the end of his article. But on the other hand, its content contrasts with the anti-Jewish diatribes which had been common in *La Civiltà cattolica* up to that point, diatribes which the Italian Jesuit review had muted starting with the preceding issue, which appeared in mid-July 1938.[49]

La Civiltà cattolica, *Jews, and Anti-Semitism*

It is considered proper, these days, to emphasize that the theological anti-Judaism handed down by Christian tradition since the Patristic period has nothing in common with anti-Semitism. This dissociation generally serves to reduce to the status of simple spasms deriving from an ancient religious quarrel the episodic hostile excesses with regard to Jews that could be imputed to the Church as an institution.

On a theoretical level the distinction is perfectly justified. One is nonetheless led to question its pertinence as soon as one considers the particulars of any given historical situation. Particularly when one is examining the history of *La Civiltà cattolica* up to the Second World War, the boundary seems very fluid between the "average" anti-Semitism of the period, on one hand, and on the other the anti-Judaism constantly manifested by the editors of that review in all the battles in the course of their long-term war against what they considered to be the various political expressions of modernity: liberalism, Garibaldism, republicanism, Freemasonry, socialism, bolshevism, etc. The following are a few examples, limited to the period between the two world wars, which will bring us to Father Enrico Rosa, whose expert opinion on the draft of *Humani Generis Unitas* was requested by the superior general of the Jesuits.

On 12 October 1922, discussing the "worldwide revolution and the Jews," an anonymous writer drew up the following clinical balance sheet of his period:

The world is sick. [. . .] Everywhere peoples are in the grip of inexplicable convulsions [. . .] and the filthy element, as uninterested in work as it is avid for money and unattainable pleasures, seems to be amusing itself in a frenetic and tragic dance of tumults and strikes, waiting to proclaim the communist republic tomorrow, while the politicians, the wise men of the nations, frightened, frantically search for a peace that is no more than a perpetual disillusion. Where are we going? [. . .] Who is leading? [. . .] Who is urging on this rabble of parties, leagues, and lodges, and guides this movement of universal revolution which is turning human society's head from one end of the world to the other? [. . .]

Who? The Synagogue, the author answers, after having "demonstrated" that in Russia, the source of world subversion, and in the communist International, all the levers of power were in the hands of "Jewish intruders."[50]

In the same vein, on 25 September 1936, another anonymous writer formulated the "Jewish question"[51] in the following terms:

Two facts that seem contradictory are both verified through the Jews dispersed in the modern world: their control of money and their preponderance in the socialism and communism [that] constitute a grave and permanent peril for society.

In order to explain this link between finance and revolution, the author espouses the point of view of a French anti-Semitic essayist, Léon de Poncins:[52]

> Socialism is not always an end in itself; it can be a weapon and a means of destruction that promotes the goals of international finance [. . .]. The supreme Judaic ideal seeks to transform the world into a single corporation with equal shares; the whole earth must become the capital of this corporation, which is supposed to make the work of all creatures flourish; then Israel, aided at the outset by a few puppets, is to provide the dictatorial board of directors of this corporation. The quickest method for succeeding is brutal and dictatorial communism. The goal is to substitute for European and American capitalism, which is still limited and relatively fragile, worldwide pan-capitalism as absolute political power. Communism is the shortest path. In fact, Soviet terrorism has erased the past and State pan-capitalism has begun to reconstruct in its own way, with the "five-year plan," on the terrain thus cleared, and this has cost it no more than a few million human lives.

As for solutions, the Jesuit writer asserts that he cannot go all the way with Léon de Poncins, who saw three kinds of solutions—assimilation, Zionism, and the ghetto:

> [. . .] The first would be the best. It is impossible because the Jews have been, are, and will remain Jews [. . .]. Zionism would be a satisfactory solution, but it does not seem a durable one, [particularly] because the Jews, uniquely endowed with the qualities of parasites and destroyers, have neither the aptitude nor a liking for manual labor [. . .]. There remains the third solution: the ghetto, that is, a

special legal status for the Jews. This is the solution Christian nations adopted before the French Revolution [. . .].

This solution is too vague to please the writer, who prefers another one, which had been proposed by Father Joseph Bonsirven, S.J.:[53]

Judaism, considered as a whole, is constantly developing and taking on new strength. It has resisted all efforts to absorb it, and all dissolving factors, and it continues to grow numerically: a unique example in the history of peoples.

This perpetuity, in spite of hostile conditions, shows us that Israel is the eternal people. Must we not see in this perpetuity and constant development the will and secret design of Providence? What does it still want to make of this people that it chose and endowed with its gifts? "The gifts and the call of God are irrevocable." What role in the religious history of the world is meant for it? A mystery.

But here is the other mystery, the supernatural truth announced by St. Paul, a prophecy full of promises: "A hardening has come upon part of Israel, until the full number of the Gentiles come in, and so all Israel will be saved [. . .]. For if their rejection means the reconciliation of the world, what will their acceptance mean but life from the dead?" (Romans 11: 25, 12, 15).

The same theme reappeared, practically in the same terms, in May 1937, in a series of three articles on the "Jewish Question" in relation to Zionism, conversions, and Catholic apostleship.[54] In the first of these articles, the anonymous writer, basing himself especially on "the clear and illuminating exposition of the illustrious English Catholic writer" Hilaire Belloc,[55] asserts at the outset that it is "an obvious fact that the Jews are a disruptive element because of their dominating spirit and their revolutionary tendency. Judaism is [. . .] a foreign body that irritates and provokes the reactions of the organism it has contaminated.

"The whole question consists in finding the most appropriate way of getting rid of the irritation and re-establishing, on a durable basis, the social organism's equilibrium and tranquillity. There are only two possible solutions: elimination or segregation. Elimination can be achieved in three ways: in a clearly hostile manner, through destruction; in a hostile but less cruel manner, through expulsion; in an amicable and kindly manner, through absorption. The first two ways are contrary to Christian charity and natural law. The third has proven impossible, historically. Segregation can be achieved in a hostile or amicable manner. In a hostile manner, without taking the foreign element into account, but considering only the contaminated organism and its interests. This manner is not in accord with charity, and moreover does not eliminate the frictions that provoke the irritation. The amicable solution takes the segregated element fully into account, and seeks to serve the interests of both parties. For the term 'segregation,' which is demeaning (as was the old word 'ghetto'), Belloc wants to substitute that of 'recognition,' in order to signify a civil and charitable arrangement [. . .], considering that this is the only practical and efficacious means of resolving the Jewish question."

This "segregation, or distinction," the same author explained a month later in his third article, has to be "adapted to our time [. . .] and brought about, not through officially decreed legislation, but through the habit of living together, which would then lead to wise legislation arising from experience [. . .]. It is not possible to find a purely political solution, that is, one founded on the temporal interests of this or that particular nation, since the latter inevitably gives rise either to anti-Semitism, which is more or less violent according to the differing interests of each of the nations, or to the disruptive ascendancy of Judaism. There thus remains only the Christian solution, which is founded on two cardinal virtues: charity and prudence.

"Charity, practiced while one is trying to convert by prayer or apostleship in accord with the best-suited modern methods, produces a rapprochement and understanding that opens the way toward a civilized common life among Christians and Jews, and to more numerous conversions. At the same time, prudence tempers these relations, so as to eliminate any danger for Christians, and to head off the two forms of disruptive Jewish dominance: materialistic-financial dominance and revolutionary dominance, without resorting to anti-Semitism. Any form of anti-Semitism is condemned by the Church, and we must recognize that it is not accepted by the majority of civilized nations, which, even if they do not say so explicitly, still preserve many principles of Christian civilization which they have inherited from preceding generations. Politics will be able to bring about a solution—if not a definitive solution, at least a provisional one—to the Jewish question, more quickly, more broadly, and more durably, in the degree to which it is inspired by Christian charity and prudence."[56]

On 24 June 1938, in discussing a book by a "non-Catholic German" refugee in Switzerland, a reviewer reminded readers of "the Jews' continual persecution of Christians, particularly the Catholic Church, and their alliance with Freemasons, socialists, and other anti-Christian groups,"[57]; a perspective that on 8 July—a week before the *Dichiarazione della razza* mentioned above was made public—received special attention in a long study devoted to "the question of the Jews in Hungary." This time it was not a question of proposing a theory of "segregation," but rather of approving its concrete application in a country represented as being "the most solid and indestructible fortress of Christianity." The "supremacy" of Jews had become particularly "disastrous for the religious, moral, and social life of the Hungarian people [because] all Jews, or nearly all, in intellectual and leadership circles are unbelievers, free-thinkers, or revolutionaries, or else freemasons and organizers for freemasonry. Anti-Christian in moral and intellectual life, capitalists in economic life, Jews are socialists or socialists' supporters in social life, maintaining connections with socialist labor unions and their leaders. In short, their rule of life (or rather their practical moral law) is success in the world by any means whatever."

While it is true that the "low birth rate among them (the result of their low level of morality)" makes it possible to hope that their number will diminish considerably over the coming years, "the Jews still remain today the masters of Hungary." The solution? Anti-Semitism, although "the anti-Semitism of Hungarian Catholics [is neither] vulgar and fanatical anti-Semitism, nor racist anti-Semitism; it is a movement defending national traditions, the true freedom and independence of the Magyar people. In the Hungarian program for the social movement proposed by Catholic Action (an organization of 250,000 persons), point IX on the 'solution of the Jewish question in accord with the interests of the Hungarian nation' declares that: 'Jews, who have not thus far accepted the ideal historical conception of the Hungarian nation, do not have the right to influence the country's intellectual life in the press, in literature, or in artistic life; this same principle must be applied against all Hungarians who side with the Jews. We have to break liberalism, which is destructive to our economic life, by way of the corporate system which will subject capitalism to the general interests of the nation. We demand that the government forbid [Jewish] foreigners to enter the country, because we cannot accept new persons at a time when our compatriots have nothing to eat. We demand in addition that all those who entered without permission [Jews having succeeded in entering through illicit favors] be deported, and that officials who helped them break the law be punished.'

"We want, in short, to defend the nation against the current danger of a still greater Jewish invasion coming from Germany, Austria, and Romania, and against the liberalism that is in complicity with Judaism and its disastrous domination, without persecution, but by forceful and effective means.

"Up to this point, the only defensive law was that of the *numerus clausus* passed in 1922, which forbade Jews to enter the university in numbers greater than their 5% of the population.

"Since then, a law has been proposed that introduces the *numerus clausus* into economic life, and another concerning more particularly the press, where Jews may not represent more than 20%, as well as in the liberal professions, banking, industry, commerce, etc.; in short, in the economic, intellectual, and moral life of the nation. In fact, this number is not so small, compared to the 5% of Jews in the population as a whole; but for the moment, we want to proceed gradually, without persecution, while promoting, if possible, a peaceful exodus of the Jews from Hungary, which they have abused, so that Dante's hope might be realized: 'How happy Hungary would be, were it no longer to allow itself to be abused' *(Paradiso* 19:142–43). We will not go into the details of these proposed laws; we note only that they are inspired by the noble Magyar traditions of chivalric and loyal hospitality, and limit themselves to what is strictly necessary, which many people consider insufficient.

"One detail in particular should be noted: the law also considers as Jews those who were baptized after 14 August 1919, with the exception of war veterans. This date makes it possible to call attention to conversions that were not sincere but made out of self-interest (there were about 16,000 at the time of Hungary's national reaction to the Bolshevik revolution and the fall of Belà Kun.[58] This arrangement does not meet with the approval of certain Catholics, because it seems to make difficulties for a good number of sincere conversions; others reply that, on the contrary, it is intended to favor the sincerity of conversions. We do not consider ourselves competent to offer an opinion on this question. The latter cannot be resolved except in conformity with the Christian and chivalric traditions of the nation, which is presently under the government of a man of superior quality, the president of the Ministerial Council, Belà Imredi, a fervent Catholic and a skilled and steady politician."[59]

The articles which we have just quoted did not go unnoticed by the Nazi propagandists of *Der Stürmer*, or by their Italian counterparts of *Il Regime fascista*, who were often able to take advantage of them—not without malice. "We confess that in both planning and execution, fascism is far inferior to the rigor of *La Civiltà cattolica*," *Il Regime fascista* remarked ironically on 30 August 1938. Mentioning, in addition, a study published by *La Civiltà cattolica* in 1890, it observed that "modern states and societies, including the healthiest and most courageous nations in Europe, Italy and Germany, still have much to learn from the Fathers of the Society of Jesus."[60]

Here we come to Father Enrico Rosa, whom the general of the Jesuits asked, on 8 October 1938, to offer an expert opinion on the "abridged" French version of *Humani Generis Unitas*. In the course of these tension-filled years, Father Rosa had several times crossed swords with one or another Nazi or Fascist propagandist who, he believed, had besmirched the honor of the pope and of *La Civiltà cattolica*.[61] We will cite only one of his articles, "The Jewish Question and *La Civiltà cattolica*," published on 22 September 1938, three weeks after the promulgation of the first anti-Semitic decree in Italy (the expulsion of foreign Jews), and two weeks after Pius XI's famous declaration, according to which "anti-Semitism is inadmissible. We are spiritually Semites," and at the very moment—give or take a few days—that John LaFarge was delivering the drafts of *Humani Generis Unitas* in Rome.

In the article in *Il Regime fascista* mentioned above, the Fascist journalist had manipulated articles that appeared in *La Civiltà cat-tolica* during the last trimester of 1890 in order to turn them against Pius XI's recent declarations concerning racism. Father Enrico Rosa thus entered the lists to re-establish the "truth" of these quotations and the "true thought" of the 1890 author.[62] Did he also want to use these fifty-year-old articles to discreetly criticize Fascism's racist policies? If that was the case, his method seems ambivalent, since it ultimately led him to defend a segregationist solution to the Jewish problem.

"Like our predecessors," he wrote, "we absolutely insist on showing justice and charity toward Jews as well, while at the same time being convinced that they will not do the same toward us, as they have certainly not done in the persecutions of the Church that they have unleashed or promoted in the past, in concert with the freemasons, to whom they have lent powerful support, as well as with other subversive and anti-Christian groups, particularly from the 'great' French Revolution up to our own time.

"That has never led us, and will never lead us, to act toward them in the same way, but only to prevent them from doing harm, and to protect others from their omnipotence, and that for the common good, particularly the moral and religious good, as well as for the salvation of the Jews themselves."

If the 1890 articles dealt with the "causes," "effects," and "remedies for the modern Jewish invasion of Europe," it was solely concerning the remedies that Father Rosa entered into polemics with *Il Regime fascista*. With regard to the remedy that "would be the most radical, but would not be in accord with the Christian spirit: the seizure of property and the expulsion of people," the author of 1890 offered the following commentary:

> In order to be legitimate, the seizure would have to be decreed by the person who normally exercises public authority in the nation; and secondly, it would have to be carried out in conformity with

certain norms of Christian justice and charity. [. . .] Not all Jews are thieves, agitators, deceivers, usurers, freemasons, crooks and corrupters of morals. Everywhere, there is a certain number of them who are not accomplices in the evil actions of the others. Why should these innocents be subject to the punishments deserved by the guilty ones? [. . .] Justice and charity would in any case have good reasons to give against the cruelty of these too-draconian measures.

The author of 1890, Father Rosa continued, even rejected the remedy complementary to the first one, that is, the "generalized expulsion of Jews as foreigners." But Father Rosa, who quoted his earlier counterpart at length, conceded that the latter maintained the following:

"If the Jews are on our soil, they have not come to it innocently, but rather in order to take it away from us Christians, or to plot against our faith," since ultimately "they are an enemy whose goal is to appropriate our land and deprive us of heaven." But such a remedy would not be possible in a generalized way, especially if it had to be applied in all civilized countries; "indeed it would contravene God's plan," which requires the preservation of Israel, even though it is dispersed, as a "concrete argument for the truth of Christianity." And "even if this measure were applicable, it would not correspond to the Roman Church's way of seeing and acting." On this subject the author [of 1890] offered the example of the popes and Catholic princes, and mentioned the testimony of two converted Jews, the Lemann brothers. The latter pointed out that "the popes have always kindly authorized residence in their city, and this wandering people, even though it could have abstained from going there, always went there, even describing Rome, out of gratitude, as the paradise of the Jews." If that was the case, it was because those Jews, who had more good sense than modern Jews, recognized that the laws of separation or "interdiction" adopted with regard to them were aimed at defending them as much as protecting Christians, by preventing any sort of mutual offense and every kind of reciprocal violation of their respective rights.

It is precisely this latter point that our periodical stressed in 1890, by opposing the leadership of liberalism and of freemasonry, which was prevalent at the time, in order to find "the only means of making the residence of the Jews compatible with the rights of Christians." This means would be, according to our periodical, "to subject this residence to laws that simultaneously prevent Jews from seizing Christian property and Christians from seizing Jewish property." It was therefore not a question of odious laws, but of just laws, not persecuting laws but mutually advantageous laws, as was pointed out at the time.

It is true that this seems contrary to the full "civil equality" without any limitation that liberalism boasted of granting Jews. Our polemicist [of 1890] recognizes this. But against the arguments of inveterate liberals, he recalls the *pensée* of Pascal, one of the antiliberal writers of the past, for whom the fact of "wanting to establish a common law among different social estates is like trying to level different heights to the same size. What is equitable and necessary, on the contrary, is respect for all the different rights," such as what differentiates nationals from foreigners. And among the latter we must count, on their own admission, the Jews, since "the cosmopolitanism of their race is admitted by the Jews themselves."

Our predecessor in the past century therefore believes that the complete civil equality liberalism accorded the Jews, which thus linked them with the freemasons, not only is not due them, given that they have no right to it, but "is even pernicious, for Jews as well as for Christians." He is therefore of the opinion that "sooner or later, through love or through force, we will have to redo what we have been undoing in the earlier legal systems for a hundred years, out of love for a so-called new freedom or for a false progress. And it is perhaps the Jews themselves who will be obliged to beg that we remake what we have unmade. Now the well-foundedness of this prediction is evident. For even today, "the omnipotence to which revolutionary law had raised them is hollowing out beneath their feet an abyss whose depth is comparable to the height of the summit they had attained."

One must observe how much what was denounced in 1890 corresponds to reality and has been confirmed by a half-century of experience, namely that "the equality that anti-Christian sectarians have granted Jews, wherever the government of the people has been usurped, has had the effect of bringing Judaism and freemasonry together in persecuting the Catholic Church and elevating the Jewish race over Christians, as much in hidden power as in manifest opulence.

And yet neither the Church nor any Catholic leader of the people or Catholic government—that is, those who have had to suffer most because of the Jews—have, currently or over the past fifty years, taken any violent measure of reprisal or combat against the Jews, in spite of their omnipotence. These violent measures have been carried out, just recently, by Protestant and Nazi Germany, and earlier, by Czarist Russia, and then by communist and internationalist Russia, whose revolution nevertheless owed a great deal to the Jews, as is well known and as our periodical has proven.

What precedes shows clearly that our periodical's writer, even though he was strongly moved by religious persecution—which was raging at the time in Italy and was attributed, in large part, even if in an exaggerated manner, to the close alliance between freemasonry and anti-Christian Judaism—was careful not to propose with regard to these evils which he deplored any remedy or opposition that was not fully in accord with the supreme principles of justice and charity. It is therefore completely evident that his thought was not properly interpreted, and still more that it was entirely deformed by those who presented his ideas as a program of vengeance and reprisals, and even of all-out war, an interpretation that would be entirely legitimate if one limited oneself to the purely human and self-interested concerns of politics. On the contrary, it was a forceful and duly motivated appeal for vigilance and for effective and peaceful defense against both the dangers and the civil, religious, and moral disorder with which Judaism threatens modern society.

It is undeniable that the form and style, more than the thought-content, may, almost fifty years later, seem somewhat harsh, particularly now that the battle being waged as much by the freemasons as by the Jews may seem somewhat attenuated, at least in form, if not in substance. But whatever might be its defects of style and form, they do not affect the power of the reasoning, nor, consequently, the value of the conclusions.[63]

In turn, we have to observe that beyond all questions of form, in spirit these articles have much in common with the "politico-Statist" anti-Semitism Gustav Gundlach spoke of in 1930, which is "permissible when it combats, by moral and legal means, a truly harmful influence of the Jewish segment of the population in the areas of economy, politics, theater, cinema, the press, science and art."[64] And it is probably in virtue of a distinction similar to the one Gundlach made between this "permissible" anti-Semitism and the anti-Semitism condemned by Christian doctrine that *La Civiltà cattolica* was able simultaneously to make such remarks on the "Jewish question" and to denounce Nazi, and then Fascist, racism.

Confronting the Anti-Semitic Laws (Fall–Winter 1938)

On 4 August 1938, Italian newspapers had announced that from the start of the next school year, foreign students "of Jewish race" would not be admitted into educational institutions, at any level whatsoever. On 1 September, the Italian ministerial council decreed in addition that "non-Aryan" foreigners residing on the territory of the empire and its colonial possessions since 1 January 1919 had to have left it within a maximum of six months; those who had acquired Italian citizenship after that date would be stripped of it. The next day, the council also decreed that teachers and members of institutes, academies, and so on, who were "of non-Aryan race" would be struck from the rolls starting on 16 October. On 10 and 11 November, the council of ministers recapitulated the measures already adopted and decreed new ones, which went into effect immediately: Marriages between Italians and "non-Aryan" foreigners were forbidden, or, if they had already taken place, were officially annulled, along with their civil effects, and erased from official records; the official records of Italian citizens who "belong to the Jewish race" had to carry a notation to that effect; Jews were excluded from military service; they were not allowed to own large tracts of land or large industrial enterprises; they could not employ servants belonging to the "Aryan race"; Jewish teachers were dismissed from their posts in teaching establishments at all three levels, from institutes and academies of science, letters, and arts; the registration of Jewish students was forbidden in establishments attended by "Aryan" Italian students—with the exception of students "of Jewish race but Catholic confession," who were allowed to attend elementary and secondary schools run by ecclesiastical authorities; foreign Jews who had taken up residence in the kingdom or its colonial dependencies since 1 January 1919 were expelled, whether or not they had been naturalized after that date. Other measures were promulgated in the course of the following months, forcing Jews in particular to give up to "Aryans" the majority of their real and commercial property, gradually restricting "their activity in all domains of national life," declaring null and void any testamentary clause that designated an inheritance or legacy to a member of the Jewish race, permitting "Aryans" with a Jewish-sounding surname to adopt a different one, and so on.[65] Contrary to what *La Civiltà cattolica*'s writer still hoped on the preceding 29 July,

Fascist Italy had just followed Nazi Germany's lead with respect to anti-Semitic legislation.

How did Pius XI react? On 6 September, he improvised an address delivered to the participants in a pilgrimage organized by Belgian Catholic Radio. Almost always, only the final words of this address are noted: "We are spiritually Semites." Thus it seems to us necessary to quote it here *in extenso*, as it was taken down at the time by a Belgian prelate, Monsignor Picard. Paging through the missal that was given to him, the pope focused on the Canon prayer *Supra quae propitio*...[66]: "This prayer," he observed, "is one we say at the most solemn moment in the Mass, after the Consecration, when the divine Victim is actually offered. Abel's sacrifice, Abraham's sacrifice, Melchizedek's sacrifice: in three marks, in three lines, in three steps, humanity's whole religious history: Abel's sacrifice, the Adamic age; Abraham's sacrifice, the age of Israel's religion and its prodigious history; Melchizedek's sacrifice, the anticipation of the Christian religion and its age. An awe-inspiring text: every time we read it, we are moved irresistibly: *Sacrificium patriarchae nostri Abrahae*. Note that Abraham is called our patriarch, our ancestor. Anti-Semitism is not compatible with the thought and the sublime realization expressed in this text. It is a deplorable movement, a movement in which we, as Christians, must have no part."

"Here," the writer notes, "the pope did not succeed in containing his emotion. He wept as he quoted the passages from St. Paul that show our spiritual descent from Abraham": " 'The promises were made to Abraham and his offspring.' The text does not say, as St. Paul remarks, 'to his offsprings, referring to many, but to his offspring, referring to one, which is Christ.'[67] The promises are realized in Christ and by Christ, in us who are parts of his mystical Body. By Christ and in Christ, we are the spiritual offspring of Abraham.

"No, it is not possible for Christians to take part in anti-Semitism. We recognize that anyone has the right to defend himself, to take steps to protect himself against anything that threatens his legitimate interests. But anti–Semitism is inadmissible. We are spiritually Semites."[68]

These words, emotional and moving, are clear: "Anti-Semitism is inadmissible," it is a "movement in which we, as Christians, must have no part." From this point of view, Pius XI has just caught up with the Holy Office's decree of 1928. But it is the last time he spoke this way in public—moreover, it was a long time before any pope spoke this way again—and he confined himself to theology, and made no explicit statement regarding the new discriminatory legislation. Finally, since this declaration had "no official character,"[69] it was not quoted by the Italian Catholic press.

On 10 November 1938, only a few hours apart, two events occurred that are revelatory: in Germany, Kristallnacht, followed by new anti–Semitic laws; and the promulgation of a new series of anti-Semitic laws in Italy.

The first of these events[70] aroused a wave of indignation and protest throughout Europe. The Catholic world also took part in this reaction, although it was still somewhat ambivalent.[71] As for the hierarchy, while the bishops did not adopt "any concrete official position,"[72] the cardinals of several large European cities nevertheless spoke out, and were quoted by the Catholic press. *La Documentation catholique*, for instance, published these statements together, thus amplifying the effect of a collective protest against racism. If one reads them attentively, however, significant differences among them are discernible.[73]

In a very long speech addressed to "the priests, during the ecclesiastical retreats,"[74] Cardinal Joseph-Ernest Van Roey, the archbishop of Mechlin, takes up the question from the point of view of "the mystery of the blood in the economy of salvation." After following point by point the letter from the Sacred Congregation of Seminaries and Universities which had been published the preceding 14 April, he opposes to the racist doctrine of the purity of blood a "very different [one], which is very true and well-founded, on which the economy of our salvation rests as an essential element": that of the redeeming and unifying blood shed by Christ. In conformity with tradition, Cardinal Van Roey situates the essential reasons for the "fundamental unity of the human race" in the original sin of Adam, the First Father, on the one hand, and on the other, in the remission of this sin brought about by the "blood of the covenant" shed "superabundantly" by the New Adam, that is, Christ the Redeemer. Through "our mystical incorporation into Christ," he adds, "the unity and equality of all men are realized." And he concludes by reminding the priests that "at the present time, the dogma of the redeeming blood of Christ must frequently be made the object of religious instruction and preaching," that they must redouble their efforts to ensure that "all parish life [tends] to bring the faithful, in as great a number and as often as possible, to the divine Eucharist."

On 17 November, Cardinal Jean Verdier wrote to Cardinal Van Roey to offer him his respectful congratulations and to ask his "permission to echo these luminous words." But the archbishop of Paris refers more concretely to the current situation than did his counterpart in Mechlin when he predicts that: "Racial differences will engender, in the world and even within a single country, legal differences that favor only the stronger party. [. . .]

"This consequence, alas, is not only of a theoretical order. The deeds we are witnessing and which so profoundly offend our human sensibility and disconcert our reason say very loudly that individuals and peoples are already acting on these strange convictions!

"Very near us, in the name of the rights of the race, thousands and thousands of men are hunted down like wild animals, deprived of their property; they are veritable pariahs who seek in vain within civilization for asylum and a bit of bread. There you see the inevitable result of racial theory.

"And if recently a crime, a stupid one to be sure, and which cannot be too greatly condemned, has overexcited all the passions of a people, it is very certain that these violent attitudes are due above all to the new philosophy that is being propagated and exploited."

In a speech given in the Milan cathedral on 11 November, and which had a considerable effect in Italy, the archbishop of that city, Cardinal Ildefonse Schuster, who was nevertheless known for his Fascist sympathies, contrasted the ancient Roman empire, as he saw it, with what was being built at the time he spoke: "Today, in the name of this myth of the twentieth century, the descendants of Abraham are being banned from Imperial territory, at the same time that the universal revealed religion is being attacked. Tomorrow, by virtue of the same principles, will they not also try to repeat against the descendants of Augustus and Varus the massacre of the Roman legions in the Teutberg forest? [. . .]

"Many Fathers of the Church have attributed to the Roman Empire the providential mission of delaying these terrible times of international conflict that are to precede the end of the world. In fact, if there has been an imperialism that was anti-Racist, and therefore truly universal and cosmopolitan, it was that of Augustus, the founder of the *Imperium*. [. . .]

"For the old patrician concept of the *agro italico*, a simple territorial domain, or the patrimony of the descendants of Quirinus, is substituted another which is eminently political: Rome extends its confines beyond the circle of the walls built by Servius Tullius to enclose the immense universe within a *unica Polis*.

"Therefore if there is an anti-imperial and anti-Roman concept, it is indubitably that of the racial myth of the twentieth century; it pushes us violently two thousand years backward in the history of the world [. . .]."

But toward the end of his speech, Cardinal Schuster makes a brusque, somewhat ambiguous return to the current situation in Italy, omitting even—intentionally?—any mention of the Jews in a quotation from St. Paul that is nevertheless archetypical: "When in the Church at Corinth, several groups were vying for pre-eminence, [...] the Doctor of the Gentiles, scandalized by this sectarianism, wrote to them: 'Perhaps you have cut Christ to pieces?'

"National distinctions in politics and in commerce, fine and good! The Church does not engage in politics or in the social economy. But racial distinctions within the Christian Church, no; because Christ cannot be divided.

"In the constitution of the mystical Body of Christ that is the Church, there no longer exists—this is Paul speaking—neither Greek nor Scythian,[75] but on the contrary the new man, *nova creatura*, who is Christ himself living in the Christian [...]."

Cardinal Cerejeira, the patriarch of Lisbon, was still more ambiguous when on 18 November, opposing true Christianity to those who want to strangle the Church and Catholic Action in the interests of totalitarian conceptions of the world and who sometimes clothe themselves in Christian garments, he exclaimed: "[...] In the dream of those who await the earthly reign of Christ, achieved under the sign of the sword, we seem to discern the resuscitation of the Judaic ideal of a national Messiah imposing his domination over all people by triumphal force [...].

"To do that is not to put the kingdom of God above all else (as the Gospels command). It is rather, like the Jews, to want the kingdom of God to adjust itself to the temporal reign of particular or national interests and individual conceptions [...]."

But he nonetheless proclaims that a living Catholicism "cannot fail to denounce the error of the pagan cult of strength, ambition, violence, harshness, hatred (of which the scandalized world had a cruel example in the ignominious vexations inflicted on Jews), as opposed to the spirit of Christ [...]."

Finally, *La Documentation catholique* quotes another very brief extract from a speech given by Cardinal Michael Faulhaber in the Munich cathedral on 6 November, an extract which, in spite of its character as a protest against Nazi racism, closes this series of quotations on a strangely discordant note:

> The people of Israel are related by blood to Christ through the intermediary of the Savior's Mother. But relationship by blood alone does not suffice in the kingdom of God. The Precursor exclaimed before his auditors: "Do not presume to say to yourselves, 'We have Abraham as our father'; for I tell you, God is able from these stones to raise up children to Abraham" (Matthew 3:9). The Savior himself was told during one of his sermons: "Your mother and your brothers are standing outside, desiring to see you." To which he replied: "My mother and my brothers are those who hear the word of God and do it" (Luke 8:20). Christ thus rejects relationship by blood and demands relationship by faith, which consists in accepting the word of God [...]. Therefore there is no point in asking whether Christ is of Jewish or Aryan birth. We should rather ask whether we have become part of Christ through baptism and faith. In Jesus Christ, St. Paul says (Galatians 6:15), Judaism and non-Judaism no longer count for anything, but only the new man. The Old Testament was based on the relationship of faith, the New is based on the relationship of faith; thus sin against faith proves to be more serious than sin against blood.

In Rome, meanwhile, Pius XI spoke "not a single word of protest throughout November and December."[76] The *Osservatore romano* published daily reports arriving from Germany, but rather than commenting on them, it hid behind the authorized positions of the cardinal-archbishops just mentioned.[77] *La Civiltà cattolica* did the same thing. In its number for 25 November, the Jesuits' periodical devoted two pages of its "contemporary chronicle" to Kristallnacht and to the new laws definitively excluding German

Jews from the life of the nation. But at the end of this purely
descriptive article, one finds this obscure commentary:

> All this disorder reveals the danger of a system that seeks to make
> responsible for a crime all the members of a race or all the members
> of the criminal's religion, and the lukewarm reprobation of the *brevi
> manu* excesses in the streets, concerning which it is said only that
> such destruction reduces the value of the planned confiscations. Ul-
> timately, if "today, in the name of this myth of the twentieth cen-
> tury, the descendants of Abraham are being banned from Imperial
> territory, at the same time that the universal revealed religion is being
> attacked. Tomorrow, by virtue of the same principles, will they not
> also try to repeat against the descendants of Augustus and Varus the
> massacre of the Roman legions in the Teutberg forest?"[78]

Catholic reactions to the anti-Semitic laws promulgated by the
Italian ministerial council on 10 and 11 November 1938 were
quite different. The pope, while abstaining from any public statement, wrote personally to the head of the government and to the
king, and the Italian Catholic press gave these missives a great
deal of publicity. But as the press reported, these limited protests
concerned only the prohibition of marriages between "Aryans"
and "non-Aryans," a measure contrary to canon law and, therefore, to the Lateran accords. In this respect, we shall cite in its
entirety the *Osservatore romano*'s article on 14–15 November,
which set the tone for the Catholic press as a whole.[79] According
to the Vatican daily, "the very recent legislative arrangements
concerning marriages" are:

> [a] *vulnus*[80] inflicted on the Lateran Concordat, which established in
> article 34 that: "The Italian State [. . .] grants the sacrament of mar-
> riage, which is regulated by canon law, civil status [. . .].
> Everyone knows that the Church of Jesus Christ is catholic, that

is, universal. According to divine precept, the news of the Gospel was given to all peoples: *Euntes docete omnes gentes* ["Go therefore and make disciples of all nations"]. All people, no matter what their race, are called to be sons of God, living parts of the living Christ, citizens of the Kingdom of the Divine Redeemer on earth that is His Church. Twenty centuries of history demonstrate this glorious and marvelous universality. So that race has never constituted a criterion for discriminating among Catholic believers. The Church has turned toward men of all races: it has instructed them when they were ignorant; it has civilized them when they were savage; it has improved them when they were already civilized. At the cost of long, often perilous and difficult labor, the Church has always sought to tear down the barriers that spiritually divide humanity and to create and develop feelings of brotherhood and love in each individual.

But at the same time, the Church, as mistress and guardian of the true faith, has always taken care to protect believers against the danger of losing such an invaluable gift. And since among the gravest risks run by a believer is precisely marriage with a person who is not a Catholic, the Church has tried to prevent, through its wise legislation, such dangerous unions. For centuries, the canonical impediments to such marriages have been two in number. The first prohibits marriages between Catholics and the unbaptized (Jews, pagans, etc.). The second forbids marriages between Catholics and baptized non-Catholics (heretics, schismatics[81]). The Church lifts these impediments only when very grave considerations are involved and when it is assured that the non-Catholic will not constitute an obstacle to the Catholic spouse's faith, and that their offspring, without exception, will be baptized and brought up in the Catholic faith.

The decree-law approved by the ministerial council at its meeting on the tenth of this month prohibits and declares null and void any marriage between Italian citizens of Aryan race and persons belonging to other races. There is no exception; no dispensation is provided for. So that the difference between the very recent Italian law and canon law is clear. A difference that is more difficult to discern when it is a question of marriages that already confront obstacles, that is, the obstacles constituted by the Church's prohibition, which, as has been said, rarely permits a Catholic to unite in marriage with an unbaptized person or with a baptized person who is not Catholic.

Very different, however, is the case where two Catholics of different races are involved. It is true that the Church, as an ever-loving mother, usually advises its children not to contract a marriage that may produce degenerate offspring; in this sense it is inclined to support, within the limits of Divine law, the efforts of the civil authority that tend toward the realization of a very proper goal. The moral and social reasons for such an attitude are evident. But the Church suggests, warns, counsels; it does not insist or prohibit. When two believers of different races who have made up their minds to marry present themselves to it, in the absence of any canonical obstacle the Church cannot, because of the difference in race alone, refuse them its assistance. This is required by its sanctifying mission; it is required by the rights that God has given and that the Church acknowledges in all its children without distinction. So that on this point a general and absolute prohibition on marriage is in opposition to the doctrine and the laws of the Church.

That is not all. In 1929 the Italian government signed a Concordat with the Holy See, by which, according to article 34, it bound itself to recognize a marriage celebrated religiously as having civil status. This is a solemn commitment: a commitment that is accepted, recognized, observed. For that reason, for about ten years, these marriages which the new decree prohibits have been canonically performed and transcribed in the civil records, always without difficulty. Today, however, what was agreed upon in a bilateral pact is being violated: the *vulnus* inflicted on the Concordat is unparalleled. It is all the more painful in that the Holy See has felt obliged to make its observations known in a timely manner, doing what it could to avoid this happening. The August person of the Holy Father himself intervened directly by addressing two handwritten, paternal letters, one to the Head of the Government, the other to the King–Emperor. Nonetheless, the new legislative provisions were adopted without the Holy See's agreement: to its great regret, the latter has felt obliged to present its protests, as we know it has already done. It is true that the recent decree-law will in reality affect only a few dozen marriages per year, since on the territory of the Kingdom of Italy, where the Concordat's provisions are in force, religious marriages between persons of different races are very rare, and this rarity is also favored by the lack of inclination, which is common to both Catholics and Israelites, to marry a person of the other race. It is also true that even under these new rules, more than three hundred thousand marriages in accord with religious rites and with full civil status will continue to be performed in Italy each year: indeed, this fact, which is a genuine consolation for the Church, is extremely useful for the good of the State, which has wisely sought, by signing the Concordat, "to restore to the institution of marriage, which is the basis of the family, a dignity in accord with the Catholic traditions of its people."

But all these considerations do not diminish the painful surprise of seeing a commitment made in the Concordat weakened, even if it is permissible to hope that an understanding might be reached to avoid a divergence that, even though it would concern only a limited number of cases, takes on, as we have shown, the status of a question of principle in a very important way.

Thus, more than the future condition of Italian Jews, it is the *vulnus* inflicted on the Lateran Concordat that seems to have particularly attracted the ecclesiastical institution's attention. In passing, let us point out that in paragraph 130 of the draft of *Humani Generis Unitas*, and before that, John LaFarge in his *Interracial Justice*,[82] had dealt with interracial marriages in practically the same terms as those in the article quoted above.

Pius XI returned to this subject again in his address on

24 December 1938 to the cardinals present in Rome and to other religious figures who had come, as they did every year at such a time, to give him their Christmas and New Year's greetings:

> Now at the same time that Christmas eve is at hand, another eve is also at hand, to which, from several quarters, We have been asked to devote a comment and an allusion that seem necessary: the eve of the tenth anniversary of the Conciliation. [. . .]
>
> We must unfortunately say, in obedience to sincerity and apostolic truth, as well as for the edification which, because of Our age, we owe to everyone, We must unfortunately say that the desired anniversary, in view of the manner in which it is coming or in which it is made to come to Us, cannot bring us the serene joy for which alone We would like to make room in Our heart, but brings Us rather genuine and grave preoccupations as well as bitter sadness.
>
> Bitter sadness, in truth, when it is a matter of true and multiple vexing measures [. . .] against Catholic Action, which is known to be the pupil of Our eye. [. . .] When one observes the zeal of the lower officials, it appears all too evidently that, although Catholic Action is clearly provided for in Our pact of Conciliation, broad—or rather concealed—signs of permission and encouragement must be proceeding from high offices in order that these vexations might not cease to occur in various places from one end of the peninsula to the other. And this is not only in small or insignificant localities.
>
> Yesterday, Turin, Venice, and Bergamo were mentioned; today, it is Milan, and precisely in the person of its Cardinal-Archbishop, who is guilty of a speech and a teaching that are precisely connected with his pastoral duties, and which we can only approve.[83]
>
> But it is We who are reminding each and all today that only what is Christian is truly fully human, and what is anti-Christian is inhuman; whether it is a matter of the common dignity of the human race, or a matter of the dignity, the freedom, the integrity of the individual. [. . .]

And there is not only the bitter sadness felt by the old Father's heart on seeing his very dear Catholic Action mistreated; there are also the genuine and serious concerns that have been aroused in the Head of Catholicism, the Guardian of morals and truth, by the offense, the wound inflicted on Our Concordat, and precisely in what has to do with holy marriage, which, for a Catholic, means everything. [. . .]

And thinking once again about the recent apotheosis prepared here in Rome itself for a cross that opposes Christ's Cross,[84] about this wound inflicted on the Concordat, and about all the other things to which We alluded earlier, it did not seem to Us excessive to hope that at least some consideration would be given to Our white hair. On the contrary, they went ahead in a brutal fashion[85] [. . .].

This *vulnus* is mentioned again in the homily given by the Patriarch of Venice, Cardinal Adeodato Piazza, on the occasion of the Feast of Epiphany, 6 January 1939. A significant homily, moreover, in which the rejection of racism coexists with the most traditionally "anti-Judaic" representations of Jews. The Church, Cardinal Piazza says, taking his cue from the *Osservatore romano*, "is distressed by the *vulnus* inflicted on the monument of wisdom that is the Italian Concordat. And we hope, from love for the Church and country, that this pact will be soon and loyally reestablished in each and all of its points, so that one might celebrate with unalloyed joy the anniversary of a historical event which the head of the government himself has described as having an 'immense scope' [. . .]."

But the archbishop of Venice also denounces the "false theories of race and blood" as well as neo-paganism, whether communist or Nazi, which he characterizes as "aberrations of the modern world," "denials of Catholic doctrine," "morbid applications of a pantheistic materialism," and "a public affront to the merits and virtues of other peoples." Then he adds: "Thus, the legitimate concern with preserving the hereditary purity of the source must necessarily be kept within these two limits: not denying the common origin and the moral connection of the great human family; and not ignoring or violating the links of the superior unity in Christ."

Speaking next of the Church, "Mother of Saints," the archbishop points out that "only the elect among the peoples who, at the stable in Bethlehem, constituted the first fruits of the reign of Christ, belonged to the Church and still belong to it, whereas the Hebraic class of officials, absent from the scene, is present at the crucifixion in the posture of accusation and hatred.

"It was an authentic Jewish sinner, the leader of the apostles, who, a few weeks after the *deicide*, speaking of Christ in the Sanhedrin, formulated the condemnation against the Synagogue: 'This is the stone which was rejected by you builders, but which has become the head of the corner. And there is salvation in no one else, for there is no other name under heaven given among men by which we must be saved' (Acts 4:11–12).

"Nonetheless, Peter, like his companions and the other converted Jews who formed the pillars and the first kernel of the early Church, did not think it good to close the doors to his compatriots, who were guilty of having killed the Master, because he remembered the precept He had given: 'Go therefore and make disciples of all nations' (Matthew 28:19); 'Go into all the world and preach the gospel to the whole creation' (Mark 16:15).

"To say simply that the Church protects the Jews, is to assert what is not true; for the Church, properly speaking, protects by divine mandate only the freedom of its universal mission, which is to communicate its supernatural good to each and all. To say that the Church is today setting itself in opposition to its past is similarly an anti-historical and arbitrary assertion: the Church has

never engaged in racial battles and could not have done so without renouncing its origins, its goal, its divine mission. It is true
that it had to defend itself as well as its faithful, and not rarely,
with the means it had at its disposition, against dangerous contacts
and the Jewish invasion, which seems in truth the hereditary mark
of this people. But one must also recognize, if one does not wish
to lie, that in the reactions too often provoked by Jewish arro-
gance, one may find, in the Church, suggestions and examples of
balance, moderation, and Christian charity.

"The Church, above all, has never ceased to pray in order to
hasten the final conversion of the Jews, and its hopes are not in
vain: there are souls that go by this path toward sincere union
with Christ[86] [. . .]."

The Mysterious Secret of Pius XI's Speech

To the extent that our knowledge is reliable, Pius XI's final concerns seem once again united with certain of the main themes
developed in *Humani Generis Unitas*.

The old pope Ratti died during the night of 9 February 1939,
carried off by another heart attack. Only a few hours after his
death, Cardinal Eugéne Tisserant later asserted, two documents
were still on his desk: the draft of *Humani Generis Unitas* and the
speech the pope planned to give the next day to the Italian bishops on the occasion of the tenth anniversary of the Lateran
accords. According to Cardinal Tisserant, these documents "disappeared" almost immediately.[87]

These assertions have been partially confirmed by two very
different sources. The first is the testimony given in 1972 to the
National Catholic Reporter by Father Walter Abbott, S.J. According
to Abbott, a note from Monsignor Domenico Tardini[88] accompanied the draft of *Humani Generis Unitas* found on the pope's
desk shortly after his death. Pius XI, Monsignor Tardini's note

explained, ordered that the draft of the encyclical be transmitted to him without delay. Still according to Abbott, the draft reached the pope on 21 January 1939.[89]

The second source is none other than Pope John XXIII, who in early February 1959, on the occasion of the twentieth anniversary of the death of Pius XI and the thirtieth anniversary of the Lateran accords, made known, in a letter to Italian bishops, "long extracts" from Pius XI's last speech.[90] "When death, our sister, came to him," John XXIII wrote, "[Pius XI] was still writing the words of the speech in which he said farewell to his Italian bishops, words that the latter were supposed to repeat later in their dioceses. Unfortunately, his weary hand stopped, motionless, unable to finish. [. . .] In order to give you some idea of this manuscript, We find it sufficient to mention the emphasis that it puts on the great responsibilities borne by the bishops' consciences with regard to both the Seminaries and episcopal discourse."

On the subject of the seminaries: "Our sole intention, venerable Brothers in the episcopacy, is to ask you, as We do with all Our heart, to come always to Our aid for the greater good of these diocesan and interdiocesan seminaries [. . .] by sacrificing, sometimes with a magnanimous heart and voluntarily, *corde magno et anima volenti*, some subject particularly useful to the diocese [. . .] by supporting the severity of the rectors in matters of admission and graduation, remembering that a special and redoubtable responsibility weighs on them [. . .]."

Here it is impossible not to think of the last part of *Humani Generis Unitas*, and about John LaFarge writing to Father Talbot on 11 August 1938 that the encyclical which he was still drafting "will contain, if the draft is allowed to pass, a stiff blow towards the end, in favor of Catholic higher education."[91]

Concerning papal and episcopal discourse, in the time of fascism: "You know, dear and venerable Brothers, how often people discuss what the pope says. People pay attention to Us, not only in Italy, to Our speeches, to Our audiences, usually in order to alter the meaning and even inventing it from beginning to end, in order to make Us say foolish and absurd things. There is a press that can say anything it wants against Us and Our concerns, even by recalling, and falsely and perversely interpreting, the recent and ancient history of the Church, going even so far as to stubbornly deny persecution in Germany, a negation that is accompanied by the false and slanderous accusation of engaging in politics, as Nero's persecution was accompanied by the accusation that the Church had caused the burning of Rome: and they are allowed to do this because our press cannot even contradict or rectify their assertions.

"You cannot expect that what you say will be any better treated. [...] Take care, very dear Brothers in Christ, and do not forget that very often there are observers and informers (call them spies and you will be right) who, through zeal or in order to be appointed to offices, listen to you in order to denounce you without having understood anything [...]."

"After these words," John XXIII said in 1959, "the dying Pontiff's manuscript dissolves into confused and trembling lines." However, Pius XI "returns to the current topic that had motivated what he was writing, namely the tenth anniversary of the Lateran accords." Before we quote this speech, it must be understood that it was to be given in St. Peter's in Rome, that is, "over the earthly and glorious tomb, and over the relics of the Lord's apostles who first brought the Gospel to Rome and founded there the universal Church," practically all of whom were martyred. "[...] Exult, glorious remains of the apostle princes, disciples and friends of Christ [...] you too, prophesy, sacred and glorious remains such as those of the patriarch Joseph. Prophesy the perseverance of this Italy in the faith that you have preached and sealed with your blood. Holy remains, prophesy a total and firm perseverance against all the blows and all the snares, near or far, that threaten and combat this perseverance. Prophesy prosperity, honor, especially the honor of a people conscious of its dignity and of its human and Christian responsibility. Prophesy, cherished and venerated remains, the coming or the return to the religion of Christ by all peoples, all nations, all races, all of them united and sharing the same blood in the common bond of the great human family. Prophesy, finally, remains of the apostles, order, tranquillity, peace, peace for this whole world, which, while seeming to be in the grip of a homicidal and suicidal madness of weaponry, wants peace at any cost, and, with Us, implores the God of peace to grant it, and has confidence that it will obtain it."

Conclusion

*"Having begun from a historical legend with the
intention of discovering the truth, we have arrived
at a region shrouded in darkness and silence."*

—ÉMILE POULAT

What happened, ultimately, in this non-event, that might
change already acquired knowledge of this period, or simply to lead us toward new questions? What happened that does
not simply confirm what historians have already written about it?

In a number of statements made public in the course of the
last two years of Pius XI's pontificate, authorities of the Catholic
Church in Rome characterized racism as foolishness with regard
to modern science, apostasy or religious heresy with regard to
Christian doctrine, and the expression of a tendency to totalitarianism incompatible with natural law. On various occasions, Pius
XI himself stressed that it was necessary "to respond to such an
aberration with the rejection it deserves" (*Mit Brennender Sorge*,
March 1937), that "the human race is a single, great, universal
human race" (end of July 1938), that "race has never constituted
a criterion for discriminating among Catholic believers" (mid-
November 1938), and that "only what is Christian is truly fully
human, and what is anti-Christian is inhuman; whether it is a
matter of the common dignity of the human race, or a matter of
the dignity, the freedom, or the integrity of the individual"
(Christmas 1938). A few hours before he died, he once again
prophesied the union "of all peoples, all nations, all races [...],

sharing the same blood in the common bond of the great human family" (February 1939).

In almost all these statements, racism is never discussed in isolation but is always considered as a phenomenon reflecting the more and more serious decline of the contemporary world under the leadership of the modern spirit. From his predecessors, in fact, Pius XI had inherited a crucial question for the Church, that of modernity. And his pontificate, more than theirs, was caught in a powerful tension between the dream of restoring a Christian order and the necessity of realistically adjusting the pursuit of this dream to the conditions created by modernity itself. All the great stimuli he gave to the Church were colored by this "obligation to transform enough—to 'modernize' enough—in order once again to move, if possible," toward a wholly Catholic society.[1] This is the case, for example, in his attitude with regard to the state, which was not very different, doctrinally, from that of Leo XIII. In his realism, Leo XIII, without abandoning the attempt to re-create a Christian society, and even to re-establish the temporal power of the papacy, had dissociated the future of the Church from "all the old legitimisms, from toppling thrones and fallen governments, as well as from the governments that [had] succeeded them," and sought to win people over in opposition to the modern state.[2] Pius XI had accentuated this tendency, beginning a policy of concordats with states in order to safeguard Catholic Action's freedom of movement, to preserve the influence of Catholic education on the youth, and to bring the working classes into Christian organizations that could compete with those of the socialist or communist labor movements. In addition, to restrain the modern state's tendency toward omnipotence, he proposed a model of society founded above all on the protection of the rights of the human person and on collaboration among free private corporate associations (*Quadragesimo Anno* and *Non Abbiamo Bisogno*, May and June 1931, respectively; *Divini*

Redemptoris, March 1937). Moreover, from his first encyclical[3] to his statements in July 1938, including along the way his increasingly adamant condemnation of *Action française* (1926–1927), Pius XI always contrasted the unity of humanity, instructed and guided by the Church, to the disintegrating effects of "immoderate nationalism." In the 1930s, he spoke out against racism in the same way, and for the same reason (*Mit Brennender Sorge*, March 1937; letter to the Sacred Congregation of Universities and Seminaries, April 1938; statements made in July 1938). Ultimately, from one end of his pontificate to the other, he never ceased to remind people that the evils of society came from forgetting God and Jesus Christ, who were "excluded from legislation and public affairs," and to contrast unity in Christ and the re-establishment of His reign[4] with everything that fragmented the human race, which exacerbated discord in social relations, conflicts in international relations, and divisions within each individual. The reader will see that all these themes are included to some degree in the draft of *Humani Generis Unitas*.

That being the case, one still cannot help wondering whether protecting the ecclesiastical institution and preserving the freedom of action of Catholic organizations was not the chief motivation for the condemnations of racism mentioned above, which were nonetheless presented by their authors as having universal bearing and value. In March 1937, for example, in *Mit Brennender Sorge*, wasn't it because racism was presented above all as the instrument of a "war of extermination [...] against Christ and His Church" that German Catholics were exhorted to "free their consciences from any cooperation with such machinations" and to oppose it with a "heroic courage [...] even at the price of the greatest earthly sacrifices"? In April 1938, wasn't it because racism was identified "with the grave persecution that is raging [...] against the German Catholic Church" and characterized as a "pernicious doctrine [seeking to] pervert minds [in order] to draw them away from true religion" that Catholic universities were urged by the Sacred Congregation of Universities and Seminaries to "apply all their efforts and their activity to the defense of the truth against the invasion of error"? Starting in mid-November of the same year, wasn't Italian racist legislation prohibiting marriages between "Aryans" and "non-Aryans" strongly criticized because it had been above all "a *vulnus* inflicted on the Lateran Concordat"?

One is led to ask further questions when one notices that the anti-racism proclaimed in Rome during this period has a genuine shortcoming with regard to anti-Semitism: *none* of the statements listed above mentions Jews, or makes anti-Semitism a specific object of commentary or condemnation. Anti-Semitism was made the object of a separate statement, and, in the period considered, *a single* statement, the one which Pius XI concluded, on 6 September 1938, by affirming that "anti-Semitism is inadmissible. We are spiritually Semites." Yet this statement was not official and did not impose any practical obligation on Catholics. Isn't it significant, in this regard, that the drafters of *Humani Generis Unitas* made no mention of this when they recalled the condemnation of "the hatred that is commonly designated today under the name of 'anti-Semitism' " issued by the Holy Office in March 1928?

But here a new question inevitably arises: Did this 1928 condemnation impose an obligation on Catholics, both clerical and lay, in conscience and in acts, or was it received only as an element strictly subordinated to its current object, namely the dissolution of the Friends of Israel? One remains perplexed when one thinks, for example, about the articles on the "Jewish question" that *La Civiltà cattolica* continued to publish during the following decade. To be sure, the Jesuit periodical always took care to dissociate itself explicitly from the various expressions of racism and anti-Semitism, and to indicate that the spirit of justice and charity ought to prevail in the search for a solution to the "Jewish problem." But in the very exposition of this "problem" and of the responses to it, the borderline between anti-Semitism and doctrinal anti-Judaism seems very fluid, very permeable—unless we believe that the Catholic mentality of the period adhered faithfully to the distinction established in Gustav Gundlach's 1930 article, between two varieties of anti-Semitism, one "national and politico-racial," which he rejected, the other "politico-governmental [...], permissible when it combats, by moral and legal means, a truly harmful influence of the Jewish segment of the population in the areas of economy, politics, theater, cinema, the press, science, and art."

In short, it seems that up until the eve of the Second World War, the authorities of the Catholic Church in Rome did not succeed in coming to grips with the reality of anti-Semitism, no doubt because they could not get beyond the limits of a mental framework delineated by both a traditional interpretation of New Testament writings and a world-view in which Israel was associated with all the misdeeds of modernity. Concerned above all with the Church's mission, and thus with the Church itself, didn't these authorities themselves produce, at least with regard to the Jews, "the amalgamation [of] considerations of law and utility" that *Mit Brennender Sorge* reproached the German government with producing?

Then it would be tempting to believe that if Pius XI commissioned in 1938 a draft of an encyclical whose specific aim was to condemn racism and anti-Semitism, it was because he had realized the urgent necessity of making up for the shortcoming mentioned above, because he was convinced that a distinction like the one Gundlach made between a forbidden "politico-racial" anti-Semitism and a permissible "politico-governmental" anti-Semitism was no longer either moral or pertinent, or that segregationist solutions for the "Jewish question," such as the ones *La Civiltà cattolica* proposed, could no longer be defended by Catholics. It would also be tempting to believe that if he selected John LaFarge, it was largely because LaFarge had made himself the advocate, in his fight against racism in the United States, of anti-segregationist solutions. A careful reading of the draft of *Humani Generis Unitas*—to the extent that the draft faithfully reflects the pope's orders, which the documents available to us do not allow us to establish—and of Pius XI's last statements does not, however, allow us to transform these hypotheses into certainties.

The Argument for The Unity of the Human Race

From the very first paragraphs, the writers of this draft lay the responsibility for contemporary disorders at the door of the spirit of modernity. The latter had stripped man "of everything that constitutes his proper dignity, that is to say his spiritual nature," and proposed a purely mechanical conception of individual and collective relations, which was supposed to ensure humanity's unlimited progress. However, incapable of keeping its promises with regard to well-being, equality, economic prosperity, order, and security, it had led a "dissociated and macerated" humanity to demand that the state reestablish the unity of the human race. Now, the state had abusively extended its functions and increased its power to an exaggerated degree, "rejecting radically all subordination to a higher form of organization of the human community," that is, to the Church. In order to reconstitute the lost unity of humanity, the state had organized itself around a single factor of social cohesion: the nation, the race, the proletariat, or the state itself, which, posited as absolute and imposed on everyone in a mechanical way, had inevitably led to a leveling and standardizing collectivism. Encroaching increasingly on the independence of individuals, it forced them to join enormous organizations, set up by totalitarianism itself, in which they sought as best they could the representation of their interests and the security of existence they lacked. Governmental regulation of the economy endangered the existence of the middle classes and the various self-governing professional communities. The worker, whose labor was no more than the expression of "the acquisitive instinct," became a kind of government worker for the benefit of the racist, national, governmental, or proletarian collectivity. Authority, henceforth conceived as a simple technique of forming a single will, was imposed by the double action of legal constraint and the standardization of public opinion by all available means, both oral and written. Thus the brutal and monotonous conditions of life and thought were accentuated. Ultimately, "the average man of our time," transformed into "a passive and inert being," "without any ideas of his own, without any will of his own," who is in danger of being "at any moment seized and carried away by blind mass movements," will give rise to the modern mass man. In short, guided by the godless spirit of modernity, people of our time have tried to rebuild the Tower of Babel, unaware that they are threatened by the same final fate that befell their Old Testament predecessors.

To this disintegrative movement, pregnant with further catastrophes, the drafters opposed their Christian vision of "the unity in plurality of humanity." So far as unity is concerned, they base it on several foundations: "a community of nature among all men," that is, a single "specifically human type both as to mind and as to physical qualities"; original sin, which was able to affect all men in all ages only because humanity was fundamentally one; humanity's redemption, brought about by Christ's sacrifice, which saves all men because the Redeemer took on a true human nature; the relations of all men with God; life on the earth "on which Humanity lives"; time; the Church, which perpetuates Christ's action "in the temporality of our social life"; "the natural right to the use of the earth's external goods"; work and the necessity of working; the family and the State, stable and ubiquitous institutions "indispensable to Humanity." As for the plurality of humanity, the drafters see its manifestation in the formation of innumerable "groupings" determined by the location and conditions of life, professional occupations, and diverse interests.[5] Four types of such groups are examined in greater detail—the state, territorial nationality, the nation, and race—but if we go by their manuscript annotations, they added a fifth: the Jews, to which they apply various criteria for deciding whether or not they contribute to internal unity and the freedom of the human person, to solidarity among groups, to the goals and values that constitute the internal unity of humanity, and to imprinting the mark of God "more deeply in the world," as well as making "man, or men [. . .] increasingly [. . .] resemble God."

Up to this point, the encyclical's theoretical and stylistic coherence is practically complete. On the other hand, in the two subsequent sections, entitled "Race and Racism" and "The Jews and Anti-Semitism," various ruptures, and even contradictory propositions, lead one to think not only that they were probably written by a different main author but that the topics dealt with may have caused problems for the writers, or even led to disagreements among them. Thus the first fourteen paragraphs of the section on "Race and Racism" seem to be no more than an amplification, and sometimes a mere repetition, of the Sacred Congregation of Universities and Seminaries' letter of 13 April 1938. Next, in the "famous paragraphs 126 to 130," to which LaFarge seemed to be particularly attached,[6] the same theme is repeated in a much more concrete manner that is virtually analogous to what LaFarge had written in *Interracial Justice*. In fact, if there are noticeable differences among peoples due to the influence of the environment, "they afford as yet no basis for an essential difference between the individual races in the capacity for religious, moral and cultural life. [. . .] Logically, therefore, the existence of more perfectly or less perfectly developed races implies no race question, whether we consider it from the standpoint of biology or of the theology in the sense of a divine election or rejection." And the text draws the conclusions for the behavior of colonizing nations with regard to their colonies, as well as for certain prejudices artificially maintained by Christians in some parts of the American continent. But the text remains prudent: in paragraph 130, while it expresses the wish that "relations among social groups might be governed exclusively by interracial justice and charity," it nonetheless points out that "there are also such actual, even if not unchangeable and rigidly normative, circumstances in the relations of the races. The races will observe them in their own interest..."[7]

Concerning Jews and Anti-Semitism

The subsequent section on "The Jews and anti-Semitism" is marked by still more obvious ruptures. First of all, the drafters brusquely leave the terrain of historical, sociological, economic, or political analysis, on which they had remained from the outset, in order to pass over into that of theology, and to develop at length the traditional themes of Pauline apologetics and narrative. Secondly, they abandon individual categories such as "the human person" or "personality," to which they had accorded a great deal of attention in their critique of the totalitarian state, henceforth referring only to an undifferentiated collectivity: "Israel," the "Jewish people," "Jewish teachings," etc. Finally, if this section was ever meant to establish obligations with a view to concrete social action, it must be noted that the incoherence of these obligations makes them practically inoperative.

Thus, after having pointed out that "the struggle for racial purity ends by being uniquely the struggle against the Jews," that thereby "millions of persons are deprived of the most elementary rights and privileges of citizens in the very land of their birth" and "denied legal protection against violence and robbery," which constitutes a "flagrant denial of human rights," the drafters emphasize that however "unjust and pitiless" it may be, "this campaign against the Jews has at least this advantage, [...] that it recalls the true nature, the authentic basis of the social separation of the Jews from the rest of humanity [...]. The so-called Jewish question is not one of race, or nation, or territorial nationality, or citizenship in the State. It is a question of religion and, since the coming of Christ, a question of Christianity." This assertion is followed by a long exposition of the traditional teaching of the Church regarding Jews. Here we will not offer a critique of this exposition or an inventory of the numerous expressions that were later to lead Jules Isaac to describe this traditional teaching as "the teaching of scorn."[8] But we will point out all the same that it leads to the conviction that "blinded by a vision of material domination and gain, the Israelites lost what they themselves had sought," that "this unhappy people [destroyed] their own nation," and that this irrepressible destructive and self-destructive impulse has pursued the Jews like a divine curse, which they themselves have called down on their heads, long after New Testament times. This seems, moreover, to have been the conviction of the drafters themselves when, departing from traditional teaching, they return to the "realities of history" in order to follow the effects of the "historic enmity of the Jewish people to Christianity."

But here the text leads the reader, who finds himself more and more perplexed, into an oscillation between paradoxical, if not contradictory, propositions. First, it asserts that, being aware of the "dangers to which contact with Jews can expose souls," the Church has always been able to take "energetic measures to preserve both the faith and morals of her members and society itself against the corrupting influence of error," nor is "this need diminished in our own time." Next, it emphasizes that the Church "is in no wise concerned with the problems concerning the Jewish people that lie within [. . .] purely profane spheres . . . [and] leaves to the powers concerned the solution of these problems. She insists only that no solution is the true solution if it contradicts the very demanding laws of justice and charity." There is no doubt why the text rejects measures that might be inspired by anti-Semitism. The latter is moreover clearly rejected, for doctrinal reasons—the Holy Office's decree of 28 March 1928 is cited—but also because it is powerless and ineffective ("persecution, instead of obliterating or lessening the harmful or anti-social traits of a persecuted group, merely intensifies the tendencies which gave rise to them"), and, ultimately, it is merely a pretext for "a war against Christianity," and "embarrassing the Church through involving her in the machinations and struggles of profane politics." Finally, after a discreet appeal for individual conversions of Jews and for prayers to hasten "the day when again Jew and Gentile will be united in their Father's house," this section ends with an exhortation to defend "the natural rights of individuals and of families," to take "care of the miserable who appeal for charity and mercy," to make "a vigorous condemnation of anti-Semitism and racism," and to "reject the gross errors of materialism."

In other words: It is not the Church's affair if states, taking its attitude in the past as their inspiration, take forceful measures to protect individuals and society against the dangers involved in contact with Jews, on condition that these measures are not incompatible with justice, individual and family rights, and charity, and that they are not inspired by racial anti-Semitism.

Those are not the ideas John LaFarge defended in *Interracial Justice* in 1937, with regard to American blacks, but rather those that Gundlach formulated in his 1930 article on anti-Semitism, set forth here in almost the same order and reproducing the internal contradictions we have already pointed out in chapter 3.

Whether or not this corresponds faithfully to Pius XI's commission, we have to observe that in any case it contains nothing new.

If for a moment we suppose that Pius XI did in fact receive the draft of the encyclical, that he had the time to read it attentively, and that he did not find it satisfactory, nonetheless from October 1938 to February 1939 he said nothing, so far as we know, that might have opened up new perspectives on Jews or anti-Semitism. Nothing at the time of the promulgation of the Italian anti-Semitic laws or Kristallnacht in Germany, nothing in his 1938 Christmas address, nothing in the notes that remain from what was to have been his final message to the Italian bishops. It is probably for that reason that Gordon Zahn suggested, in 1972, in the *National Catholic Reporter*, that "it is unwise to make too much of the 'intrigue' which delayed and finally prevented its appearance."[9]

Finally, in *Summi Pontificatus* (20 October 1939), his first encyclical, Pius XII, we are told, included parts of *Humani Generis Unitas*. In fact, we find in it, virtually unchanged, the enumeration of the foundations of the unity of humanity.[10] There are also many concerns—about the rights of all people, the importance of religious instruction, and so on—that are so common to the two popes that they probably owe nothing to the drafts of *Humani Generis Unitas*. What is not found in Pius XII's encyclical, on the other hand, is the slightest explicit reference to racism, not to mention anti-Semitism. But at this point we enter another discussion, the one concerning Pius XII's "silence," which it was not our intention to take up.

Let us conclude. On the eve of the Second World War, the doctrinal anti-Judaism traditionally professed by the ecclesiastical institution retained all its normative power. It was even reinforced by contextual factors that were wholly secular in nature. In fact, as a result of the breakdown, in the course of the nineteenth century, of the whole world of which the Church saw itself as the principal as well as the unifying ideological and political center, the institution had gone on red alert against modernism and modernity, in which it always saw a plot, concocted above all by Jews, to undermine the Christian order of international society.

Consequently, Catholics were hardly educated for a well-equipped and effective resistance to anti-Semitism, no matter where it came from.

In this context, the preparation, starting in June 1938, of an encyclical denouncing particularly racism and anti-Semitism, appears in itself an important event. Not that any written document, even an encyclical, would have sufficed to overturn the mentalities and attitudes of the faithful, of the clergy, or, indeed, even of the hierarchy. If we suppose that a pope, in this case Pius XI or Pius XII, had suddenly appealed to the Church for a crusade against the perils that threatened Jews at that time, we may well wonder whether such an appeal would have been acted upon. Wouldn't this change of direction have seemed too abrupt, too radical, too brutal, even to be understood? To set in motion that kind of transformation took precisely the genocide perpetrated by the Nazis, Jules Isaac's efforts, John XXIII's inspiration, the Vatican II Council, and so many other shocks that jolted the Church over the half-century that separates us from the death of Pius XI.

Moreover, the document in question, *Humani Generis Unitas*, was not, with regard to Jews, the vehicle of a revolutionary turnaround; far from it—at least in the form in which we have it. Nonetheless, it asserted that Christianity was incompatible with racism and anti-Semitism, and condemned the particular attacks on the natural rights of Jews. If only for that reason, it is unfortunate that this encyclical project was never carried through to completion.

Humani Generis Unitas

THE COMPLETE TEXT

Foreword

In a letter written to Father Francis Xavier Talbot on 18 September 1938, John LaFarge indicates that he hopes to leave Paris for Rome on 20 September, "taking with [him] the completed work. Unfortunately, we still have to retype to make it presentable." The documents that are in our possession or that we have been able to consult show that LaFarge left Paris carrying several copies of the draft encyclical, written in English, French, and German, and covered with deletions and annotations.[1] In Rome, LaFarge made the whole "presentable" by putting it in the form of an "abridged" French version, the first page of which bears the following annotation, in LaFarge's hand:

HUMANI GENERIS UNITAS
Pope Pius XI—The Ineditum
(cf. declaration in his address quoted by
Osservatore Romano, August, 1938)

Authentic and complete (French) text.[2]

Hence we have chosen to publish this version.
To try to establish as precisely as possible the role played by

each of the three men who collaborated in producing this work, let us review the documents at our disposal:

—an English version covered with manuscript annotations, deletions, interpolations, cross-references, bracketed passages— additions that all appear to us to be in LaFarge's hand;

—a shorter English version, corresponding exactly to what remains of the longer one once the emendations burdening it are eliminated—we consider this version a fair copy of the first;

—a French version corresponding exactly to the "short" English version, one of them—but which one?—clearly being a translation of the other.

When compared with the other two, the longer English version appears to be a working copy. It obviously consists of three fragments, of which the third was written on a different type-writer:

—The first fragment (fifty-five pages, numbered 1–55) runs from paragraphs 1 to 70. On the flyleaf, LaFarge has written by hand: "Translation not yet made of paragraphs *77 to 110 inclusive*. NB—1) Translate "Nationalité Terrienne" by *territorial national-ity*—when word first appears, add word *people* in parenthesis. 2) Extensive *totality*—or *totality of extension* is preferable to exten-sive *totalitarianism*, etc."[3]

—The second fragment (nine pages, numbered 1 to 9), which begins with the subtitle "Race and Racialism," runs from para-graph 111 to paragraph 130.

—The third fragment, which runs from paragraph 131 to the end (paragraph 179), is much more chaotic—the pagination changes several times, and there are numerous deletions, correc-tions, interpolations, references, and handwritten or typed addi-tions.

Examination of the annotations in this copy seems to show that the first fragment is a translation of an earlier text, probably written in French (or possibly in German). However, the direction of the translation appears to be reversed in the last two fragments: they seem to have been first written in English, and later translated into French.

To compare our own observations with the conclusions at which Edward Stanton and Johannes Schwarte arrive in their doctoral dissertations: Although Stanton did not have the German version at hand, after a detailed analysis of the three copies at his disposal[4] he concludes that within the final text there are two clearly distinct parts: "The first 75 pages of the final English version (up to the treatment of race and 'racialism') are the work of the specialist Father Gundlach; the remaining fifty pages are the work of Father LaFarge; Father LaFarge corrected various passages in the work of the author of the first part of the document—A comparison between the French version and the two English versions shows that the emendations proposed in the first section were in fact incorporated into the final French and English versions—Of course, it does not necessarily follow that these changes are due to LaFarge alone, or to LaFarge and Gundlach. The third member of the team played a role as well [though] nothing allows us to discern a clear contribution on the part of Desbuquois."[5]

According to Johannes Schwarte, the German version, entitled *Societatis Unio*, is the final version. In his view, this text, to which he did have access, differs from the English and French versions only with regard to the paragraphs on racism and anti-Semitism. Whence the hypothesis he proposes: that it was Gundlach who reworked a first draft written by LaFarge, repeating, in the paragraphs on racism and anti-Semitism, the ideas he had already set forth in 1930 in the *Lexikon für Theologie und Kirche*.[6] Schwarte bases this hypothesis on an examination of the documents to which he had access and the testimony he had collected while working on his dissertation. The testimony of Heinrich Bacht, for example: "As I remember it, all the work of elaboration fell on Father Gundlach, if only because the good Father LaFarge was absolutely not an 'intellectual' capable of that kind of work. That was also why, after he had been given this wholly unexpected mission, he went to Father General Ledochowski to explain the difficult situation in which he found himself. Father LaFarge did of course attend our editorial discussions. But his most important contribution, if I remember correctly, was to maintain a good work climate; and that is why he sometimes invited us out, Father Gundlach and me, when the occasion to do so arose. It is undeniable that from his social work among people of color in the United States he brought us valuable objective information. But Father Gundlach's great socio-philosophical visions were not his cup of tea."[7]

Anton Rauscher reported that Gundlach had told him that he had reworked a first draft by John LaFarge that was "too pragmatic, not sufficiently principled."[8]

According to Paul Droulers, who bases his remarks on the memories of the Parisian Jesuits Gustave Desbuquois and Barde, "[LaFarge] set himself up in Paris at the offices of the *Études* and came over for long conversations with Desbuquois, so that a genuine friendship grew up between them, and Desbuquois, who admired LaFarge, said that he was fulfilling 'a giant's task.' Gundlach joined him and redeveloped the outline in his own manner. Overworked, Desbuquois had asked Barde, who was interested in international and interracial questions, to work more closely with them, but Barde, who was rather reserved, came only once or twice to the editorial discussions: he found Gundlach's philosophical considerations too abstract and unsuited to the theme, according to him. . . ."[9]

Here we offer two additional subjects for reflection. First, in his thesis, Edward Stanton asserts that he received indirectly from Father Anton Rauscher the following information regarding "Gundlach's papers." The latter were supposed to consist of: "1) A handwritten draft covering about half the projected encyclical; 2) a typed copy of the whole of the text, with a complete table of contents; 3) a few typed pages, often including many corrections, of a French text, whose author is not indicated; 4) three typed pages of a manuscript [?] by Father Gundlach, containing the draft of a preface to the text and a few commentaries on 'a request made by the pope that an encyclical on nationalism and race be drawn up.' "[10]

Finally, we should explain that the German version we were authorized to peruse in Mönchengladbach was presented as a complete text, without any correction, and seemed to us to correspond faithfully to the "long" English version mentioned above.

From all the preceding, it seems most likely to us that the "abridged" French version is inspired by Gundlach up to paragraph 76. The rest probably resulted from discussions and compromises among the three writers, although we cannot establish what contribution Desbuquois made.

What follows is, then, the "abridged" French version of the draft entitled *Humani Generis Unitas*.

TRANSLATOR'S NOTE

The present English translation of the draft encyclical is based on the French text, using the extant English versions as a guide. The first of these versions, which the authors assume to have been made by John LaFarge, is incomplete; Thomas Breslin has informed me that he himself probably made the second one, and also translated the passages not translated in LaFarge's English version. Since there are many minor divergences between the French and English versions, and since the French text is the only complete one known to have been prepared by LaFarge and his team, I have elected to follow it here. I would like to express my gratitude to Thomas Breslin for making the relevant microfilmed materials available to me, and for his help and support at various stages of my work.

Humani Generis Unitas

1. THE UNITY OF THE HUMAN RACE has been forgotten, so to speak, because of the disorder in contemporary social life, in relationships among individuals as well as in relations among groups and nations. This disorder is found in factual reality, but it is still more evident in people's minds. That this is so is clearly shown by the variety of remedies proposed for curing the illness.

In one place we find rigid doctrinaires proclaiming the sovereign value of the unity of the nation, in another a leader rousing people's souls by an intoxicating appeal to the unity of the race; whereas eastern Europe throws out to the whole world the promise, tinged with terror and blood, of a new humanity in the unity of the proletariat.

To the often incompatible demands of these various collectivities—nation, race, and class—we must add the obligations imposed, in the name of the unity of the state, on the political community proper.

The Church's right to speak based on her pastoral mission

2. Therefore, at a time when so many contradictory theories are leading to increased disorder in human life in society, the

Church has a duty to speak to the world. She often did so in the course of the past century; now as then, her purpose is to remind so-called purely human wisdom, which has gone astray, of God's Wisdom, the wisdom in which the Spirit of Truth and Order speaks, and which alone provides the legitimate foundation for the principles of our social life.

3. In so doing, the Church is not encroaching on foreign terrain; she does not seek to engage in "politics," pursues no personal interest; she is carrying out the pastoral mission of teaching with which she was entrusted by her divine Founder. This teaching mission concerns not only the immediate or mediate content of Christian revelation, but also everything required to enlighten and direct consciences in everyday life. In fact, to the full extent to which human actions and intentions can have moral value, and thus involve the glory of our Creator and the salvation of His creatures, they are subject to no rules other than those of the Gospel itself, of which the Church is the guardian and interpreter. That is why the Church continually intervenes in matters that concern social life. She is only carrying out a sacred duty.

Right to speak acquired through its history

4. But it is appropriate to observe here that in taking a position on these questions, the Church can appeal to still another right she has acquired through history. The Church, as a supernatural society of souls, provides the world with an example of a unique community: the most unified, most ample, most durable social reality on earth. In fact, for many centuries the Church has provided unity for vast and important parts of humanity. And if it is true that her beneficent action is much less clearly felt in our modern, secularized society, who would dare to deny that what remains of our aspiration to the union of peoples, and of the

consciousness of their duty to unite, is due to the Church's earlier motherly education?[1]

5. Whether or not they are aware of it, civilized peoples in the West still live by the teaching and principles with which the Church, acting like a true mother, endowed them in the past; and in turn they have transmitted this teaching and these principles to other peoples all over the world. Thus the Church is fully justified—not only by her nature and proper function, but also by her actions in history—in considering herself the true principle of life for human society; and she is fully justified in condemning as a violation of divine order the disastrous secularization of society. And especially today, when there is such great disorder and discord among men, before all the world the Church stigmatizes this secularization as a criminal attack on the unity and happiness of the human race.

6. Nonetheless, the Church prefers to speak as a loving mother, inviting all peoples as her children to regain contact with their ancestral spiritual homeland, from which the blindness of their leaders, philosophers and heads of state has led them away. Let them understand that by abandoning it they have lost all hope of genuine unity under the gentle yoke of Christ—gentle, even though, for both individuals and peoples, it can be burdened with the Cross. Let them see, on the other hand, what a desperately heavy yoke weighs on them, a yoke of ideas and social systems that are unfortunately often wholly outside the true divine order.

PART ONE: HISTORICAL EXPOSITION OF THE
ORIGINS OF THE DISORDER FROM WHICH SOCIETY
IS NOW SUFFERING

7. This being the case, the Church will speak. First, to clarify the precise state of affairs, she asks: How does it happen that our contemporary world is suffering, to the point of paralysis, from

such a lack of unity, such an absence of sure guidance, when it is a question of re-establishing order in the life of humanity and of peoples?

I. The Mechanistic-Atomistic Conception of Human Society

If we go back to the beginnings of the period in which we now live, and follow its gradual development up to the present day, when it reaches its culmination, we find that originally there was a spiritual attitude entirely opposite to the one that now prevails. Then, reason felt sure of itself, to the point of believing itself exempt from error; it claimed to have discovered the true principles of every kind of knowledge. By using these principles, reason planned to establish an enduring order of life in society that would obey the law of uninterrupted progress in order to arrive at universal well-being in permanently assured peace. As man's inventions increasingly put at his disposal the gigantic power of steam and electricity, which his technology sought to exploit in ingenious ways, he imagined that he had discovered the universal secret of mastery, order, and efficiency in all domains. And he automatically applied the method and the maxims of his technology to problems of social life. In conformity with that method, he thought that once these questions had been broken down into their constituent parts, and the relations among these diverse parts and their interactions clearly determined, he could then let the social organism, which was also governed by determinism, function mechanically. Moreover, by further pursuing the study of the physics of society man believed it would be possible—taking into account the varying needs of the place and time, and acting at the right moment—to rebuild the institutions and arrangements of collective life from the ground up, the way he would like them to be.

False idea of man and of reality

8. Two conditions had first to be fulfilled, or more precisely two obstacles had to be cleared away before men could begin with full confidence this task of adjusting and reconstructing social life. First, a new conception of human nature and of all that is essential to man had to be developed; next, it would be especially important to clarify the content of what we call the real, the constitutive being of reality itself. In fact, no attempt was made to see in human nature a living, intimate, indivisible unity, spiritual through and through, and whose various constituent elements are coordinated and associated. Human nature was reduced to a single element, or at most to a purely extrinsic combination of several elements. And man's essential reality was seen only in its exterior shape or outward aspect, which amounted to saying that it is simply this or that, now one thing and then another, but always undergoing successive changes.

Neither was there any attempt to penetrate human reality's inward structure, to grasp the essential, immutable, and thus intangible, relations and connections of Being, Finality, and Value. Consequently, it was erroneously assumed that the particular reality of human life in society, precisely as it has emerged from historical evolution, was merely a collective, wholly external phenomenon, whose appearance varied with time and place. The inner principle that maintains the living unity of social life and directs its manifestations in accord with its nature and goal remained undiscovered.

Denial of the spiritual soul

9. To locate the common source of these two false assumptions, we have only to rely on the conclusions of sound philosophy and the teachings of Christian Revelation in order to

determine the doctrinal point denied or at least ignored by those who are taken in by the erroneous theses of materialist or positivist philosophy: What characterizes and distinguishes man is his spiritual soul. From this spiritual nature proceeds man's drive toward unity and order in his life. That is why human nature is marked by an indestructible unity of inner life, including the ordered hierarchy of the elements that make up its being; that is why human activity, whether involving understanding or will, cannot and must not remain content with the surface and multiplicity of things, but delve into their inner reality. And it is once again for the same reason that men do not live together like animals, in space and time. As men, together they must achieve more than a mere conglomerate; they must realize a genuine community of life, in which the requirements of their being are fulfilled and the values of their nature are put into practice.

Effects on society and on the dignity of the human person

10. Hence the initial error of making these two false assumptions and failing to recognize the true nature of man was pernicious, even though seductive. The ground seemed to be cleared for building new political and social structures, taking into account only external needs and ignoring historical elements persisting from the depths of the past.

11. It followed from these assumptions that man would be stripped of what constitutes his special dignity, namely his spiritual nature. And in fact no attention was paid the essential tendency of man to seek unity in his life, to develop his personality and his responsible autonomy.

All that was left standing amid these ruins was man's ability to perceive the phenomenal aspect of things and their change, governed by so-called purely mechanical laws, and the sole possibility of reacting by choosing extrinsic means and ends.

What a mystification it was to adorn that simple capacity with the noble name of "intellect"! Of the essence and spirit of man, of that spirit made in the image and likeness of God, nothing more was retained. Because of this basic error, sociology was henceforth wholly incapable of becoming a solid normative science for man.

Bankruptcy of the mechanistic-atomistic conception

12. And yet was there ever a time in greater need of reliable guidance for social development? For as we have already pointed out, in our period there is an extraordinary mobility and incessant variability in the conditions of life. The industrialization of old countries, which were previously almost entirely agricultural, along with the colonization of immense new territories, have torn great numbers of men away from their ancestral land or from their traditional environment; these uprooted people have been thrown into the maelstrom of nomadic life, finding work where they can, but not able to become genuine craftsmen. Attachment to one's native soil and to family traditions inherited from earlier generations were considered factors without any significance for the social order.

Deceptive promises of material well-being

13. In fact, didn't everything seem to justify proceeding in this way? Men were confronted by vast economic and technological prospects capable of providing the same forms of well-being for everyone, and in enormous quantity. Didn't this suggest that we should ignore the characteristic differentiations of the human person as such, and see men only as atoms similar to those constituting inorganic matter, and with elementary instincts—particularly the acquisitive instinct—that were the same in all

individuals? The facts seemed to support this way of seeing things: the ease in moving about, exchanging goods, gaining credit, and communicating news had undergone prodigious development; space was no longer an issue, so to speak, in the functioning of human societies. In short, wasn't the conquering drive toward progress so indisputable that attachment to the past, to tradition, seemed no obstacle in the race toward a future characterized by infinite possibilities? Similarly, didn't reckoning with the slow pace of time and the overlapping of generations seem superfluous, now that everyone, everywhere, felt this new need to live at top speed?

14. Today, we see that the modern Tower of Babel has suffered the same fate as the one in the Bible. We will not dilate here on the fallaciousness of assuming that equilibrium in social life is spontaneously and automatically produced. At present, this much has become clear to Us: in place of such an equilibrium, a humanity has been constituted—precisely by giving the will and power of individuals free rein—that from decade to decade, with increasing rapidity, and in every domain, has broken down into countless separate groups competing for supremacy. And what this humanity claimed was its main organizing agent has produced, because it was directed solely from the outside and toward the outside, only overt conflict on one hand, and on the other, an unstable social equilibrium or a system of armed peace.

Bankruptcy of equality

15. Moreover, we have now discovered that the hypothesis of the perfect equality and interchangeability of men is equally fallacious, even within this new social system. Whereas in the interest of social order men were once differentiated and classified by their spiritual and moral qualities, by their professional knowledge and overall social value, today they are increasingly classified

solely in terms of the amount of capital they possess: a wholly superficial principle of classification, or rather a simple fact usually resulting from accidental circumstances.

16. Finally, We regard as equally fallacious the hypothesis of an economic prosperity continually developing through its own mechanical operation alone. In fact, while humanity, to an unprecedented extent, had access to raw materials, while manufactured products were accumulating in enormous numbers, while men were offered the hope of an ever higher standard of living, at the same time there was a steady growth in the number of men who had no share or only a relatively modest share in this material progress, and who in spite of their fully legitimate desires were not able to find work, and thus could not satisfy these desires, since they had no means of acquiring anything whatever.

Loss of internal unity

17. But all this is well-known, and We have already discussed it on several occasions in recent years. What We wish to stress here is the undeniable fact that as a result of the changes we have mentioned, human society has gradually lost all inner coherence, all internal cohesion. Where could it have found this constitutive unity connecting all its elements? It sought only a material, generalized well-being. This goal, considered in itself, in its materiality, and involving only a purely exterior kind of happiness, was already wholly incapable of uniting men in the inner recesses of their souls. But in addition, the more time passed, the more this goal receded into the distance.

Dissociation of men through the acquisitive instinct

18. Unqualified praise was showered on the efficient operation of a purely acquisitive instinct in social life; an instinct of a lower order and which, moreover, does not constitute the basis of hu-

man nature, but is really no more than a particular manifestation of human nature, or more precisely of a mutilated human nature. If not integrated into man's spiritual nature and governed by it, this instinct, far from being an agent of unity among men, can on the contrary only brutally dissociate them and hurl them into a pitiless struggle for existence in which victory hardens the soul and defeat drives resentment to madness.

19. Labor ceased to be a genuine professional bond, consolidated by a common professional spirit and a feeling of shared dignity, with the same good will. This community of souls was replaced, as already noted, by the juxtaposition of haves and have-nots that resulted from the unrestrained exercise of the acquisitive instinct.

Even by private property

20. The institution of private property itself, which was by nature and origin intended to provide a way of making better use of worldly goods and to increase unity within human society, has become, to an unprecedented degree, a source of discord, envy, and obstacles to the rise of the best men, fracturing and tearing apart the social fabric.

21. Finally, space and time, whose power to separate men from each other seemed to be diminishing as technology and economics progressed, have recovered their ability to separate, and have even ignited battles of unparalleled violence for the possession of territories or markets, while also arousing an unanticipated rivalry and mutual incomprehension between the present generation and the preceding one.

Recourse to the state

22. After what we have just said, it is hardly surprising to find that wretched humanity, feeling itself fragmented and torn

asunder by these tendencies that pull it simultaneously in every
direction, has sought support in the social institution of the state.
The latter is in fact the institution best suited to resort to external
constraint in the interest of order, and moreover this preserves its
God-given spiritual and moral character. However, by seeking
help above all from the state, and what is more, from a state
conceived as a purely material power, humanity received nothing
very beneficial either to itself or to the state.

Unifying function of the state

23. For the sole aim of the state, by its nature and proper
function, is to secure the common welfare of its members. Yet
what was asked of the state, precisely when the mass of citizens
were suffering most from instability and internal dissociation, was
to provide a foundation for unity and order in accord with certain
principles—more or less false—of a so-called social morality. This
request implied a practically unrealizable and moreover anti-
natural extension of the state's functions.

Excessive growth of the state's power

24. It was therefore to be expected that states, urged to extend
their functions abusively, and precisely because they were encountering difficulties and failures of increasing magnitude, would
seek abroad diversionary successes of another kind in order to
preserve their prestige and maintain their own existence.

The result was to strengthen the temptation felt by anyone
who holds power to increase it excessively, and this in turn led,
in a way entirely characteristic of the relations among modern
states, to a violent and constant tension, to an unacceptable but
forcefully expressed assertion of the state's absolute sovereignty,
radically rejecting any subordination to a higher form of organi-

zation of the human community. And this is what ensued: the distribution of humanity into different states (which, given man's natural tendency to form such groups in order to perfect his spiritual and moral life, is in the divine plan a way to develop the life of the whole by differentiating it) itself became a new and discouraging source of division among men.

25. That is not all. The relations of individuals and groups with the state deteriorated in the same way. As we have already observed, the state and the state alone was seen as the ultimate resort; it was therefore increasingly asked to further the interests of individuals and groups. The state, in this regard, was considered and used as a simple instrument for services benefiting individuals. Thus the state, along with its institutions, became an arena in which selfish individual and collective interests battled each other for control of the state's power. Later on, the nature of the relations between citizens and the state was entirely corrupted. The state's primary aim and its moral goal is to secure the common good, to serve the interests of each and every one without distinction, and in that very way to establish union among all men. However, matters being as we have just described them, men's spontaneous, natural tendency to come together in a state thereby itself became, contrary to its proper orientation, a principle of deep division.

Summary of the failure

26. If we now sum up these bleak observations, it appears beyond doubt that in our time the story of the Tower of Babel is being repeated. With the assistance of the resources of modern technology and economics, the passion for acquisition has gradually taken a large part of humanity in its grip; it has erected a gigantic pyramid out of every man's yearning for enjoyment and an ever increasing standard of living; everywhere, unlimited by

space or time, by profession or nationality, a single language expresses the same appetites...A deceptive unity! For we must all
finally acknowledge that the proud edifice will never reach its full
height today, any more than it did in Biblical times, and for the
same reason: the builders no longer understand one another, and
this is its characteristic mark. The impossibility of mutual com-
prehension—which in Babel resulted from differing languages—
signifies for us, as it did for the people of that earlier time, that
the community of men has lost its true spiritual unity, that the
active elements of disorder described above have erected cruel
barriers between the members of human society, dug deep
trenches—in short, created division. Among us as well, the attempt has been made, using great supplies of material, to build
an edifice of dominating height; and once again, because spirit,
and The Holy Spirit itself, has been outrageously denied, another,
far more valuable edifice has been overthrown, the living edifice
of a humanity united in its common soul. For there can be a truly
united humanity, a truly real humanity, only insofar as it is full
of the spirit, or we should rather say, the Holy Spirit; and this
humanity can remain united only insofar as it takes its inspiration
from the Holy Spirit, obeys its laws, and determines its goals and
the hierarchy of its values in accord with it.

Effects on human personality

27. In any event, not only the unity of the social aim has
perished, but also man's personality itself, the sense of the rights,
dignity, and value of the person. Corresponding to social dissolution there is a parallel decline of the individual members of
society. The latter, losing their lofty status as persons, are now no
more than simple parts of a whole, numbers in endless files of
other similar numbers.

28. This is hardly unexpected, after all that has been said

above. The same factors that by their very nature ought to con-
nect, structure, and create unity in social life, but which for the
reasons indicated have had the opposite result, cannot fail to have
the same catastrophic effect on personality. There again, they are
acting contrary to their true mission, which was to secure and
enrich the human person's value and dignity. This mutilation and
elimination of personality were inevitable, to the very extent that
labor became no more than the expression of the instinct to acquire material goods, and the amount of wealth a man possessed
almost the only determinant of the respect and importance accorded him. Mutilation and elimination of personality were all
the more inevitable because men were also becoming more es-
tranged and more opposed to each other in social life, striving to
prevent or at least limit the development of others, whether individuals or collectivities. At the same time, the uprooting of so
many men from their traditional environment, such as we see in
the case of great numbers of peasants, was depriving them of the
natural conditions of improving themselves and their position in
society. The state's activity accentuated this disastrous breakdown
of personality by encroaching more and more upon the independence of individuals, forcing them to enter into enormous,
constantly growing organizations in order to seek the security
they lacked elsewhere, stifling the individual and reducing his
normal opportunities for personal development.

Diminution of personality as a result of social forces

29. Yet labor in a regular profession should have marked every
individual's deepest being with a character peculiar to him; property should have provided everyone with solid assurance of security; rootedness in a particular environment, determined by his
attachment to tradition, love of country and sense of nationality,
and nourished by history, should have oriented every individual's

thought, will and feelings; in everyone, citizenship should have increased consciousness of responsibilities, or better yet, made him happy to feel responsible; eagerness to organize associations should have been merely the manifestation of a firm resolve to help each other and not of poorly disguised indolence and fear. Had this been so, each man would have increased the real wealth of his being, grown in value; he could have become a person in the full sense of the word, worthy and capable of legitimate autonomy.

30. Unfortunately, things turned out otherwise. We have seen that the forces acting within society, far from coordinating its constitutive parts and providing an inner armature, far from constructing in this way an organic whole of gradually increasing vigor, have on the contrary dissociated and separated the elements of society. They have committed the same crime with regard to the human person. And what remained of man after he had been ravaged in this way was a singularly diminished creature who had abdicated his power of making decisions and acting for himself, who was inclined to allow himself to be pushed and carried along by events, an almost passive and inert being, an elementary molecule lost in the mass of a body—in short, a reed shaken by the wind, as the Scriptures say.

By the standardization of human life

31. That is not all. Man's misfortune was completed by another disintegrating force, so-called uniform living conditions. Cities spread their suburbs out over what had earlier been purely farmland; industry's assembly-line products have been standardized, forcing a specific form on the consumer; even leisure and recreation have been standardized. In short, uniform ways of life have today reached the countryside as a whole, promoted by contacts and multiplying relationships with cities. The brutal and

monotonous uniformity of this state of affairs would not have come about had the present development not led to the depersonalization of man that we have deplored. For all these reasons, we are currently confronted by a frightening phenomenon: the ordinary man of our time is in constant danger of being caught up and carried away by blind mass movements. Without ideas of his own, without a will of his own, as soon as the incessant, insistent propaganda proceeding from the press, radio, movies, public meetings, or anywhere else goes to work on him in order to rouse his enthusiasm for a cause or a man, or on the contrary to inflame his opposition to someone or something, he immediately joins the crowd, shares its passions, and participates in its acts. This is, let us acknowledge it, a lamentable sign of the absence of personality and independence, especially when one thinks of all the energy and material resources that are spent today on educating young people and adults in order to make them worthy of being called men.

32. This should not be considered surprising. The most advanced and ingenious teaching methods could not give man what the development of our times constantly seeks to take away from him: namely, the solidity and richness of a strong personality, personal judgment, a sense of running his own life—all basic qualities that allow man not only to remain open to ideas and influences from outside, as he should, but especially to develop within himself the will to judge them independently and to act independently, rather than letting himself be manipulated by others.

The true Christian

33. Confronting today's world, the true Christian stands as straight and strong as a tower. Even if he happens to lack a full education, which is certainly not a negligible advantage, he

nevertheless dominates from above the dismal crowd of men who are prey to every external force. His faith, his union with God and the Spirit of Truth and Order, have given his inner life unity, solidity of character, and the calm assurance of soul, that all proceed from the Spirit. If these evolutionary factors, repeatedly mentioned above, were all to come together to create an environment that favors man's healthy development, the values we admire in rare men who bear the plain stamp of the Christian—namely personality, character—would then be every man's lot, for the full realization of his being and his personality.

II. Effects of the Mechanistic-Totalitarian Conception on Human Society

34. No truly informed person, We think, would challenge the correctness of Our explanation of the current evolution of society. This evolution is marked both by the way the unity and inner connection of human society are slipping toward an interior rupture, and by a similar slippage of individuals toward the mass into which they are absorbed. Any remaining doubts on this subject must be abandoned when confronted by clear evidence of the desperate, not to say fierce, efforts being made to re-establish unity, any kind of unity. These efforts were particularly noteworthy after the Great War; then, as We mentioned at the outset, the most diverse formulas called for unity: the unity of the nation, the unity of territorial nationality, the unity of the race, the unity of the proletariat—and, crowning them all, the unity of the state.

35. Let Us leave aside for the moment a consequence not noticed at that time, namely that the number and incompatibility of these various formulas alone, and particularly the efforts to put them into practice, inevitably further increased the division among men and within humanity; We will not dwell on the way these formulas drove men into different, violently opposed camps.

What is most important here is to determine if all these formulas are suitable for avoiding the catastrophe that is threatening us, for re-establishing the unity of the human race and the value of the human person in all their truth and assurance. Unfortunately, our experience up to this point offers no grounds for hope.

a) Effects of the totalitarian system on human unity

36. First of all it is clear that under the domination of some of these formulas, people have become accustomed to denying that concrete humanity constitutes a genuine unity; or at least to minimizing that unity by opposing it to other concrete realities, for example race, nation, or class; then it is claimed that anyone who still refers to the unity of the human race is a mere fanatic, an intellectual living among abstractions. There is no need to mention here what We will explain later on: that the unity of the human race is known to us both through reason and through divine Revelation. Our natural powers of understanding can already discover that there is a human nature identical in all men and in all times; this unity is also founded on the supernatural truth of the Redemption, just as it is presupposed by the very fact of original sin, and found in the supernatural relation of all men to their Redeemer, Jesus Christ.

Threats to human unity posed by the foreign relations of totalitarian states

37. While these developments are already deeply disappointing, even the most summary consideration of the effects they have already produced suffices to destroy any remaining optimism. Wherever their proponents have begun to put these formulas into practice on the social level, we find them claiming for their respective fundamental ideas a primacy of rank and value, a primary

and absolute right in every domain of life, in order to shape men in accord with their aims. Everywhere, they are seen at work outside their proper territory, and thus in the rest of the world, cleverly undermining, when not attacking directly, the sense of the great human community, its goals and its institutions that are indispensable for social life. At most they leave in peace certain types of collectivities regarded as deserving favor because they already represent some similar tendency, whether nationalist, proletarian, racist, or some other.

38. Leaving aside the fact that this way of proceeding is inconsistent with the principle on which these formulas are based, and also that interested and opportunistic considerations are involved, it has to be clearly stated that the sharply defined will to be oneself first and foremost, without regard for others, itself elicits in the larger social group steeped in it a dynamism that has a divisive effect on the rest of humanity. For this dynamism seeks to annex morally, by every suitable means, groups belonging to other states, but which it considers to be its spiritual relatives; henceforth, it is easy to foresee the immediate consequences that will flow from this. We thus find ourselves confronted by forms of imperialism. The specific type does not matter: in every case efforts to establish this kind of unity accelerate humanity's evolution toward dissociation, rather than promoting the union of men.

Threat to internal unity posed by states founded on totalitarianism

39. From this point of view, what now remains from the internal structure of the social systems We are to examine? In response to the capital question of unity, a question that requires so much circumspection, all these systems tend to offer a solution that is all the more mechanical because they categorically refuse

to acknowledge that a solid and communitarian social organization has a proper and natural function in the establishment of unity, and thus the right to contribute to it. Each system posits at the outset a fundamental idea considered as absolute, and seeks to make every form of life and every right flow from it. Even leaving aside for the moment the highly debatable question of the legitimacy of this conception, We can affirm this much: The unity sought in this way is equivalent to the purely mechanical unity of a machine, or at most to the unity of a vegetable or animal organism; it is not a genuine unity, and does not deserve to be called a human social unity, in the full sense of the word. In fact, true human social unity requires, really to come into existence, unity within variety, that is, it requires that the unity of the whole, the agent and guarantee of the spiritual and moral Good of the whole, be constantly asserted as a force of union and organization among the diverse constitutive elements, and constantly interpenetrate them in order to lead them to collaborate in this union.

It is thus highly improper to use the expression "social unity" when it is claimed that in both principle and fact internal social factors cannot have their own role in the establishment of this unity, and when it is also claimed, on the contrary, that the form and content of the life of these factors are exclusively determined by each system's fundamental idea, considered as a sovereign absolute informing every aspect of social life.[2]

Tendency toward economic collectivism

40. A grave danger thus appears in concrete reality: This extensive totality, with its erroneous concept of social unity, tends fatally toward a leveling and standardizing collectivism.

Moreover, economic activity within the political frontiers of these states is directed exclusively toward developing and ensuring

their respective communities' material life, as if this were its supreme and sufficient principle. Morality, basing itself on the natural order of things and the hierarchy of values, proclaims that
economic activity in a given state must have as its primary goal
the material well-being of families in harmony with the overall
prosperity of states, and that thereupon rests the development of
any civilization. But this teaching is scornfully rejected as tedious
and vulgar social eudaemonism.

41. In addition, it is clear that in societies in which unity has
taken the form of this abusive totalitarianism, the various independently administered occupational communities, and their associated collaboration, are considered in theory a form of harmful
pluralism whose existence is undesirable; in practice, after making
many attempts to move in other directions, they revert to the
state when they have to resolve labor conflicts or regulate the
conditions of labor in the interest of social order. The state settles
matters directly. To be sure, in certain cases and under certain
conditions, and when the common good requires it, this direct
state intervention in social matters is itself in conformity with the
principles of natural law; indeed, sometimes it is the only way of
establishing or re-establishing order. Nonetheless, a twofold doubt
then arises. Are we not unduly sacrificing private groups and organisms based on nature by depriving them of their role? Moreover, and this is still more serious, does a social group of the
totalitarian type just described understand the term "common
good" in the objective sense assigned to it by natural law?

Mutilation of the state

42. This question regarding the common good entails consideration of another, still more important factor in social life: the
state. The state's raison d'être is, in accord with its natural goal,
to provide for the common good on an ongoing basis. Now social

unities of this kind, namely states, as soon as they tend toward an unlimited extensive totality, threaten to strip the state of its essential attributes and sovereign power. If this happens, the state is transformed into a wholly mechanical administrative bureaucracy, a simple instrument of the racist or nationalist collectivities involved. Thereby the state's own nature as a state is mutilated, in violation of natural law; in addition, in relationship to the concept of the common good, a clear inner contradiction arises between this concept and the state's own activity, with regard for example to legislation, the determination of rights, and administration. In fact, in this case, the state's own obligation, which we have already said consists in taking the good of the whole body of citizens as the normative goal of its action, is completely abandoned and subordinated to the interests of the collectivity. As a result, the state's essential duty, which derives from its very nature—namely, to ensure equality of rights for all citizens without exception—is henceforth absolutely unrealizable, even in the most reduced form.

43. In summary, this is what emerges from these observations taken all together: on one hand, the tendency in practice toward a leveling, standardizing collectivism, on the other, at the very core of social life, a profound inability to achieve social unity within an authentic and legitimate diversity. All this creates a tension that, joined with the overheated dynamism of outward expansion, imperils the unity of the human race's social life.

Proletarian states

44. Substantially the same thing can be said about social unities or states that base their extensive totalitarian activity on the "unity of the state" or the "unity of the proletariat." However, we should note that in the first case (that is, totalitarianism based on the unity of the state) the state's inner moral nature is completely

ignored. In the second case, we are justified in asking what is meant by this "unity of the proletariat" that is supposed to be the origin and foundation of social totalitarianism. Is it chiefly a psychological complex composed of all the abandonments and uprootings, all the insecurities of existence? In that case we find ourselves confronted with at most a deep despair that leads the masses to react in a brutal manner; a clear and tragic proof of the disorder. If it is on the contrary the finally acquired sovereignty of a class in accord with the aims of Marxist socialism, then it is no clearer how the principle of class struggle and dictatorship based on force which is at the foundation of this system can become a principle of internal order, of harmonious unity within human society. In what We have already said or written on this subject, notably in our encyclicals *Quadragesimo Anno* and *Divini Redemptoris,* We have repeatedly pointed out the way in which Marxism has deprived humanity of its liberty, destroyed all dignity of the human person, and shown itself utterly incapable of establishing any form of human unity.

45. Let us therefore conclude that the formulas for achieving unity that have been promoted in our time are of no avail in strengthening the internal fabric of humanity. They aim directly at provoking a terrible catastrophe, or rather they hasten its arrival. Another question arises: What protection is afforded personality, a value which is intimately associated with the unity of humanity and therefore faces the same peril?

b) *Effects of the totalitarian system on personality*

46. Here again, as in the case of humanity and its unity, We cannot fail to be disappointed in advance. For what do we see, without being able to doubt it? Paralleling and in connection with the social systems of extensive totalitarianism, we rather frequently find a certain systematic depreciation of man's personality, a mis-

trust toward it expressed in both speech and writing. Oh, yes! People spread the view that if one stresses the value of personality and its freedom, one is merely following in the wake of Liberalism, a doctrine held to be void of all sense of community and purely individualistic.

47. We will not undertake here an analysis and critique of these ideas, which have already been examined in the light of the teachings of our faith and a sound philosophy; let us leave this to specialists. But insofar as the Christian position on this subject is concerned, it is clear—and every Catholic ought to have learned this from his catechism—that affirmation of human personality and its peculiar value is as old as the creation of man, as old as the august mystery of the redemptive sacrifice on Golgotha, and therefore as old as the supernatural link uniting human personality with the One God in Three Persons, through the sacrament of Baptism.

48. Why then should we be astonished that as a result of such tendencies to fundamentally depreciate the value of personality, the latter's fate within extensively totalitarian social unities, when compared with its former fate, does not seem to be improving? This is all the more the case because in this conception we observe a parallel and logically consistent depreciation of the value of human labor, considered in both its individual and social aspects. In the case of countries subjected to the influence of either collectivist doctrines or concepts of extensive totalitarianism regarding the unity of social life, man is considered first of all as a worker, and still more, and exclusively, as a sort of government employee working for the benefit of the racist, nationalist, statist, or proletarian collectivity. And then the great questions whose solution already involves so many difficulties, namely the choice of an occupation, of an apprenticeship, of independent control over the profession, of the freedom to establish oneself in a profession, of opportunities to rise in society—these questions run

the risk of being grossly simplified to the detriment of morality and human dignity, when some form of totalitarianism erects the monstrous structure of collective labor.

The fate of private property

49. Anyone who wishes to foresee the full development of the consequences of these systems has only to consider the fate of private property in such a situation, even though it is an institution positively founded in natural law. Through its dynamism, extensive totalitarianism tends to take an increasing number of measures that will in fact lead to a broad socialization of the means of production, even if that socialization is not juridically acknowledged.

What is the result? The danger that private property will be abolished, contrary to the strict requirements of morality and natural law, whether it is considered in itself or as one of the social institutions, and to the full extent that private property should in fact be the material foundation on which the activity of individual persons and families is to be established and peacefully and freely pursued over the whole field of human civilization.

The fate of the middle class

50. That is not all. There is moreover, and principally, a danger to the existence of that broad stratum of independent middle classes constituted by active and thrifty families, composed of peasants and artisans as well as industrialists and merchants. History teaches us that these middle classes are the natural support for the internal stability of the state; the source of healthy development, healthy growth of spiritual and material strengths; the fertile territory on which elites of all kinds, distinguished by their personal gifts and capacities for action, are born and naturally rise, without there being any need for artificial measures or purely

external policies. And ultimately we arrive at that dismal state of affairs in which more and more men, finally becoming the majority, depend directly or indirectly on the collectivity for their existence. That is a situation which, given the dynamism of extensive totalitarianism, can bring along with it, and, alas, has already brought about a limitation of freedom that strikes a blow at the personality deep within it, and moreover puts a terribly heavy burden on consciences struggling with the moral duties of marriage and the family that their Christian faith enjoins upon them.

Right of association suppressed

51. Confronted by such facts, a clear judgment must be made. Extensively totalitarian societies are far from arresting man's slide toward this mass existence in which his personality is dissolved. In this kind of society, in fact, man no longer relies on powerful private organizations to make up for the weakness of his individual existence; he cannot do so, for within these same social unities, a natural law attaching to human personality, the right of association—implied by the very collectivizing institutions that so vigorously oppose any form of autonomy for individuals or groups—is rendered powerless. That is why man is forced to seek the representation of his interests in strong organizations emanating from totalitarianism itself and remaining enclosed with it, organizations that are hardly more than the arms with which totalitarianism, which intends to judge, regulate, and direct absolutely everything, holds the masses in its grip.

Manipulation of public opinion

52. In addition, there is something that was already beginning to reveal itself in earlier developments but is now completely evident: the regimentation of public opinion. This is carried out

in all sorts of ways: by the spoken and written word, by the theater, cinema, and radio, by art and even by science, by schools and the trades, and even—a repugnant development—by pressure put on the poor through the assistance offered to them. And the result of all this is the modern mass man, who no longer has any opinions of his own, any will of his own; he is merely a passive instrument in the leader's hands. It is practically impossible for him to undertake any initiative at all, no matter how limited; yet without this spirit of initiative, man is incapable of acquiring the personal culture that is a vital element in the human community.

Destruction of the true notion of authority

53. This brings us to one of the most important points in modern social life: authority. In the course of earlier contemporary development, this question was obviously ignored, to the point that the current constructors of new social unities dare to attribute their superiority to their stress on the principle of authority, conjoined with the totalitarian principle. But we have noted that totalitarianism is incapable of establishing true unity in men's social life; similarly, among the new architects of authority, a purely negative conception of authority leads away from true unity rather than toward it. And in fact their conception of authority is purely negative. It includes this thesis that the formation of will within these social unities excludes, without exception, any personal cooperation on the part of its members; indeed, the very formation of this will must be accomplished in such a way as to avoid relying on the positively and freely expressed will of its members; however, it remains understood that any measure taken by members on their own, any initiative on their part, will not be allowed.

Fallacious use of the term "authoritarian"

54. Today it is common to call "authoritarian" methods of shaping will in social unities. This is a fallacious use of the term, and the more literally it is understood, the more fallacious it is. For it gives the impression that its "authoritarian" constructions are particularly concerned with the principle of authority in social life. In fact, what is directly involved here is a specific technique for shaping will in the interest of social life, and not at all authority itself, in its authentic essence.

55. In the kinds of societies termed "authoritarian," what is at issue is not safeguarding authority as such, but rather, in the given case, shaping a *unified* will for the benefit of social unities, with a full guarantee of success, and with minimum friction and maximum speed. These two results, and particularly the first one—namely, the shaping of this unified will in a state—have encountered various dangers in the course of the contemporary development We have described. Reviewing the social history of our time, we can always point to the trials and perils so-called democratic institutions have faced in their attempts to shape a unified will.

56. There is no doubt that finding a way of operating with the minimum of friction and the maximum of speed is genuinely important; but it remains to be discovered whether it is wise to adopt this mode of operation in every situation, and whether, by trying to force success in this way, one has to sacrifice other elements in men's life that are more important, or at least deserve serious consideration. To justify this way of proceeding, appeals are made to the example of the conduct of war; emphasis is laid on a principle which, it is said, is absolutely inevitable: that it is important above all to act, preferable to run the risk of failure than to do nothing at all. But there is cause for serious reservations when we see the model for governing a

people or a state sought in a situation as abnormal as that created by war.

Peace is the normal condition of life

57. Yes, our cries of pain must rise up toward the God of peace; today, it seems, it is no longer everywhere considered abnormal to live social life under conditions resembling those of wartime. For here and there has arisen the objectionable practice of giving civil life the appearance of war, as if peace were in itself nothing but preparation for war. Anyone who steadfastly holds that peace is the normal condition of social life will think otherwise: he will say that because stability is necessary for life, the exercise of authority in framing laws—insofar as this is a patient weighing of arguments for and against, and the continuity and interconnection of the laws is maintained—constitutes the most active element in shaping the unity of will in the state.

Authority, taken in isolation, is not the principle of unity

58. This naturally leads us to make another observation, namely that the examination of these so-called authoritarian modes of forming the collective will not only has a certain technical aspect, but also raises questions regarding the essential basis and thus the very morality of human life in society. These types of governments, precisely by virtue of the fact that they abhor discussion and reject any contribution made by public opinion, demonstrate their small regard for personality and its normal capacities. This mental attitude leads them to scorn still more any actual participation by members of the state, and to cede, totally and without reservations, the task of forming the collective will to the person who holds authority, and to him alone.

59. This complex of ideas and this actual conduct rest upon

the following false conception: The principle of authority, taken in itself and in isolation, is the principle of the unity of social systems. This is an inadmissible conception. For it is not when taken in itself and in isolation that the principle of authority is the principle of unity, but rather when it is closely connected with the fact of the natural union of all the members and with their obligation to unite in the interest of the aim assigned to the whole. It follows that authority's field of action and power are in each case determined, founded, and limited by the quality and essence peculiar to this aim. It further follows that the principle of authority, precisely insofar as it exercises its natural function of creating unity, logically presupposes in every case the obligatory union of the members, as such, because of the common goal they are to seek. No doubt the proper function of the principle of authority, through which it guarantees unity, is its leadership function; nonetheless it should also be observed that there exists still another function that creates unity, which is permanent and fundamental and results from the common goal that must be pursued: namely, to foster and cultivate, among members of the community, the simultaneously spiritual and moral sense of their responsibility with regard to it. By neglecting this, social unity is transformed into a simple aggregate of these same members, formed by constraint and discipline.

Authority derives from God

60. The close connection between the function of the principle of authority and the dignity of the members of the community as persons is still more evident if we consider the fact that human authority in itself is derived from God.[3] By assigning it this lofty origin, one strongly emphasizes the dignity of the human person. Human authority in itself entails relationships of subordination between one man and another, spiritual and moral

relationships affecting men as persons; but these very relationships, because of the dignity of the person, and especially because of his essential non-dependency, are so particular that they cannot result from the will of men, whether taken separately or collectively, and they can be grasped in themselves only as the exercise of God's own authority, communicated by God to man.

This inner connection between the origin and essence of authority in itself, on one hand, and the dignity of the human person on the other, is of the greatest importance; it sets the limits of the proper authority of social systems as such, and reduces to their correct proportions the reckless exaggerations that are current today and ultimately damage legitimate authority. The fact that measures are or seem to be useful and even necessary for realizing collective values within a social system does not suffice to justify immediately, and for this reason alone, granting to the authority involved the power to take these measures. For even then we have to consider the inner nature of authority, the origin and essence of these relationships of subordination among men, which are so particular.

And in that way set its proper limits

61. Taken in themselves, these relationships of subordination cannot result from the will of individual men, nor from that of men grouped together in a social whole. If that were not so, then the consideration of what is said to be the common good in a given social system would not merely delimit authority's scope, but also confer on it full and total sovereignty. In other words: Any measure taken by the authority that was, or was claimed to be, connected with the so-called common good of the social system in question could derive its moral justification immediately from that common good itself—a common good, let us note, that has nothing to do with the true *common good* of a well-

ordered society. Human authority taken in itself does not proceed from the social bond, considered without reference to God, who has indivisibly united society and authority; and the reason for this is that human dignity does not allow us to seek any other foundation for these relationships of subordination of one man to another that are established in exercising authority.

62. Therefore any action on the part of human authority that is taken, or said to be taken, with a view to the common good cannot derive its immediate, moral legitimation from this fact alone. And it follows logically that this limitation of the authority's sovereignty in human social systems as such can be applied to all actions directly affecting the human person and its essential rights. The legitimacy or illegitimacy of such actions must in no case be established merely by considering the so-called common good of the social system in question, but must be solidly based on their full accord with Divine moral law.

Practical consequences of the false doctrine of authority

63. And now what do we find in practice? That the mere assertion or assumption that something is useful or necessary for the supposed common good of the state or collectivity—national, racial, or proletarian—suffices to provide human authority with an immediate moral justification for measures that attack the very core of the human person's rights. On this basis, the human person's right to exist is assaulted: it is destroyed in the mother's womb, or its life considered to be without value; it is robbed of its bodily integrity; on insufficient grounds it is exposed to grave dangers to the health of the soul and the body; the right to punish by death is based on destructive premises, on the sole, direct interest of the supposed common good of the state or of some other collectivity, and this right is capriciously exercised, since under the same circumstances and for the same reasons, in one

case the punishment of a murderer is held to be unjustified and in another the murderer is honored as such.

64. On the basis of these same assumptions, other rights of the human person are attacked. Men are unhesitatingly stripped of their freedom, and with still less hesitation, the sanctity of home and hearth are violated. The freedom to marry, to educate children, and even the practice of conjugal rights is limited, with no authorization and in direct connection with the interests of the national, racial, or proletarian collectivity. And worse yet, attempts are made to deprive individuals of the right to decide in accord with their consciences, to make their own choice before God: the decision is to be made by society conceived in a totalitarian manner.

Decline of authority itself

65. This being the situation, we often hear complaints that freedom has perished.[4] For Our part, We too complain, and say that true authority has perished. And We then urge all to remember what has just been clearly explained: In the immutable truth that all human authority proceeds from God, the dignity of the human person is affirmed and emphasized. Authority's consciousness of its divine origin cannot be maintained if the dignity of the human person is violated in the manner described.

66. We have already explained the deplorable consequences this way of proceeding has produced in the area of education, when those holding authority pay no attention to the positive factor in social life constituted by the responsibility of the members of society in the pursuit of the common goal, or acknowledge its role only when it suits them to do so.

If today, remaining faithful to themselves, those in authority still refuse to accord any active role to man's personal dignity, to his spiritual and moral responsibility, even though it is so bene-

ficial for social life as such, then even in this case the external
aspect of a collectivity united by firm discipline, acting by fits and
starts, could never lead Us to conclude that the rightful requirements We set forth and defined have been fulfilled. Behind this
facade is concealed both a mortal threat to the human person and
what would ensue from its demise: an authority that is denatured,
as a spiritual and moral power, an authority that has been transformed into brute force.

Risk of a complete catastrophe resulting from the abandonment of the spirit

67. Our modern society is thus diseased; and the new formulas
for achieving unity, the new types of unity, far from curing the
disease, can only aggravate it. For they dissolve, along with the
concept and ideal of life, which have themselves become mechanically dissociating, the internal coherence of human social
life, and, in a parallel way, the natural components of social life's
constitution as well as its natural foundation, the unity of the
human personality. In the final analysis, they threaten to lead
humanity to catastrophe through their mechanistic, atomistic
conception of the human race, and by their radical abandonment
of the spirit, and ultimately of the Holy Spirit.

Regarding these forms of extensive totalitarianism's unity, let
Us mention one last bit of evidence that points in the same direction. Because it was de-spiritualized and employed purely mechanical procedures, thought could no longer perceive the various
natural factors involved in the building of society and their essential interdependence, as well as the unity within plurality; it
could no longer move on to the true unity and totality of a
complete system of the world, including an intensive totality,
that is, an authentic unity in an authentic plurality. Of spirit it
retained intelligence alone, which precisely no longer deserved to

be termed intelligence in its deep sense, that is to say, in the sense of spirit; yet in recent years intelligence has had to be all the more prepared for the attacks made upon it.

68. The social forms of extensive totalitarianism demonstrate their lack of spirituality in that they place special emphasis on a single factor in the social edifice—race, the nation, the state, the proletariat—and accord it such decisive preponderance that other factors lose all meaning and value of their own. To be sure, unity is thus produced, but a purely mechanical unity, obtained only by the extension of this single factor: and then one also has only a simple extensive and mechanical totality. True, internal, profound unity is destroyed and along with it the visible stamp of a social edifice full of spirit and informed by spirit.

69. This same lack of spirituality has brought about the destruction of the internal unity of the human person and of personality. Thus it is hardly surprising that among contemporary men, and especially the younger generation, resistance to a reality stripped of all its objective values has stiffened. Such a reality could only produce weary, skeptical men without shared convictions who carelessly abandoned everything—even all properly human values.

That being the case, there remained and still remain only two choices: either a return to the spiritual, or a strong and open commitment to what is not spiritual, namely the pressure of temperament and instinct, affective sensibility, or vigorously aggressive action as such. Doesn't the second alternative amount to an attack on the very heart of human life, or rather on the heart of all social reality?

The reality of the human person, informed by spirit, which defines and asserts itself in the intimate unity of the various manifestations of its life and its responsible exercise of freedom, and which moreover is opposed to the view of the individual, *qua* member of society, as nothing more than a member—this reality no longer counts, for only the collective concentration of a material-sensate current of life is to constitute the final and definitive unity and reality.

In addition, man's natural sociability itself is nothing more than the essential and therefore necessary manifestation of his person as informed by the spirit; but it has been transformed into something entirely different: a simple mechanical, organic process, like those we see in plants and animals, in which individuals are concentrated or mass-produced in accord with a certain type and common development. When this occurs, the abandonment of the spirit is definitive.

70. Because they have turned away from the spirit—that is, ultimately, from the Holy Spirit, the foundation and source of all unity and all order—the men of our new times have likewise sought for the past century to build their own Tower of Babel, and, of course, without God's help. "Let us glorify our name," these builders of society have said in their turn. And, as before, their enterprise has ended in appalling division and destruction. Men no longer understand each other. Now as before, the Divine Spirit, the Eternal, has descended upon men as an avenger, saying: "I shall confound their tongues."

PART TWO: THE UNITY OF SOCIAL LIFE

71. After the preceding examination of the errors into which the society of our time has strayed, we Christians are still more firmly convinced that true unity among men can come only from the spirit, inspired by the uncreated Spirit whose Divine Person has been poured "into our hearts" in "mysterious fullness," and who at the birth of the Church made all Christians "of one heart and mind," achieving the miracle of making it once again possible for all the representatives of the most diverse peoples to communicate in a single and unique language. This Spirit is the spirit

of unity, since He Himself is the love of the triune God in all its fullness. Wherever He is poured forth, there unity is poured forth; where His fertility is allowed free rein, inner unity is created. Illuminated by this uncreated light that is "the spirit of God who dwelleth within us," enriched by the gift of His grace fortifying our faith, making steadfast use of the natural faculties of the created spirit given to all men, we recognize that in truth humanity constitutes a unity. This is clearly not a unity in the way an individual person is a unity, and still less in the way a machine or a vegetable or animal organism is a unity. It is something else entirely: a unity of order, that is, the unity of a large number of members, each one distinct and personally responsible, with his own destiny, but all of them together internally organized toward common goals. To be sure, a unity of this kind is possible only by virtue of the spirit that produces it. This unity in plurality is what humanity is. Let us consider humanity first in its unity, and then in its plurality.

I. The Unity of Humanity

The unity of nature

72. The unity of humanity is based in the first place on a foundation that can be discovered through our natural powers of understanding. This foundation, this solid ground that supports the whole of humanity, is our common human nature. Certainly, men and groups of men are not interchangeable in a mechanical fashion, like atoms. On the contrary, we see a complex of diverse characteristics and qualities of soul and body. Individuals and groups vary greatly in the way they react to developing events, in their way of thinking and dealing with things; and they are often perplexed as how to choose between extremes. But we

always find different ways of thinking, intermediate attitudes and opinions, never absolute, irreconcilable oppositions. In primary impressions and affective states there is a certain general norm of thought, a certain sameness of feeling, a certain commonality in the fundamental tendencies and direction of the will. Wherever we look, in any period in which we encounter men, whether in our own time or in the most remote past, whether we are concerned with modern civilized man or so-called primitive man, we always find the same human nature. Even those who attempt to deny this bear witness to its truth, for what are they trying to do by denying it, if not to understand the life of these souls, which they claim is so different from our own? This attempt is doomed to fail unless it is acknowledged that the spiritual life of these primitives is ultimately identical with ours. We are led to conclude that all men share a common nature: whether we study the various categories of men distributed at the present time all over the globe, or move backward along the line of human development to primitive man, we find the same specifically human type, identical in both mental and physical characteristics.

Revelation's testimony; Original sin and human unity

73. Thus science seems to confirm the truth of the Old and New Testament's teaching regarding the unity of the human race. No one who professes the Christian faith can doubt that the account of man's creation in Holy Scripture teaches the unity of the human race. We must affirm this single, unifying stream of bodily life—the blood stream, as it is called—that God set in movement in the world, and in which all men are plunged, is such a powerful agent of unity—even though it acts not by itself but by virtue of a formal decree of God—that were it not for this stream of life the melancholy heritage of original sin would not be passed down through the generations. Thus every time

parents, even those who possess sanctifying grace, exercise their holy function of awakening new life, since they are themselves bearers of this stream of life, their very act inevitably endows the child with membership in a community subject to supernatural death. Fortunately, however, this state of death can and must be promptly replaced by a new state of divine life, through holy baptism, in whose waters we are born anew.

Unifying work of the Redemption

74. Moreover, by virtue of the same divine decree, deliverance from the bonds of original sin could be accomplished only after the Redeemer, Jesus Christ, in the womb of his blessed Mother, had himself shared in this blood stream through which all men come into being, and become "like one of us, and in all things save sin." As the fathers of the Church said, "What was not assumed by Him was not healed." That is, humanity has been redeemed only because the second Person of the Holy Trinity took on, through the hypostatic union and through Mary's true human motherhood, a genuine human nature.

Mystery of the blood

75. And this is the true "mystery of the blood." That is why and how blood and blood relationship underlie the reality of the community of men, "the great human family that extends beyond the borders of all races and countries,"[5] and which links all men by that which is deepest in them, namely by their relationship to God. It is sad to observe that today there are men who still want to be Christians, at least in name, who do not admit this mystery of the blood, which is nonetheless one of the foundations of our Christian religion. Such men grossly exaggerate the role of accidental and in any case very superficial accidents of blood and

blood relationships in the formation of social groups larger than the family. And they do so to the point that, in opposition to all experience, and still more in opposition to the teaching of our Catholic faith, they absolutely reject the unity of the human race and seek to erect insurmountable barriers between the different communities of blood and race. They even go so far as to formulate the proposition that human races, because of their natural, immutable characteristics, are so different one from another that the most inferior race is more remote from the most developed than from the highest animal species.

Men are united by their life on the earth

76. The human race is united not only by a common nature, but also by the necessary, twofold force that accounts for the extension and evolution of human life, that is, by space and time. Doesn't unity also result from our life side by side on the same earth, over which all men of all times go as pilgrims toward their eternal destiny, and over which passes the endless "caravan" of which Saint Augustine speaks?[6] Man's joys and sorrows, his successes and defeats, are always borne by the same earth, it constantly offers material energies to the new generation and receives the dead; on it rest and will always rest men's houses and homes; in its own way, it stamps the deepest recesses of men's souls with its own beneficial stability, which, as people say, "attaches them to the soil"; it binds men together through their sense of being neighbors and through their common love of their native land, and makes them long for the place where they were born even when they are far away. All men everywhere show the influence of having lived side by side in space, on the same earth. May we not find therein the basis of a genuine unity in which all men can understand each other?

That is what all men of all times feel with regard to the earth that bears us all. That is why everywhere on the earth, in accord with a holy custom that cannot be too highly recommended, they plant the cross, the sign of the most intimate community; for the same reason, the Church has always and everywhere blessed, with ancient, unchanged formulas, the earth on which humanity lives, the earth that the first and second Adam both trod.

Men unified by time

77. We have just seen how space, in virtue of men living side by side, leads to union among them. The same is true of time, which also acts to unite men and marks each of them with a seal of unity. Men's lives, succeeding each other, give rise to tradition; and through them history comes into being. Many people see precisely in this relation through time the very reason for what is called the nation or national cohesion.

The Church's sense of history

78. The Church is particularly aware of the important role time plays in uniting men, and of the social efficacy of tradition and history in the life of humanity. The Church is in fact rooted in the temporal, precisely because of her divine, spiritual element. God became man, not at a random moment in history, but at a very specific moment: "when the fullness of time was realized." When human history had reached that point, then God, through the incarnation of His Son, entered our history, entered the temporal life of men living together, not as a stranger, but as a member of the family.

Historical vocation of a Catholic nation

79. As a result, His action, a source of life and grace, perpetuated by and in the Church, an action that is subject to the laws

of history, has continued since that time, maintaining the constructive activity of tradition and unity. Thus the Church, whatever her very special nature may be, finds herself here in accord with all other types of society, since by their very nature they are all rooted in history, in tradition, in the temporality of our social life; and the same can be said of the Church's accord, both internally and positively, with nations. If there are state-systems that call themselves Catholic because they are based on a dynasty or a crown anointed by the Church, this is the result of a historical encounter with the Church that was not merely a positive fact, as in the case of other nations, but also a religious fact. If this encounter took place in history, that is because in the view of the Church and of these states history was and is above all, since the incarnation of the Son of God, the history of God and of the work of His grace. And what a magnificent, profound, and fruitful unity could spring from that! On the other hand, what a lamentable decline resulted from the misuse or waste of special graces given to the community, when this consciousness on the state's part evaporated, and the state's Catholicism became merely a political formula used by the rulers.

For its part, the Church gives a sacred character to the unifying value human life possesses in virtue of the fact that it is realized in time, itself drawing a perpetual renewal of life from this value all during its march through history. In addition, in every age and for every generation, the Church has acted as a true mother. She is, to use Saint Augustine's expression, "a child to the children, firm with the young, and good and tender to the old."[7]

Union through the use of external goods

80. The development of this human nature common to all takes place not only in space and time, but also in connection with all the external elements of our world. Considering the latter, we perceive another important factor of unity among men.

Among the rights of the human person is the natural right to use the external goods of the earth. If order and peace are to reign in communal life, no doubt the exercise of this right must be constrained by the institution of private property; but it does not follow that it is therefore, in itself and as such, rejected or abolished; on the contrary, it acquires a broad function as an agent of unity among men. From this right possessed by all derives the duty—even in a social system of private property—to facilitate as much as possible the mutual exchange and circulation of products and persons. Apart from human nature's profound tendency to sociability, this general right to the use of goods also entails in theory that peoples have an obligation to facilitate the exchange of people and goods even across their frontiers, in both directions; and in any case to avoid systematically hindering such exchange.

Wasting goods harms families

81. The general right to use goods within a given system of property is all the more justified because the permanent purpose of the goods of the earth is to guarantee the life-security necessary for all individuals, and still more, for all the families of humanity. Because it does not serve this end, massive waste of these goods is contrary to the natural order, even if it does not in any way infringe upon the right to private property. We saw this kind of waste during the disastrous four-year-long World War, when immeasurable material wealth was squandered. Why then should we be surprised that this terrible outrage committed in common against what supports the life of families has still not been repaired?

The wate of war

82. We are faced by the threat of another war, which would bring on a far more massive waste of material goods—a waste

that has already begun through expenditures for armaments. We will not argue here that such a war would not be economically beneficial to any of those who participated in it, because this purely utilitarian point of view is not a conclusive argument against war. Rather, We want to protest this impending war, in the name of millions of families throughout the world and in solidarity with them; for by restricting still more narrowly the effective exercise of the natural right of all to make use of this world's goods, war inevitably destroys the very foundation of the unity of humanity's physical life established by the Creator. We further protest the war, in the name of all men, and more particularly in the name of the many fathers and mothers who are already so burdened with heavy cares, and who all over the world are praying and repeating in every language, and above all at the Holy Sacrifice of the Mass, Our Father's request: "Give us today our daily bread."

Unity through work

83. Men neither want nor ought to wage war; they want to work, and should do so. This vocation to work constitutes a further element in their unity, in which all men come together. Because of their sameness of nature, their spiritual and moral development, as well as their physical improvement, are linked, among us, with work; in the present order of things, after the loss of that happy order of things that preceded original sin, the natural vocation to work was confirmed by God's command: "You shall earn your bread by the sweat of your brow." Consequently, the obligation to work is first of all every man's personal duty, a duty that is embodied, in a new and special way, in actual paternity and in the preparation for the honor of being the father of a family.

84. As a result, the obligation to work, as We noted at the beginning of Our Letter, is not primarily the exercise of a

function imposed by some authority—a state, nation, racial group, or individual man; it is simply a direct obligation attaching to personality, and therefore makes the sum of all men in all times and regions a vast community of workers. The needs of society require that professions be differentiated; distributed among them, men work together, each one in his place, at a common activity; some work as leaders or teachers, others labor under their direction.

85. When labor is carried out in this way, within an occupational framework, it is capable of binding workers together in a genuine community of life, which can extend beyond the limits of space, time, and differences of age. Once, when everything was not so narrowly regulated by the state, there were periods in which those who worked at the same trade collaborated greatly to their mutual advantage, undeterred by differences in living conditions or citizenship. They saw in the general obligation to work a call to carry out the *opus Dei,* to accomplish and perfect, in the same spirit, creation in all its lines, for the glory and honor of the Creator. And when all these companions in labor throughout the world gathered, under the protection of the same heavenly patrons, on the occasion of certain feasts, at the foot of the altar to witness the Holy Sacrifice, this was not merely a pious ceremony carried out by a random group, but rather the union of all participating in the Sacrifice of Christ. They knew that Christ, the artisan of our redemption, had thereby supernaturally elevated all forms of human labor, had raised and established all the partial activities of men in a single *opus Dei*. "Through Him, with Him, and in Him is due to You, God, Almighty Father, in Union with the Holy Spirit, all honor and glory." That is why our hearts go out to the countless Catholic occupational associations that are increasingly realizing, in forms adapted to our times, the true unity of the kingdom of work, in order to heal the schism between classes and the disunity among professions.

The family and the state: unifying factors

86. The richness of human life's variety, which characterizes and supports humanity as a whole, is not limited to the unifying elements already set forth. It includes as well two other unifying factors which, as durable and stable institutions, further contribute to the unity of humanity. These social organisms, which are at the same time living societies, are the family and the state. In any period, wherever we see the spiritual and physical life of man flourishing, we always find the family and the state; they proceed from human nature itself, which was created as both spiritual and corporeal. By internal, natural necessity they are indispensable for humanity, which must, in order to fulfill its spiritual and religious goal, constantly add new members well prepared to play their role, and establish a stable order within its community of life and work.

Religious character of the family and the state

87. By their origin, because they proceed from the nature common to all men as it was created by God, and by their inherent goal of achieving the unity of humanity which the Creator also intended for His honor and glory, these two societies, the family and the state, have always worn the halo of a religious consecration. As for the family, in Paradise we already see it in its initial state of happiness; from that time on, marriage was the foundation of the family, and had the character of a religious pact. Even among pagans, the memory of this has been preserved in various forms; when Christ our Lord came he raised the marriage contract between man and woman to the dignity of a sacrament. The matrimonial community's lofty origin also sanctifies the family society, into which, moreover, the Man-God himself consented to enter during his sojourn here below. He even submitted

to the sacred yoke of authority within the family, an authority proceeding from God, "the husband being the head of the family and the wife the heart." By his example, He both ennobled and confirmed the duty of obedience to parents, a duty in which an original law of human nature is expressed, a law the Creator has inscribed within men's hearts.

88. Similarly, the religious character of the state results from the fact that its authority also proceeds from God, and that person who holds that authority is acting as a "servant of God." Furthermore, this fact also shows that the organization of men into states, considered independently of original sin, is a necessary consequence of human nature as it was constituted by the Creator. Being a citizen of a state fundamentally implies a religious duty and a religious dignity. So-called primitive peoples retain a dim consciousness of this: solemn ceremonies mark the initiation of young people into the tribe, which is like an embryonic organized state. Among the most highly developed pagan peoples, we also find various manifestations of this religious character recognized in the community of the state. It is therefore neither to the honor nor to the advantage of the modern state in a Christian country, and it is naturally also not the fault of the Church, if the majority of present-day states rarely or never agree to recognize overtly the religious character of the state's constitution, or even completely deny it.

True scope of the notion of the family

89. After this explanation of the importance of the family and the state for the unity of humanity, it will be easily seen that absolutely everywhere men are aware that when the family and the state come under attack, the very foundation of their life in common is threatened. In fact, in our own time, the family, as a psychological, juridical, and economic unity, is very gravely affected, as can be clearly seen from many passages in Our Letter.

If in spite of everything the family still appears to be the cell most capable of resisting the social body, that is the proof that it is rooted in the very heart of human nature. Of course, human nature must be understood here as completely involved in the internal unity of its spiritual-corporeal life; for it is only when it is understood in this way that it is the root of the family, and not when it is understood as simply a certain source of physico-organic characteristics, considered in themselves and independently. Only because it is the internal unity of a life that is both spiritual and corporeal is human nature the root of the family— which should henceforth be conceived as the "spiritual womb" in which human society takes form. The family in fact provides all the elements necessary for human life in society, all the formative, necessary influences, with regard to both the soul and the body. All considered, this amounts to saying that the members of a social community are what their families are. The importance of the care we ought to have for the family in its full and true scope follows from everything we have just said. On the other hand, despite the grandiose words used, a false conception of this care for the family is drawn from the erroneous proposition that "It is from the blood, the seat of racial characteristics and their principal source, that proceed all man's intellectual and moral qualities." Here, in contradiction to the teaching of the Catholic faith, sound philosophy, and experience as well, human nature, the family, and of course also marriage are considered solely in their corporeal aspect. Consequently, this way of conceiving care for the family leads toward a disastrous result and disastrous means of achieving it that are sometimes and in some ways wholly scandalous with regard to morality.

Sickness of the state

90. It is not only this development of the family that worries men today; the development of the state is an equally great cause

for concern. In this development we are in fact justified in seeing a threat to the foundation of human society and its unity. In the first part of Our Letter We have explained the source of the modern state's sickness; the latter consists in the fact that the state is in some ways too small, and in other ways too great; the authority of the state is pushed too far in some regards, and destroyed in others. In addition, if energetic measures are not taken, the state faces a terrible crisis, a crisis in the very idea of the state, and one which will end up being the true crisis of human social life.

Essential remedy for the state

91. As regards the domain of the state's activity, salvation must first be sought in this direction: the Church must return to her essential functions. By doing so, she will ensure the proper development of the social organizations that are constituted, founded on the common appurtenance of men to a place and a profession; organizations which, as natural though not essential societies of life in common, have in principle an inherent right, not derived from the state, to govern themselves, and normally must be recognized by public law. When that happens, the state is relieved of a burden, and the development of men in their natural capacity for life is furthered at intermediate stages; this permits them to shape a unified social will without anything unreasonable being required of individuals.

Relations among states

92. Relations among states are currently deteriorating as well. We have expressed Our view on this several times earlier in the first part of this Letter. We have discovered a very precise cause for this deterioration, namely a dynamism peculiar to the modern

state. This dynamism constantly attacks the already rather weak links between states, and threatens to break them altogether, thus completely destroying the unity of the human family that includes all men and all peoples. We, who through Our God-given office are the father of all men, do not wish and must not allow this to happen. For all peoples are brothers in justice and love, not only by virtue of their nature—this much, to the shame of our present-day civilization, was acknowledged even by pagans such as the Stoics—but also, especially, and far more profoundly, in their brotherhood through the Redeemer of the world.

Court of justice

93. This fraternal unity of peoples must be given visible expression by establishing a Court of Justice with its own authority, in appropriate cases, over all peoples. In the event of conflicts between peoples, this Court of Justice would have the power to summon them before its bar for a fair trial, or to make known its opinion, and if necessary, to render a decision binding on all parties to cases under its arbitration. Eminent Church doctors such as Saint Augustine, Saint Thomas Aquinas, and Saint Robert Bellarmine, and great theologians such as Francis of Vitoria and Francis Suarez, have set forth the principles of international law; they unanimously affirm that because the social nature of man is capable of constant improvement, it requires from within such a common institution among states. If sovereignty is properly understood, no infringement of the sovereignty of individual states will result from such an institution.

Undoubtedly, this institution presupposes that all men share the same spiritual attitude, and this is clear from the failure of the efforts that have already been made. This attitude can take root only in Christian teaching, which includes true natural law, and of which the Church must be recognized as the depository and distributor, continuing in the role that she has already so often fulfilled in her mission of peace.

II. The Plurality of Humanity

94. Thus humanity, because of the supernatural and natural principles on which it is founded, constitutes a genuine unity which is invested with the Holy Spirit, the spirit of Order and Love. In the kingdom of this spirit on our earth, "citizens are united with citizens, peoples with peoples, and in sum, all men are united in the memory of their first parents, not only by a bond of sociability, but also by a bond of fraternity," as Saint Augustine splendidly put it.[8]

False internationalism

Hence Christians must not allow themselves to fall into the kind of humanitarianism found in all the possible forms of an internationalism that mixes and confuses all sorts of things and peoples. The reason is that humanity assuredly constitutes a genuine unity, but a unity within a well-ordered plurality. And for the same reason, it appears that humanity finds its origin and mode of development in the spirit, and first of all, in the Holy Spirit, which cannot produce, approve, and sanctify a social life in which there is neither order nor unity in plurality. And the same father of the Church, Saint Augustine, rises up in opposition to precisely this state of mind, which mixes and confuses everything absolutely indiscriminately, and considers only the absolute character of being a man. Once again, Saint Augustine calls upon the Holy Spirit to establish the foundation of relationships within humanity, among persons and among groups. Speaking of the terrestrial realm of the spirit, he exclaims: "it is certain that we are not obliged to provide all things to everyone, but we are obliged to love everyone, and injustice toward anyone is unacceptable."[9]

The fact of plurality

95. If we abstract from persons and families as constituting the primary, intangible, original, and stable element of social life, plurality in humanity is manifested through the formation of countless groups. We are concerned here only with groups that form one body with human nature and the unfolding of its life. The formation of such groups is dependent upon the common characteristics of man's physical or spiritual attributes; it can also be dependent upon certain general conditions that result from man's life in space and time. In addition, the basis for the constitution of groups is provided by being involved together for a long time in the same sort of work, and also by having the same conditions of life on the economic and social level. Further, human nature, by its essential, irresistible disposition to live in states, provides the occasion and inner impulses for forming various social unities. Finally, by Divine decree, Christ, "the cornerstone the builders rejected," is Himself at the origin of the formation of a society. This multiplicity of groups, which moreover intersect each other in various ways, conceals within it, by the diversity of the interests involved, the danger of fractions and conflicts. But anyone who considers the unity of all men, first of all in humanity, and then in the Holy Spirit, the Spirit of true order and of love, must be prepared to give, not everything to everyone, to be sure, but to each his own, and thereby help avoid the danger We mentioned.

The formation of separate groups

96. In the very formation of groups a process of particularization, separation, differentiation occurs. But we must always insist

that this is never anything but a particularism *within the overall human unity*; unaided reason declares it and Christian revelation teaches it very firmly, as We have already repeatedly shown. This being the case, it is appropriate, in discussing this particularism in connection with its intimate and necessary relationships to humanity as a whole, to establish in very general terms a few doctrinal points, both negative and positive.

Three criteria of the falsity of a human grouping

97. Let us take first the negative points. These all derive from the proposition that no group, no particular social organism, can constitute a genuine human unity unless it is connected with the general unity of humanity. Within this fundamental proposition are included, if we analyze it, three criteria or value judgments. The *first* is this: A group which, by the way it is established and its members bonded, suppresses and destroys the inviolable source of humanity itself, namely, the internal unity and liberty of the human person and the internal unity of the family, is itself marked with the sign of inherent falsity and non-value. The *second*: A group which, because of its own social type, pursues goals and proclaims values that contradict objective goals and values constituting the inner unity of humanity, is also marked with the sign of inherent falsity and non-value. The *third*: A group that claims, for its own advantage, an extensive totality, that is, one which, because of its own goal and the value it attributes to itself, seeks to determine the content of all other goals, all other values of social life, makes a mockery of the fundamental structure of humanity, with its ancient unity in its authentic plurality; such a group once again marks itself with the sign of inherent falsity and non-value.

Three criteria of a justifiable group

98. Here now are the positive doctrinal points. These all derive from the proposition that every group, every particular society, if it is truly a human unity, will bear fruit for humanity considered as a whole. This proposition can also be analyzed into three criteria or value judgments. The *first* is: The fecundity of a group is shown by a certain characteristic vigor, which is a source of consistency and solidity, and which the group provides for the families it brings together. The *second*: The special know-how with which the group grasps and realizes the general, objective goals of humanity enhances humanity's pursuit and achievement of these values and goals. The *third*: Every group, simply by living in accord with its own essence and all its demands, and by being in that way an intensive totality, supports and gives life to the internal edifice of humanity, namely its genuine unity in its genuine plurality.

One law for all

99. It may happen that, in the case of a particular group, a given goal is sometimes desirable and within reach; it can happen that a given means is useful for achieving it; but in that case, the goal does not constitute a real Good if it can be attained only by sacrificing the order of justice and love that ought to reign in this world. The basic principle and the three criteria set forth above in the negative propositions remain the primary rule, always and in all circumstances. Just as there is no special moral law for great geniuses, so there is no special rule of private morals for any people, whatever its degree of development, real or imagined, or for any other group. Hence it is clear that the negative propositions formulated above ultimately include a positive truth that repels any subterfuge, namely, that every result proceeding from

man, whether by commission or omission, must, in order to establish its final value, be measured by this rule: Does it put God's stamp still more deeply on the world, the stamp of the God of justice and love? Does it make still clearer, in the men who are acting, their resemblance to God?

When this is not the case, it makes no difference how useful and successful the results are; their realization makes no direct addition to their actual value, and it is therefore blasphemous when in such cases peoples and their leaders claim that their successes are proof of Divine benediction, as if success were a sign of particular favor.

100. These then are the doctrinal points, both negative and positive, that can in a general way be considered in relation to social particularisms and particular groups. We have been concerned to determine the mutual relationships among these groups, and to situate them within the general life of humanity. However, because of current circumstances, certain special points demand separate examination.

1. The state: its proper function

101. First of all, regarding the state. After the family, the state is the most important of the particular societies of natural social life. In accord with its origin and nature, it must be an organization that creates order to safeguard law and human well-being in society. It follows that it is the very essence of the state to recognize that all its members, without exception, have a right to equal protection of the law. And the law that it is called upon to safeguard can derive from no source other than the one from which the state derives, that is, from the order that is moral, universal, and valid for all men, including natural law: that is the supreme rule leading the state to safeguard law. This doctrine is valid in all circumstances, even when the state is composed solely

by members of a single race—a case that is hardly imaginable. If the state is to remain a genuine state, and fully realize itself in its natural function, that is, develop an intensive totality, then the following proposition must be absolutely rejected as false: "The primary source and supreme rule of all legal order is racial instinct." It goes without saying that the same would be true with regard to any given national instinct.

Mitigation of excessive state activity

102. In any case, the general re-awakening of the state's awareness of its true role, in the sense of a limit on its direct intervention, would lead it to mitigate the dynamism of the modern state, against which people are rebelling, and which is manifested within the state as well as in international relations. This would facilitate the organization of different states into a relatively effective, unified system based on international law, and this would in turn make it possible for individual states to work together to set up larger economic unities. In addition, by reducing the dynamism of the state in this way, the common, peaceful, and productive life of various groups, whether national or racial, within a single state entity would be facilitated. In fact, exaggerated direct activity of the state, especially in the area of spiritual life, has no doubt made more acute the deplorable current problem of so-called minorities and different national groups, and this hinders the pursuit of state unity, to the extent that the latter is legitimate.

When the state, conducting its life in accord with its proper function, has finally succeeded in gradually bringing back to life an awareness of moral and spiritual principles among members of its community, then it will deserve to be the object of the duty and virtue we call patriotism, and which is required by the moral order and by God.

2. Territorial nationality

103. It remains to say something about what is termed the unity of the people or association in a single community. It is clear that just as in the case of nature or race, when everyday language tries to define this kind of grouping, it does not always use the same terms. By the term "territorial nationality" (*peuple, Volk, Volkstum*) we may refer to an association of men more or less conscious of what they have in common, insofar and inasmuch as they were born on the same soil and are consequently permanently marked by the same personal characteristics.

Territorial nationality distinguished from the state

104. Such a territorial nationality, taken in and of itself, has no direct relation to the essentially political achievement constituted by the state. It would therefore be false to consider in advance as unnatural the fact that human groups belonging to different territorial nationalities may be brought together in one state, or that members of the same territorial nationality may live in different states. It would be equally false to claim that such a group has any absolute natural right or natural duty to seek political union with a state in which it is represented by a sizable minority of citizens. And it would be equally false for that state to claim any kind of sovereign power, no matter how and under whatever pretext, over a group of its own territorial nationality belonging to another state.

Territorial nationality in foreign lands

105. The falsity of such a claim also derives from the fact that it would be an inexhaustible source of concern in the world, and from a political point of view, would make members of that

community suspect throughout the world, and give other states legitimate reason to defend themselves against them with all the means at their disposal. That is why it is all the more clearly the duty of a territorial nationality that has members dispersed beyond its native soil, or which sends them to take up residence in foreign lands, to limit itself to not forgetting them, to helping them in time of need, and as for the rest, being proud to participate in a major way in the life of humanity by providing valuable men who have been shaped by their connection with the homeland. It is naturally inevitable that the new land where the emigrants have taken up residence should begin to exercise on them the formative social power it exercises on all those who live there together, and it would not even be legitimate to seek to prevent this. But the more the mother country's gift of its children is disinterested, the more it will receive in return from them in time of need. Many peoples of the old world have had this experience in recent years.

3. The nation

106. Our teaching on the relation among men in the body of the nation is similar to Our teaching on territorial nationality. Unlike the latter, the nation emerges from the circumstances of common life, not so much in the same place as in the same time. The nation is a large association of men who have common memories and whom a common tradition, particularly with regard to spiritual culture, has shaped and continues to shape. Like territorial nationality, this bond in the body of the nation has a powerful formative influence on the thought, will, and sensibility of individuals and families, and this consolidates the body of the nation itself; it stimulates and gives life to humanity's overall effort to achieve general goals, to realize the values assigned to man. That is why every citizen, exercising the virtue of piety, has the

duty to be grateful to his nation, to be attached to it, for it is above all the nation that maintains the common traditions, and it is the nation from which he proceeds and on which his life is dependent at all times.

The nation is distinct from the state

107. But just as in the case of territorial nationality, and for the same reasons, this bond within a national body does not in itself give us the direct right to conclude that belonging to a nation implies belonging to a given state. Belonging to a given state is in and of itself distinct from belonging to a nation. The opposite view, which is widespread, derives from a more or less artificial idea of the nation that relies far too much on a shared language, and takes far too little account of the bond—which is nonetheless of capital importance—between a national group and its collective historical tradition, and ultimately indicates less a nation than a state that is founded or to be founded on the basis of a shared language. We have personally experienced this. For the solution of the "Roman question" was made possible only by abandoning this false idea of the nation, which would necessarily have entailed the maintenance of the integrity of the state, and returning to the true idea of the state, which is based on history.

Nationalism

108. Consequently, all the conclusions at which We have arrived with regard to the relations with the state and with other states apply equally well to territorial nationality and to the nation. The nation has the right to fully develop its own nature, that is, to be intensively totalitarian; but it does not by itself have the exclusive right to control the legal order or the state, and still less the Church; it does not have the right to be extensively totali-

tarian. For in that case we would have nationalism. We are aware of the disagreeable overtones this word has already acquired in many languages. In it, a genuine perversion of the spirit is expressed. It is a grave criminal offense to urge men, and especially adolescents, to move in this direction, using every means at hand; and it is all the more criminal because it perverts the noble impulses of the soul that the nation and territorial nationality awaken in every man of sound mind and body. These impulses are profaned by being unjustly put in the service of politics and its goal of gaining power.

Duties to the nation

109. When on the other hand men, and especially young people, seek assiduously and faithfully to fulfill their entire duty with regard to their nation, they are acting in the right way, and fulfilling their obligations to the divine moral order, and in particular to natural law. Our Lord Jesus Christ himself did this when he taught the people of the Old Testament; it caused the Messias to weep over Jerusalem; it is in perfect accord with the feelings of the Church which, as a visible, historical society, cannot avoid encountering nations in a positive manner on the terrain of history.

Possibility of a second fatherland

110. Let us add this: Men can really give themselves another fatherland, they can really incorporate themselves into a second territorial nationality; similarly, through major events, it is possible for them to be gradually incorporated, without being forced to do so, into another complex of traditions, into another national society. To deny this would be to see man's life in common as having a rigidity which, because of its development in time and

space, it absolutely cannot have. Moreover, if it were rigid in this way, none of the existing nations would ever have been able to establish themselves.

4. Race and racism

111. When we arrive at the issue of race, we find a striking example of the harm caused by the false, sentimental, and almost mystical way of speaking that has been applied to the ideas of nation, people, and state. There is so little agreement, whether in scientific terminology or in common usage, with regard to the meaning of the terms "race" or "racial link" that we find them used today—and still more in the past—solely to designate a nation or a people. In addition, the expression "racial link" usually signifies, in modern scientific vocabulary, certain definite physical characteristics which are permanent and common to a group of human beings. In relation with the physical constitution, which is itself marked by these bodily traits, we constantly observe certain mental characteristics. If the term "race" is used to refer only to these obvious facts, and if the individual racial characteristics are not assumed to remain constant over too long a time, then the use of this term remains within the limits of verifiable observation.

Negation of human unity

112. But the term "racism" is used to refer to a great deal more than that. Then the word contradicts the negative conclusions already established in this Letter, which are based on the teachings of the Faith, on the testimony of philosophy and other branches of knowledge, and on experience as well. It contradicts them with regard to the authentic divisions within human social life. It contradicts in both theory and practice the principle that categories

or genuinely human lines of separation cannot be admitted unless they themselves participate in what forms the common bond of humanity. For the theory and practice of racism, with their distinction between superior and inferior races, ignore the unifying bond whose existence is demonstrated by the three kinds of testimony mentioned above, or at least they deprive it of any practical scope. One has a right to be surprised that, confronted by these facts, there are still people who claim that the doctrine and practice of racism have nothing to do with Catholic teaching on faith and morals, nothing to do with philosophy, and that they remain a purely political issue.

Negation of human personality

113. Our surprise at this incomprehension increases when the three criteria proposed to reinforce these negative conclusions are applied to racism. The first criterion showed that the inner unity and free will of the human person were necessary conditions for founding any genuine human society. But if the racial community is to be the source of all other forms of society, the human person's inner unity and free will have to be guaranteed. Racism does not accord the human person its rights and its importance in the formation of society. It claims that the fact that individuals have the same blood irresistibly involves them in a single current of physical and psychological characteristics. Any other explanation makes it impossible to understand the hopeless position racism assigns to the races it considers inferior. Any other interpretation fails to account completely for the mechanism of racist legislation that judges all individuals of a given race by means of the same ethnic formula.

114. How can we reconcile these views with the basic personality, with the physical, special, psychological unity represented by each individual? How can they be reconciled with the multiple

influences of the material and spiritual environment? For only tendencies and nothing more can be inherited through the blood, not definitive, already formed qualities. And the development of character—leaving aside the possible effects of man's free will— is affected by the environment, and especially as regards upbringing, at least insofar as the psychological tendencies that depend on the physical organism are concerned.

115. These remarks suffice to show that many of the primordial doctrines of Catholic faith and morals have been ignored by racism: for instance, the doctrines concerning the human person, free will, the unity of soul and body, and finally divine grace, with regard not only to its efficacy but also to its mode of operation. Racism also contradicts many truths affirmed by philosophy and modern science, which the Church cannot and will not ignore.

Negation of the true values of morality and religion

116. The same close relationship with the doctrines of faith, morals, and science appears when racism is subjected to the second criterion We established earlier in discussing the undeniable unity of the human race. We said in particular that when a group's social constitution affirms goals and values in opposition to those that objectively serve the bond of humanity, it betrays by this very fact its inner mendacity and poverty. But racism denies, practically if not theoretically, that there are objective goals and values common to humanity as a whole.

117. Let us examine racism's moral teaching, whose essential thesis We have recently been obliged to condemn. "The strength of the race and the purity of its blood must be preserved and preserved: any means that serves this end is, for that reason alone, good and legitimate." That is the rule of racist morality. We ask: Doesn't such a principle deny the existence of an objective moral

order valid for all men and all times? Doesn't it abandon that order to the arbitrary will and instinct of particular races?

118. Nevertheless, even the pagans acknowledged the existence of this universal moral order when they saw its origin in a divine and simple principle. Aristotle observes:[10] "He who asks that law govern is asking that God and reason alone govern." Cicero says the same.[11] Among the Christians, Saint Jerome says:[12] "One law, written in our hearts, extends to all nations, and no man is unaware of this law." Finally, Saint Augustine: "There is no soul capable of reasonable thought in which God does not make his law heard."[13]

119. In any case, the existence of a natural moral law, which all men carry in their hearts, and which is written by the Creator, is taught by Holy Scripture.[14] Hence the racist rule of morality is once again in conflict with Catholic teaching in matters of faith and morals. It constitutes in addition a permanent threat to the security of public and private life, and to every kind of peace and order in the world. This world has become aware of the crisis it is suffering. In the past, this crisis was already not primarily social and economic in nature, and under the influence of this destructive doctrine it has developed objectively into an immense crisis of all morality.

Religion is not subordinated to race

120. But racism is not satisfied with denying the value of a universal moral order as a blessing that unites humankind; it further denies that essential values have an equal and general role to play in the domains of economy, art, science, and above all, religion. It maintains, for instance, that each race should have its own science, which is to have nothing in common with the science of another race, especially if that race happens to be inferior. Although the unity of the whole of human culture is

important to Catholic faith and to morality, let us limit ourselves here to considering only the relations between race and religion. Concerning this connection, we have recently drawn attention to the false racist thesis that asserts that "Religion is subordinated to the law of the race and must be adapted to that law." In their research, noted scientists have compared various peoples and also the differing stages of development of peoples taken individually. They have declared that there is no direct connection between race and religion: the result of their studies is, on the contrary, to demonstrate the religious unity of humanity.

121. As soon as a philosophy succeeds in clarifying the essential elements of religion, the absurd contradiction that implies that religion could ever be the result of a purely human aspiration explodes. This is, however, the thesis that racism is forced to defend. On the contrary, religion is based on the relation between the human person and a personal Being distinct from man, and on which man totally depends.

122. Above all, our Catholic faith teaches us as a fundamental truth that there is one God for all men and for all races, "the Father of our Lord Jesus Christ" (Ephesians 1:3). The Christian religion, the only true religion, is thereby fundamentally adapted to all and ordained for all races. Anyone who denies this truth contradicts an essential manifestation of the Church's life, which is, moreover, expressed in the universal mission with which she was entrusted by her Founder: "All power over heaven and earth was given to me. Go, therefore, and make disciples of all nations, baptizing them in the name of the Father, and of the Son, and of the Holy Ghost, teaching them to observe all that I have commanded you" (Matthew 28:19–20).

The conduct of the Church, insofar as it is the continuation of the life of Christ who, as the Man-God, is simultaneously true God and true Man, is precisely and necessarily adapted to all authentic human conditions and all historical, legitimate developments of peoples and groups. It puts no people or group under any constraint in order to impose on it anything contrary to its true nature. But no one can receive the Christian religion in any way other than as a pure grace and gift, as an obligation laid upon him by God. Consequently, he cannot change it in any way, otherwise it ceases to be the Christian religion. Indeed, the loss of its objective and obligatory character would cause religion to lose completely its characteristic of universality.

Racism destroys the structure of society

123. Simple respect for reality, as manifested in its consistency, in the light of divine revelation, many sciences, and experience, does not allow the Catholic to remain silent when confronted by racism. For as a Catholic, respect for what is must always be his essential trait. Therefore it must be repeated that racism cannot stand up to the test of the third negative criterion already established. According to this criterion, any group that claims an extensive totality, that is, which judges the content of all other purposes and values from the standpoint of its own purpose and fundamental scale of values, destroys the basic structure on which humanity depends in order to achieve true unity in authentic plurality. Thereby it reveals its inner falsity and its poverty. Now, this is precisely what racism does, either in its theory or in its practice. It makes the fact of racial grouping so central to its system, assigns it such an exclusive significance and efficacy, that in comparison all other social bonds and groupings no longer have a distinct, relatively independent individuality or foundation in law. Through an abusive extension of racial values, the entire life of society is reduced to a totality whose unity is wholly mechanical. It is deprived of precisely that form that the spirit gave it: true unity in real plurality.

124. When racial value is oversimplified and made central and

exclusive, it confuses and obliterates all other notions. Through its totalitarian extension, it realizes a type of society that exactly resembles the internationalist society that racism claims to oppose and that We Ourselves are combating. Its concept of the world is too simple, primitively simple.

Young people exposed to these ideas about the world become fanatical when they accept them, and nihilistic when they reject them. Both attitudes are possible if hearts and minds have become incapable of appreciating the manifold riches of the True and the Good, riches which, in their broad extent and unity, can only be the heritage of an authentic spiritual life.

Disastrous effects on youth and on education

125. Wretched youth, wretched parents, wretched teachers, to whom the fundamental law of racist education offers no viewpoint other than fanaticism or nihilism! Let Us lay before the whole world this shameful educational principle, which We recently stigmatized as false: "The goal of education is to develop the race's characteristics and to inflame the mind with an ardent love for its own race, considered as the supreme good." For the young people whom such a doctrine threatens to lead into spiritual destitution and decay, We cannot pray too fervently to Him who is the divine Teacher, the one who in His own Person offered a perfect model that united, with incomparable breadth and magnitude, the natural and the supernatural in their totality. We shall pray to Him who said: "I came that they may have life and have it more abundantly" (John 10:10).

The diversity of races

126. Would that the world were free of this mistaken and harmful racism that erects rigid barriers between superior, inferior,

and indigenous races, and assumes invariable differences in blood! Certainly there exist today more or less perfect, more or less developed races, if they are measured by the outward manifestations of their cultural life. But these differences are determined by the environment, in the sense that, setting aside the effects of the exercise of free will, only through the influence of the environment could fundamental racial characteristics develop in one or another manner, and continue to develop. Even if we grant that these primary tendencies, or those that later emerge on account of race, set the direction and even the limits of this development and the influence of the environment, they do not provide the basis for essential differences that might arise among particular races with regard to religious, moral, and cultural life. This truth emerges from the teaching we derive from revelation as well as from philosophy and other branches of knowledge.

Influence of the environment

127. These teachings tend to demonstrate the original and essential unity of the human race, along with the fact that its fundamental tendencies are not due to primitive differences of blood but solely to the influence of the environment, including the spiritual environment. Some large, isolated human groups have been subjected to such an influence over long periods of time. In that respect the positive development of various racial tendencies, through the diversity of particular races, occurs in exactly the same way as the development of other elements shaping human communities. These tendencies put on the whole the clear stamp of a vital individuality, and enrich the life of humanity as a whole. The only influence in this fertile and positive development of different races in the world today—again, apart from the influence of human freedom—is in the favorable or unfavorable disposition of the past or present environment.

Practical consequences for colonization

128. Logically, then, the existence of more or less developed races implies no race question, whether we consider it from the standpoint of biology or of theology in the sense of divine election or rejection. In principle and in practice, the matter comes down to the influence of the environment. If the colonizing nations, urged on by political ambitions and the thirst for material gain, neglect their duty to raise the cultural level of certain human groups by means of beneficent political, social, and economic measures, and in that way fail to imitate the constant example of the Church in her missionary work, and if in certain cases they even keep the colonized peoples at this inferior level, then they are violating the elementary principles of Christian morality and natural law. These principles concerning the respective rights of the colonizers and the indigenous peoples were, moreover, set forth by the Church shortly after the discovery of the New World. In spite of the frequent, deplorable offenses men driven by avarice and political ambition then committed against these principles, the latter nevertheless left their imprint. Thus today we see that they have been adopted among the proud, powerful peoples of South America, who have a bright future. This is a living proof, let us note, of the execution of divine plans in the diversity and mixture of races. On the other hand, what would have been the result had racism exercised its destructive power without constraint in the colonization of these regions? No doubt something analogous to what would have happened to the leading role of European peoples—themselves a mixture of diverse races—had they been "purified" by racism.

129. Although not based on its more recent assumptions, racism long exercised its pernicious influence on certain parts of the American continent. There, the idea of a fixed distinction between inferior and superior races has been kept alive not so much

by the surrounding circumstances as by the artificial nurturing of prejudices. And the application of this idea is carried out by unleashing the basest human instincts in the so-called lynch law. And it is still evident in those who are and wish to be branches of Christ, members of His mystical Body, and yet who as a matter of principle or practice are not willing to acknowledge that the House of God is open to all races and is the visible expression of their brotherhood in Christ.

Recommendations on race relations

130. That is why men of good will should do everything they can to put an end to all unmistakably defamatory and discriminatory distinctions in public life, so that relations among social groups may be regulated solely by interracial justice and charity. But no one will reasonably consider as discriminatory such differences and social separations as brotherly love and prudence may counsel to the advantage of all the different races in view of their actual circumstances. Just as there are unwritten matrimonial impediments arising from differences of age, education, social conditions and origin, and even from bodily conditions, which the prudence of parents, the wisdom of those immediately concerned, and an experienced pastoral guidance have always been wont to consider, so there are also such actual, even if not unchangeable and rigidly normative, circumstances in the relations of the races. The races will observe them in their own interest, in accordance with the oft-quoted words of Saint Augustine: "we are not obliged to provide all things to everyone, but we are obliged to love everyone, and injustice toward anyone is unacceptable."[15] These unwritten matrimonial impediments between races are preferable to written ones, particularly if written impediments would attack the personal rights of individuals and the institution of matrimony as a Sacrament instituted by Christ and exclusively

subject to the Church. And rightly so, for what a fearful insult to a race and what a degradation of humanity is committed when marriage between the members of different racial groups is systematically prohibited yet none take offense at unlawful sexual intercourse between members of different groups!

5. Jews and anti-Semitism (religious separation)

131. Those who have placed race illegitimately on a pedestal have rendered mankind a disservice. For they have done nothing to advance the unity to which humanity tends and aspires. One naturally wonders if this end is faithfully pursued by many of the principal advocates of a so-called racial purity or if their aim is not rather to forge a clever slogan to move the masses to very different ends. This suspicion grows when one envisages how many subdivisions of a single race are judged and treated differently by the same men at the same time. It is further increased when it becomes clear that the struggle for racial purity ends by being uniquely the struggle against the Jews. Save for its systematic cruelty, this struggle is no different in true motives and methods from persecutions everywhere carried out against the Jews since antiquity. These persecutions have been censured by the Holy See on more than one occasion, but especially when they have worn the mantle of Christianity.

The present persecution of the Jews

132. As a result of such persecution, millions of persons are deprived of the most elementary rights and privileges of citizens in the very land of their birth. Denied legal protection against violence and robbery, exposed to every form of insult and public degradation, innocent persons are treated as criminals though they have scrupulously obeyed the law of their native land. Even those who in time of war fought bravely for their country are treated

as traitors, and the children of those who laid down their lives in their country's behalf are branded as outlaws by the very fact of their parentage. The values of patriotism, so loudly invoked for the benefit of one class of citizens, are ridiculed when invoked for others who come under the racial ban.

In the case of the Jews, this flagrant denial of human rights sends many thousands of helpless persons out over the face of the earth without any resources. Wandering from frontier to frontier, they are a burden to humanity and to themselves.

Question not of race but of religion

133. But however unjust and pitiless, this campaign against the Jews has at least this advantage, if one can put it so, over racial strife, that it recalls the true nature, the authentic basis of the social separation of the Jews from the rest of humanity. This basis is directly religious in character. Essentially, the so-called Jewish question is not one of race, or nation, or territorial nationality, or citizenship in the state. It is a question of religion and, since the coming of Christ, a question of Christianity.

How utterly misguided is such a policy toward the Jews, how harmful and ineffective for the very purposes it seeks to accomplish, can only be seen when we compare it with what the Church has ever taught and practiced in this connection, and with the lessons of history.

Position of the Church with Regard to Judaism

Teachings of Revelation

134. If we look upon the matter from the historical standpoint, we find that in the history of the human race only one people has had a calling, properly so called. This is the Jewish people,

who were chosen by Almighty God to prepare the way in history for the Incarnation of His Only-Begotten Son. "Who are the Israelites, who have the adoption as sons, and the glory and the covenants and the legislation and the worship and the promises; who have the fathers, and from whom is the Christ according to the flesh . . . ?" (Romans 4:4–5).

135. The vocation of the Jewish people culminated in a wholly unique and unprecedented historical occurrence that interrupted and transformed the history of the world. At a definite moment in time, in a definite locality, in one of the tribes of the Jewish people, through the operation of the Holy Spirit, the person who had been announced and awaited by the prophets of Israel for centuries was born from a Jewish mother: Jesus Christ. His mission and his teaching were the completion of the historic mission and teaching of Israel; His birth, life, sufferings, death, and resurrection from the dead were the fulfillment of Israel's types and prophecies. Extraordinary as was this occurrence, it was linked with another no less extraordinary and also unprecedented in history. The Savior, whom God had sent to His chosen people after they had prayed and longed for Him for thousands of years, was rejected by that people, violently repudiated, and condemned as a criminal by the highest tribunals of the Jewish nation, in collusion with the pagan authorities who held the Jewish people in bondage. Ultimately, the Savior was put to death.

Through the sufferings and death of the Savior, the work of the Redemption was wrought for all humanity; the sins of the world were taken away; the doors of Heaven were opened; man was restored by the Second Adam to the privileges from which he had been excluded by the sin of his first parents, and the spiritual kingdom of Christ was established for eternity. The Redemption opened the doors of salvation to the entire human race; it established a universal Kingdom, in which there would be no distinction of Jew or Gentile, Greek or barbarian. The very act by which the Jewish people put to death their Savior and King was, in the strong language of Saint Paul, the salvation of the world.

136. On the other hand, blinded by a vision of material domination and gain, the Israelites lost what they themselves had sought. A few chosen souls, among whom were the disciples and followers of Our Lord, the early Jewish Christians, and, through the centuries, a few members of the Jewish people, were an exception to this general rule. By their acceptance of Christ's teaching and their incorporation into His Church, they shared in the inheritance of His glory, but they remained and still remain an exception. "What Israel was seeking after, that it has not obtained; but the chosen have obtained it, and the rest have been blinded" (Romans 11:7). Saint Paul adds: "But by their offense," that is, through the Jews' rejection of the Messias, "salvation has come to the Gentiles" (Romans 11:11).

Moreover, by a mysterious Providence of God, this unhappy people, destroyers of their own nation, whose misguided leaders had called down upon their own heads a Divine malediction, doomed, as it were, to perpetually wander over the face of the earth, were nonetheless never allowed to perish, but have been preserved through the ages into our own time. No natural reason appears to be forthcoming to explain this age-long persistence, this indestructible coherence of the Jewish people.

Saint Paul's teachings

137. Addressing the Gentiles, Saint Paul clearly indicates the apparent contradiction between the unbelief of the Jews and the providential part that God's Providence has permitted them to play in the world's salvation. But he goes further still, and points out that there is no reason to despair of Israel's salvation, since the Redemption accomplished through the rejection of the

Savior and His death extends its fruits not to the Gentiles alone, but also to the very people who rejected Him, on the sole condition that this people repent and accept Him as their Redeemer. "So they too have not now believed by reason of the mercy shown you, that they too may obtain mercy" (Romans 11:31).

138. Although the Gentile world, in so far as it is converted to the teachings of Christ, now shares in the fruits of those promises which were rejected by the Jews, the Gentiles are not to boast. In a striking metaphor, Saint Paul compares the people of Israel to an olive tree, onto which have been grafted branches from a wild olive (Romans 11:16–24). The root of this tree, the patriarchs of the Old Law, is holy; and so, at least through their original vocation, are its branches. Certain branches, however—the unbelieving Jews—have fallen from the tree. In contrast to this, branches of wild olive—the pagans—have been engrafted upon the natural olive. These, however, even after their conversion to the true faith and their incorporation into the Church of Christ, are to remember three things: first, that they possess this supernatural life solely thanks to the root and sap of the natural olive; second, that they, the non-Jewish Christians, do not carry the root, but the root carries them, that is to say, Judea does not receive salvation from the Gentiles, but rather the opposite is true; third, that the Gentiles themselves, if they apostatize from the Faith of Christ, and live in presumption and blind self-confidence, can perfectly well share the unhappy lot of the fallen branches. "They were broken off because of unbelief, whereas thou by faith standest. Be not high-minded, but fear" (Romans 11:20).

139. Saint Paul, however, is not content with warning the Gentiles against undue self-confidence. He goes further, and holds out still the possibility of salvation to the Jews, once they are converted from their sins, and return to the spiritual tradition of Israel, which is properly theirs by their historic past and calling, but in which the Gentiles, through grace, have been made par-

ticipants. If and when this time of their return occurs, whether in the case of individuals—as has always happened through the centuries and continues to happen in our own times—or in the case of the Jewish people as a whole, those who come back to Christ find themselves wholly at home in their own house, more than any other people in the world.

Even in Saint Paul's own day, as at all times, there was a "remnant saved." *Reliquiae salvae factae sunt* (Romans 11:5). So, with prophetic voice, the Apostle points to the future, to the conversion of the Gentiles as the forerunner of the conversion of the Jews and their return to their Father's house: all Israel, *omnis Israel,* not as meaning each individual, but the Jewish people as a whole.

140. Israel has incurred the wrath of God, because it has rejected the Gospel. Yet even thereby it has hastened the evangelization and, as a result, the conversion of the Gentiles. Israel remains the chosen people, for its election has never been revoked. Through the ineffable mercy of God, Israel also may share in the redemption which Israel's own rejection has made available to the Gentiles, who had themselves been unbelievers. "For God has shut up all in unbelief, that he may have mercy upon all" (Romans 11:32). "Oh the depth of the riches of the wisdom and of the knowledge of God!" (Romans 11:33).

Historical results of the fall of Israel

141. But this profound paradox, existing in the invisible, purely supernatural order, has worked itself out in the inevitable occurrences of history. As a result of the rejection of the Messias by His own people, and of His corresponding acceptance by the Gentile world, which had not shared in the special promises delivered to the Jews, we find a historic enmity of the Jewish people to Christianity, creating a perpetual tension between Jew and

Gentile which the passage of time has never diminished, even though from time to time its manifestations have been mitigated.

The Church's reservations

142. The lofty concept the Church has forever held relative to the vocation of the Jewish people as seen from their past history, and her ardent hopes for their eventual salvation in the future, do not blind her to the spiritual dangers to which contact with Jews can expose souls, or make her unaware of the need to safeguard her children against spiritual contagion. Nor is this need diminished in our own time. As long as the unbelief of the Jewish people persists, as long as there is active hostility to the Christian religion, just so long must the Church use every effort to see that the effects of this unbelief and hostility are not to redound to the ruin of the faith and morals of her own members. Where, moreover, she finds that hatred of the Christian religion has driven misguided souls, whether of the Jewish people or of other origin, to ally themselves with, or actively to promote revolutionary movements that aim to destroy society and to obliterate from the minds of men the knowledge, reverence, and love of God, she must warn her children against such movements, expose the ruses and fallacies of their leaders, and find against them appropriate safeguards.

We find that in her history the Church has never failed to warn her children against the teaching of the Jews, when such teaching has been directed against the Faith. The Church has never sought to minimize the terrific force of the reproaches addressed by the protomartyr Saint Stephen against those of the Jewish people who knowingly resisted the call of grace: "Stiff-necked and uncircumcised in heart and ear..." (Acts 7:51). The Church has warned likewise against an over-familiarity with the Jewish community that might lead to customs and ways of thinking contrary to the standards of Christian life. The unyielding energy, at one time, and the mildness, at another, of such warnings and measures of self-protection correspond not to any interior change in the Church's policy toward the Jews, which remains unaltered, but to altered circumstances and to variations of attitude upon their part. The policy of the Church herself in this matter is not to be confounded with the policy of mere individuals. It is to be determined by the conduct of her bishops taken as a whole, her councils, especially the ecumenical councils, and most particularly by that of her Supreme Pontiffs.

143. While, however, the teaching of the Church concerning the relation of the Jewish community with the Christian community, as well as the Church's practical attitude in the face of the problems encountered clearly demonstrate the need for energetic measures to preserve both the faith and morals of her members and society itself against the corrupting influence of error, these same doctrines likewise show the utter unfitness and inefficacy of anti-Semitism as a means of achieving that end. They show anti-Semitism not only as pitifully inadequate, but also as defeating its own purpose, and producing in the end only greater obstacles to cope with.

Condemnation of anti-Semitism

144. That such persecutory methods are totally at variance with the true spirit of the Catholic Church is shown by the decree of the Sacred Congregation of the Holy Office for March 25, 1928: "The Catholic Church habitually prays for the Jewish people who were the bearers of the Divine revelation up to the time of Christ; this, despite, indeed, on account of, their spiritual blindness. Actuated by this love, the Apostolic See has protected this people against unjust oppression and, just as every kind of envy and jealousy among the nations must be disapproved of, so in an especial

manner must be that hatred which is generally termed anti-Semitism" (*Acta Ap. Sedis,* 20, 1928).

Ecclesiae enim Catholica pro populo Judaeo, qui divinarum usque ad Jesum Christum promissionum depositarius fuit, non obstante subsequente ejus obcaecatione, immo hujus ipsius obcaecationis causa, semper orare consuevit. Qua caritate permota Apostolica Sedes eumdem populum contra unjustas vexationes protexit, et quemadmodum omnes invidias ac simultates inter populos reprobat, ita vel maxime damnat odium nempe illud, quod vulgo "antisemitismi" nomine nunc significari solet.

Persecutions only increase the evils

145. History's long experience has repeatedly shown that persecution, instead of obliterating or lessening the harmful or anti-social traits of a persecuted group, merely intensifies the tendencies that gave rise to them. What previously was but a moderately effective and inchoate tendency of individuals or small groups is solidified by persecution into a generalized, vehemently accentuated and persistent complex of traits that thrive upon opposition. The victims of persecution believe they find eternal justification for manifesting such traits in the very measures of repression and persecution that were supposed to cure them.

Effects of persecution

146. The terrible consequences that have befallen society since those words were spoken, consequences resulting from the unwillingness of the world's rulers to listen to the Vicar of Christ's pleas for charity and peace, have amply demonstrated the ease with which destructive ideologies are implanted in the minds of peoples aroused to fury by persecution. Those who suffer injustice themselves not infrequently become the devotees of injustice.

Their bitter resentment against their own pitiable condition leads them to wreak or attempt to wreak their vengeance upon those who appear to enjoy a more fortunate position. So we find that the persecuted and oppressed of every nation or class readily lend ear to those who would profit by this resentment, and would stir up social or international hatreds in their hearts. A natural resentment against political, social, or economic oppressors becomes, under the facile nurture of modern instruments for the spread of ideas and the manipulation of public opinion, a fertile seed-ground for the most destructive ideas, whose advocates, though professing the most violent antagonism to one another, are united in their common hatred for the Christian faith.

Such a spirit, however, cannot be profitably met by a similar demonstration of hatred, which would only pour oil on the flames. Nor can it be profitably met by a reckless dissemination of falsehoods and calumnies. Though Christ our Lord suffered torments and death at the hands of the wicked Pharisees, He did not bid His followers to borrow the weapons of calumny, hatred, and pride from the persecutors, in order to deal with those unfortunate people whom the Pharisees had misled.

Attacks on religion

147. Zeal against the sin readily becomes zeal against the sinner; but zeal against the sinner soon throws off its mask and shows itself for what it really is, an assault, under the pretense of protecting society from a single social group, upon the very basis of society, an evocation of limitless hatred, a license for every form of violence, rapacity, and disorder, and an engine against religion itself.

Thus we find that anti-Semitism becomes an excuse for attacking the sacred Person of the Savior Himself, who assumed human flesh as the Son of a Jewish maiden; it becomes a war against Christianity, its teachings, practices, and institutions. Anti-Semitism attempts to embarrass the Church by giving her the alternative either to join with the anti-Semites in their total repudiation of any esteem or regard for anything Jewish, and thereby to associate herself with the anti-Semites in their campaigns of vilification and hatred; or else to embarrass the Church by involving her in the machinations and struggles of profane politics, attributing earthly and political motives to her legitimate defense of the Christian principles of justice and humanity. Like the willful children spoken of by Christ our Savior, these sowers of dissension complain of the Spouse of Christ: "To what then shall I liken the men of this generation? And what are they like? They are like children sitting in the market place, calling to one another and saying, We have piped to you, and you have not danced; we have sung dirges, and you have not wept" (Luke 7:32–33).

The Church's answer to anti-Semitism

148. To this challenge the answer of the Church is unequivocal and unchanging. Her answer is determined by no earthly policy but rather by her fidelity to the truths bequeathed to her custody by her Divine Founder, and preserved in their original purity in her bosom by the personal assistance of the Holy Ghost: truths that reveal what human reason of itself can never attain, while they reaffirm and perfect the knowledge of those truths which man's reason, devoid of passion and self-interest, can hope to reach of its own accord. Her concern is not with political victories and triumphs, not with the alignments of states and the devices of politicians; hence she is in no wise concerned with the problems concerning the Jewish people that lie within those purely profane spheres. Thoroughly aware that the great diversity of circumstances in which Jews of different countries find themselves

gives rise to very different problems in the practical order, the Church leaves to the powers concerned the solution of these problems. She insists only that no solution is the true solution if it contradicts the very demanding laws of justice and charity. Her sole care is that the custody of truth committed to her care be preserved intact and that her children be preserved against error and sin; that the principles of life taught by her Savior be carried out in their integrity; and that through her beneficent action upon earth as many souls as possible may be brought to their eternal home in Heaven. As has been well said: "Men ambition a thousand things; the Church desires but one, the salvation of souls" (E. Rodocanachi, *The Holy See and the Jews*).

Religious concern for the Jews

149. The position of the Jewish people is unique, and occupies a singular and painful place in the vast series of these historical developments. It offers the paradox of being the object of a special Providence reserved to it, above all peoples in the world; of having rejected that Providence, thereby injecting a stumbling-block of contradiction into the history of all other peoples; yet being still the object of a mysterious preservation by the same Providence of God.

The bitterness with which Christian consciousness has periodically reproached the Jewish people for their rejection of the teachings and Person of Christ, as well as for their attitude toward Christianity, and the like bitterness with which the Jewish people has responded to these reproaches, show by their very acuteness that the conflict and the issues concerned are ideological, and concern material goods less than spiritual values. The very sharpness of such reproaches testifies to the knowledge shared by all involved that man's supreme values lie in the field of liberty, with its correlative of moral responsibility for good or for evil, thereby offering a clear, if painful, testimony to the supremacy of spiritual over material ideals as the measuring rod of human worth. The lessons drawn from this testimony demonstrate likewise how utterly incapable any philosophy that ranges merely within a bodily or material sphere is of reaching a solution to such a conflict. Both sound reason and Christian Faith bid us look to spiritual means, not to violence, force, or brutally coercive measures.

Conversion of the Jews

150. The hour and manner of the return of the Jewish people as a whole to their Father's house in the Church of Christ remains God's secret. Where such a return occurs in the case of individuals, it should come as the result not of indiscreet proselytism, and not from motives that incur even a shadow of worldly expediency or material gain, but from a conviction arising out of reflective study and freely formed in a spirit of humility and self-sacrifice. Any other supposition on the part of Christians is contrary to the express precepts of the Church; any other method on the part of those who embrace the Catholic Faith leads only to evils graver than those that arise even from an open persistence in refusing to accept Catholic teachings, since it would give rise only to hypocrisy.

Call to prayer

151. Our faith, however, bids us ever look forward to the day when again Jew and Gentile will be united in their Father's house, and to pray earnestly for the hastening of its coming. Particularly do we seek the all-powerful intercession of the Holy Mother of God, herself a daughter of Israel, that thereby, in the words of the petition presented to the fathers of the Vatican Council and signed by 570 of their number, may be fulfilled the

supreme aspirations of her own sublime canticle: "He has given help to Israel, his servant, mindful of his mercy—even as he spoke to our fathers—to Abraham and to his posterity forever" (Luke 1:54–55).

Doing the truth

152. It is clearly our duty, likewise, so to live as to facilitate that return as far as is humanly possible. This we shall do by the practice of the truth in prudence and in strict justice, as well as in abundant charity. In the cause of truth, let us encourage such works as spread knowledge and do away with calumnies, lies, and baseless recriminations. In the cause of justice and charity, the present time presents such opportunities as would have seemed unparalleled in the world's history. Defense of the natural rights of individuals and of families; care of the miserable who appeal for charity and mercy; a vigorous condemnation of anti-Semitism and racism wherever these doctrines lift their heads; and cooperation for the sake of public order with men of good will who from their hearts reject the gross errors of materialism—for these ends let us make use of our opportunities.

PART THIRD: THE CHURCH'S ACTION ON BEHALF OF THE UNITY OF MAN'S TEMPORAL LIFE

153. As We conclude this long retrospect and survey of the good and evil developments of man's social nature in our day, We can only repeat once more: "The spirit giveth life." The spirit alone can shape man's manifold capacities into a loving unity in a living diversity. Thus will the social life of man reflect its Divine prototype: "That all may be one, even as thou, Father, in me and I in thee" (John 17:21).

The Church's task: to show the way

154. From what We have already written, it is clear that the life of individuals as well as the life of the various human groups is deeply involved in the countless relationships of social life. Yet these relationships cannot be truly understood if we lose sight of the significance of all human activity in its relationship with God, man's Creator and Redeemer, a significance that derives from the unchanging plan of the Redemption, the unchanging moral order, and their application to each individual's conscience. It is the task and duty of the Church, the dignity and responsibility of the Chief Shepherd and of His brother shepherds whom the Holy Ghost has placed to rule the Church of God, to show mankind the true way to be followed, the eternal divine order in the changing circumstances of the times.

Catholic university education

155. In fulfilling this task, the teaching office of the Church counts on the support of the *universitas litterarum,* of the arts, sciences, and letters bound together by an inner unity, in order to treat so complicated a subject as is dealt with in this Letter in the comprehensive and consistent manner it deserves. It is with deep sorrow, therefore, that the Church sees the disaster that in many countries has overtaken that institution, which arose from the very heart of the unity of Western civilization. However, in those countries where it is still possible, and where no special circumstances hinder its development in the service of Catholicism, We pray that Catholics will make every effort and spare themselves no sacrifices in order to provide adequate support and achieve full development for the realization of the Catholic *universitas litterarum.* In doing so, they will be laying the foundation for true Christian leadership, conferring a supreme

good on humanity, and fulfilling an apostolic service for the Church.

156. Catholic university education is unique and distinctive because of its fullness; it embraces Truth as a whole and cannot be satisfied with half-hearted participation or with any division of that whole. Catholic education is not a mere transmission of information: it is a way of life. It is a manifestation of the Church of Christ, and thus participates in its unity and universality. It participates in the Church's unity because Catholic education considers all partial truths in their relation to Him who is the living Truth, and thus makes a living whole of every object it studies: moral life, religious orientation, intelligence, sensitivity, and imagination, even physical strength and ability. Catholic education also participates in the universality of the Church, because like the Church it addresses humanity as a whole, in time and in space. In its own way, it is a genuine spiritual city of souls.

In the spiritual whole that is Catholic university education, we find a harmonious union between two deep trends in human development. On one hand, cultural development: the unfolding of intelligence and imagination within the human person, participation in the heritage of the past, enrichment of this heritage through new and original research; on the other hand, the development of Christian character. These two trends nourish, each in its own way, the life of the Christian city. Thus the Catholic scholar who devotes many years of his life to scholarly work in libraries or laboratories, expecting neither earthly rewards nor earthly honors, is making an essential and invaluable contribution to the overall life of the Church, and consequently, to the unity of humanity.

157. With respect to this unity of the human race, which is desired by God and so battered by men, how sweet it is to savor the beauty of the Church in its admirable unity and variety—a principle of unity even for the temporal life of nations and races.

We would like to consider here one aspect of the Church to which We attach great importance: Catholic Action, as an *expression and principle of unity* in the richly diverse life of the Church, and also as a principle of unity in the temporal life of peoples, races, and states.

Catholic Action: Expression and Principle of Unity

158. By nature, Catholic Action tends toward unity, because it is Truth and Life. Its countless tasks, and its activities, which are diverse both because of the circumstances in which they are carried out and because of the character of the people who are involved in them, all contribute to the building of the Mystical Body of Christ in this world, just as the individual members of the human body all work together, each in its own way, toward the marvelous unity of the whole.

The person of the priest

159. Catholic Action finds its first and most essential manifestation in the collaboration between clergy and laity, for by its very nature Catholic Action is the aid given by the laity to the apostolate of the clergy. As a result, the clergy has very precise obligations, since it is from the bishops and priests that the laity must seek enlightenment and guidance in order to carry out its apostolate successfully. Personally, a priest doing pastoral work must be a man whose inner life deeply unites him with Christ Our Lord, for it is through his example and the influence of a priestly life that he can hope to communicate Christ's life to his people. A priest's position as spiritual guide and counselor requires him to be a man of learning, versed in the sacred sciences, devoted to a life of study, and capable of fully realizing the talents God has given him. Hence the fundamental importance, for the

work of Catholic Action, of studies that enable the young clergyman to adapt the teachings of the Gospel to the particular conditions in which he is called to work.

Thus a young priest whose youth was passed in a tranquil and pious environment may have to begin his priestly ministry in a complex industrialized community that is deeply troubled by class strife and hostile to Christianity. Another, brought up in a city, may have to work in a rural parish, with a population whose interests and occupations are completely unfamiliar to him. Or his ministry may be carried out among people of a different national or racial origin, with whose psychological problems he has no experience. Confronted by such situations, the young priest will recall that souls are not saved in the abstract, but in space and time, in the providential conditions in which God has placed them. Accordingly, he will apply himself to a systematic study of the concrete living conditions of families entrusted to his care, the various economic and social and legal institutions that affect their spiritual and temporal welfare, the mentality of those who administer these institutions, the best opportunities for the young to find congenial and useful occupation, and other such matters which, though temporal in their nature, are intimately connected with the salvation of souls. Finally, the disordered state of society requires on the part of the priest a firm grounding in the so-called social sciences, so that he can penetrate beneath the surface of the multitudinous social phenomena he encounters in his work, understand their causes, and, so far as possible, devise effective remedies for the disease.

160. In truth, the extent and difficulty of the struggle against such evils demands no small courage. If Catholic Action requires such courage in the laity, how much more is it to be expected in the priest, to whom the Holy Spirit has entrusted the teaching and care of souls! In regions where the Faith enjoys comparative freedom and Catholics are numerous and lend generous support

to the sustenance and activities of their religion, pastors may be strongly tempted to follow the line of least resistance, in a spirit of opportunism, and close their eyes to the injustices and un-charitable practices of people whose favor makes their lives easier, justifying their timidity by appealing to false prudential maxims.

Furthermore, Catholic Action requires that a priest be tactful and moderate. His sense of moderation keeps him from embark-ing upon futile and unrealizable schemes; tact puts him on guard against the natural human tendency to want to control every-thing. Rather than furthering the good, domination only stifles efforts to realize it; it substitutes an individual's personal will for the generous and spontaneous collaboration that alone promotes the Kingdom of God. A priest who exceeds the limits of the authority that his functions confer on him, who represents his personal opinions as the Church's teaching and official discipline, who considers the laity as docile instruments for achieving his own ends, may be very zealous and well-intentioned, but his attitude produces, among many deplorable results, a false concep-tion of the Church as no more than a vast organization in which the individual layman counts for little, instead of a living body in which each Christian is a living cell.

The task of the spiritual shepherd of souls is not to produce docile servants, but rather to shape courageous men of initiative deeply aware of their spiritual responsibilities. The more obstacles stand in the way of achieving his true task, the more his zeal and his activity increase.

Universal ministry of the clergy

161. While the priest must be able to understand the members of his flock who belong to another nation or race, it is nonetheless desirable, in order to ensure the very existence of the Church and its essential development, that no large group of the faithful

be permanently deprived of the ministrations of priests belonging
to their own people. We have repeatedly expressed Our opinion
on this matter, not only in Our discourses, but also in an even
more effective manner, by encouraging everywhere the training
of an indigenous clergy, and by elevating to the lofty dignity of
the episcopate priests drawn from the ranks of peoples who have
only recently been won to the Faith, giving them full episcopal
jurisdiction and authority. So that all groups among our Christian
people may be thus provided, including groups of different racial
or national origin living within a larger nation, it is indispensable
that candidates for the priesthood, no matter what ethnic group
they belong to, may freely enjoy the advantages of a Catholic
education throughout their training, from their earliest years to
their theological studies.

The shaping of consciences

162. We have already emphasized the necessity of clearly and
competently teaching the people about the Church's social doctrine, the principle of true social unity. In order that the clergy
may carry out with the desired competence its role of teaching
the principles of Christian faith and morals, it is greatly to be
desired that the problem of relations among various human
groups be adequately dealt with in courses and textbooks on
moral theology. This in turn means that Catholic theologians
should study this problem very attentively, in the light of
Christian truth, reason, and experience. If consciences are to be
truly enlightened, it is imperative that all ranks and degrees of
intelligence among the faithful be armed with clear ideas regarding men's mutual responsibilities and proper ways of fulfilling
them. The existence and origin of natural rights, the questions of
justice and charity that enter into relations among racial and national groups, the value of the human personality and the spiritual

unity of the human race are not matters that can be left to a select few; they must be made known to all Christians.

The person of the layman

163. If we consider the multitude and variety of human occupations, we quickly see that each of them offers, in one way or another, numerous opportunities for furthering unity among men. We have observed with the greatest satisfaction, over the past few years, the creation of a galaxy of specialized groups that bring men together and make it possible for Christian life to flourish in the most diverse environments of age, sex, profession, or trade. We have followed with the greatest interest the development of these associations among the youth of both sexes, and We have noted their profound influence on the spiritual regeneration of the Christian community.

Specialized movements

164. It is clear that there are human groups for which the practice of Christian religion poses particular problems that cannot be adequately resolved through the efforts of individual Christians. Hence the necessity of concerted efforts to make the value of Christian life visible to these various groups. In this way all those engaged in the same occupation can profit from their common experience, counsel each other, make available the common means of achieving common goals, and enjoy the benefits of the specialized direction of spiritual guides capable of clearly and competently applying to their particular situation the principles that should inspire their individual activity.

Formation of associations

165. Thus a great variety of organizations have been enrolled under the banner of Catholic Action, each of which devotes itself to a particular phase of the apostolate of the laity. However, it should be noted that it is essential to the concept of Catholic Action that in every case the organization is only an instrument for aiding and completing the individual action of its members. The strength of an individual's action must be in the value of his action itself, the radiation of his own personal example and influence, not in the strength supposedly created by the simple juxtaposition of a large number of individuals.

These movements may become vast, imposing organizations with hundreds of thousands of members, and their splendid demonstrations may arouse the greatest enthusiasm. It remains nevertheless true that the secret of the apostolic achievement toward which these various organizations are working remains the supernatural character of the individual action of each of their members.

Organic character of associations

166. But, it may be asked, doesn't the Christian body acquire a special beauty and power from the very multitude of those who compose it? No doubt it does, but it is not by putting vast multitudes into the framework of homogenous groups that the Christian body shows its spiritual vitality. The view that the so-called power of the masses and collective pressure are signs of spiritual vitality is alien to Christianity. No less foreign to Christian thought is the view, which reflects mechanistic-atomistic ideas, that the individual derives his spiritual dynamism from the simple fact of being integrated into a collectivity made up of numerous individuals who think and act as he does. On the

contrary, the Christian collectivity, as We have already said, draws its peculiar beauty not from the number of individuals or from their simple juxtaposition, but from the *organic* character of its composition, in which different individuals and various groups each find their proper place: "of all nations and tribes and peoples and tongues" (Apocalypse 7:9).

167. We therefore consider it of primordial importance to preserve the authentic stamp of Catholic Action on all these various organizations: it must be clear that the organization, in its constitution and in the delimitation of its field of activity, in its rules and methods of work, in its services and publications, in its leadership and administration, is only an instrument and means of aiding the individual, allowing him to fully realize his apostolate as a person and a member of the Church of Christ. Thus, although the organized movement will receive, obediently, joyously, and faithfully, all the directives of the hierarchy, whose desires and directives it will seek to fulfill, and although in addition its very nature as an organized movement makes it subject it in a special way to the approval of ecclesiastical superiors, nonetheless those who belong to the organization and the superiors who sanction it must never lose sight of its essential role, in order to preserve its spontaneity and the superabundant vitality of its members, and to make of them a typical illustration of Catholic Action.

Spiritual contributions to the formation of institutions

168. The work of social regeneration undertaken by Catholic Action must not be limited to ephemeral manifestations. Its task is to build a spiritual city, and thereby to make a solid and life-giving spiritual contribution to the formation or maintenance of *social institutions* based on justice and Christian charity. History teaches that the stablest and most fruitful human institutions have

drawn their existence from the life of the Church, the mother of all civilization, as manifested in the individual lives of her children.

169. Making his spiritual influence felt on the formation or preservation of these institutions severely tests every Christian's moral courage and personal initiative. Self-interest, personal ambitions, and hopes for material gain must be relentlessly sacrificed to the common good, in order to liberate as fully as possible in each individual the energies that can be devoted to building the spiritual city. Thus while the individual's participation through his inner life and sacramental union with Christ constitute the starting point and source of Catholic Action, the realization of the Christian spirit in the socio-political and economic institutions of human society is its culmination: institutions that restore to human society its organic character.

Economic institutions

170. In Our Letters *Quadragesimo Anno* and *Divini Redemptoris,* We already mentioned the importance of providing society with sound economic institutions corresponding to the various ways economic life impinges on human activities. Only in a society whose economic structure truly corresponds to real human needs can the family more readily be freed from living conditions that wound the dignity of the human person; only in such a society can the Christian achieve his ultimate goal at the same time that he achieves his earthly destiny. This economic regeneration may lead to the creation of new social bodies or corporations that would group together all those who, in whatever way, as providers of capital, as managers, or as workers, depend on the same industry; it may also limit itself to creating new bonds of economic cooperation among the various organizations that already represent workers, management, and consumers. But the goal

always remains the same: to put unity and peaceful collaboration in the service of the common good, while at the same time satisfying individual interests as much as possible. Collaboration of this kind, clearly, truly serves society and individuals only to the extent that it is based on the authentic reality of true human needs, those of the family.

The organization: an instrument for its members

171. Moreover, these purely economic organizations must be considered in the light of the principle We invoked earlier in speaking of Catholic Action. Even when only material and economic interests are involved, it must be remembered that the organization is only a means, an instrument put at the disposal of its members. The organization does not exist in order to replace, through the magic of a fictive collective personality, the initiative, will, and intelligence of each of its members; it exists for each of its members, in order to allow each to contribute as much as he can to the common good, thanks to the advantages of mutual aid, consultation, competent guidance, and the common use of material means or intellectual abilities. Only the most lamentable disappointments, even from the standpoint of purely material welfare, can be produced by a contrary philosophy of economic organization. This has been shown by the repeated failures, in recent years, of vast enterprises of collectivization by which a government guided by militant atheism has tried to replace the moral and spiritual deficiencies of its members with the supposed efficiency of the proletarian masses.

It is not for the Church to determine the formation and type of such economic organisms. Her role here is to lay down the principles that should direct them. However, she strongly urges the faithful to study these concrete problems, not because of the material gain they might derive from doing so, but because of their obligation to realize Christian principles in human society.

Political institutions

172. Catholic Action is not concerned with politics. However, a legitimate and very natural concern leads it to ask whether the political, juridical, and administrative institutions that incarnate state power in some way respect the rights of the human person (and the principles that should govern human relations). Each believer must therefore consider himself responsible, to the extent that he participates in their creation and functioning, for the conformity of these institutions with the requirements of natural law. These institutions include the various family assistance offices and professional organizations of all kinds: labor unions, mutual aid societies, joint commissions, chambers of commerce, municipal institutions, school boards and educational commissions, leisure organizations, health boards, international commissions, colonial administrations—in short, all the public and private institutions that affect the moral life of individuals and families. Christians who participate in any of these institutions have a serious obligation to always and everywhere testify, by the words and by their lives, to the teaching of the Master of indefatigable workers for the unity of human society.

The totality of Christian life

173. After surveying at such length the mournful factors harming contemporary society and tearing it apart, let us look for a moment on the beauty of this unity itself.

This unity is not merely the sum of the individual splendors of each of its members. The Kingdom of God draws a particular beauty from the very union of all these individuals in a harmonious body. When pleasing traits are not bound together in a harmonious whole, their simple coexistence does not suffice to produce a beautiful countenance.

Analogy of the cathedral

174. The same can be said of the architectural splendor of the great monuments the past has handed down to us as testimonies to its faith and piety: each element contributes its beauty to a whole that transcends the beauty and perfection of these elements. Consider one of our cathedrals: each line rises into space as if it had its own life, thanks to the conjunction of stones each of which has its own perfection. A mosaic or stained-glass window expresses an image whose beauty surpasses the individual beauty of each of its parts. And in the creative imagination of the artist, although each element retains its own value, the arches and columns, the vaults and naves, the windows, mosaics, sculpted portals and capitals, the towers and the steeples, all come together harmoniously in the transcendental splendor of the whole.

175. And yet this building is only a material testimony, written in wood and metal and stone, to a still more marvelous spiritual reality: the incredible collaboration of countless minds and countless wills in realizing this gigantic work. They have come to this spiritual city, which the material edifice merely symbolizes, from the far corners of the earth: architects, designers, sculptors, and painters, masons, cabinet makers, and carpenters, with their apprentices and disciples. Often, they came from far away: they left their homelands and traveled a long time in order to contribute their bit of beauty to the ineffable adoration of God expressed by a new temple. All classes of society were represented: prelates and priests, monks and scholars, kings and statesmen, innumerable men, women, and children of the people, craftsmen, associations, and pious confraternities, all working together to erect a house of God worthy of Him.

176. It was not by stifling or mutilating the personalities of the co-workers that this sublime harmony was achieved, nor by submerging them in the anonymous collectivity or in the ideas and will of some brilliant architect whom the artists only have echoed in a servile manner. These ways of proceeding may at first seem productive; in fact, they lead to death. This is not how the miracle was accomplished, but rather through each artist's personal response to the call of the Spirit of God, which invited him to collaborate in the plenitude of his individualized activity. Not being lost in an indiscriminate collectivity, each man could draw from the depths of his personality the most perfect and spontaneous expression of the task that fell to him through his particular vocation. Thus, through the mediation of their common activity, they could offer God a worthy testimony of their obedience and love by erecting a temple to be a dwelling among us for the Eucharistic Christ, the eternal Oblation always present on our altars.

Thus each man could say of his participation in this great manifestation of collective worship: "In all things we have grown," following in that way Saint Paul's injunction "to practice the truth in love, and so grow up in all things in him who is the head, Christ" (Ephesians 4:15).

Through their inner devotion to Truth, a reflection of the Eternal Truth they sought to make manifest in their work, through their oblation in the spirit of charity, perfection, and total collaboration to the work undertaken for His sake, could these Christians not say they had found themselves in finding Christ? In Him and through Him, they discovered what the modern world is so feverishly searching for: the full development of the personality that each person has received as a gift from the Creator, and the unity in activity wherein the fullness of individual life may be achieved.

Perfecti estote . . . est, "Be thou perfect." With this call to both laity and clergy we conclude. It is the exhortation by which

Our Lord stirs us to become energetic, courageous, completely self-giving, integrated Christians. *Si spiritu vivimus, spiritu et ambulemus:* "If we live by the Spirit, by the Spirit let us also walk" (Galatians 5:5).

CONCLUSION: UNITY AND PEACE:
FRUITS OF THE REDEMPTION

The principles that preside over the true unity and true diversity of human life may not be well received everywhere. But the unity, order, and peace of humanity impose a great burden on us. Its weight corresponds to the value of the ransom the world's Redeemer paid with his blood on the cross, compensating at the same time once and for all for the sins of politics and the culpable violations of the principles of true human unity. We believe that this peace, which is so dear to Our heart, has a firm guarantee in the love of the Crucified, who gathered together all men without exception, and moreover, that this peace exists only in this love. In any case, it is not found where man's true value is not recognized and where, consequently, no serious attention is paid to the terrible sufferings that war causes in the hearts of mothers, wives, and children, or to the sacrifices that it entails for the combatants.

Need for reparation

178. Above all it is high time to offer reparation to our Redeemer's Sacred Heart for the sins in public life committed in relations among states, peoples, nations, and races, so that the Divine wrath does not strike us with just and terrible punishments.

The unity of humanity in the Holy Mass

179. And it is high time that We recognize, more fully and more efficaciously than before, the unity of humanity in the Holy Sacrifice of the Mass. It is in the Mass that, since the holy Council of Trent, the great and profound tradition has become the actual reality that unites us all, unites all men: the time before Christ with the day of Golgotha, the time after Christ with the perspective opened for all of us on the end of time and the consciousness of the presence of Christ at the heart of the most urgent and heart-felt aspirations of all men, namely the redemption of our daily sins by the Holy Mass through the Sacrifice on the Cross. That is why we have in this holy sacrifice an overflowing source of grace for unity and strength for peace. In the profound words of Saint Leo, which the Church recalls on the feast of the Exaltation of the Holy Cross: "Now, too, all kinds of fleshly sacrifices are at an end. There remains but the one oblation of your body and blood. It fulfills all former types of sacrifice, for you are the true *Lamb of God who takes away the sin of the world* (John 1:29). Thus you perfect all mysteries, and just as one sacrifice now replaces many victims, all nations are replaced by a single kingdom. "*Nunc etiam, carnalium sacrificiorum varietate cessante, omnes differentias hostiarum una corporis et sanguinis tui implet oblatio: quoniam tu es verus Agnus Dei, qui tollis peccata mundi; et ita in te universa perficis mysteria, ut sicut unum est pro omni victima sacrificium, ita unum de omni gente sit regnum.*"[16]

Therefore let our Redeemer's blood extinguish the passions of hatred and ambition among peoples, those firebrands of enmity, so that in harmony with the goal We Ourselves proposed at the beginning of Our pontificate, Christ's peace may reign in Christ's Kingdom.

Notes

INTRODUCTION

1. Henry James, correspondence cited in John LaFarge, S.J., *The Manner Is Ordinary* (New York: Harcourt, Brace, 1954), 23. James's great biographer, Leon Edel, said that James "was haunted by John LaFarge." See *Henry James, The Untried Years: 1843–1871* (Philadelphia: Lippincott, 1953), 166.

2. Ibid., 34.

3. Ibid., 35.

4. Ibid., 59, 76.

5. Ibid., 111.

6. Ibid., 154, 189.

7. John LaFarge, S.J., *Interracial Justice: A Study of the Catholic Doctrine of Race Relations* (New York: American Press, 1937), 144. All the later debates over integration are anticipated in LaFarge's book. Seventeen years before the Supreme Court's 1954 discussion on school integration, he made the Court's argument that separate is not equal, since education rests on a self-respect and sense of responsibility undermined by treatment of blacks as unworthy of white company (132), and he analyzes sympathetically the guilt that achieving blacks feel when they are forced to leave their brothers and sisters stranded in isolation from the larger society (116).

8. Ibid., 19.

9. Thomas B. Morgan, *A Reporter at the Papal Court: A Narrative of the Reign of Pope Pius XI* (New York: Longmans, Green, 1939), 134.

10. Benito Mussolini, Minute of Meeting with Pope Pius XI, February 11, 1932, in Peter C. Kent, *The Pope and the Duce: The International Impact of the Lateran Agreements* (New York: St. Martin's Press, 1981), 194.

11. Denis Mack Smith, *Mussolini* (New York: Knopf, 1982), 159–61.

12. Anthony Rhodes, *The Vatican in the Age of the Dictators, 1922–1945* (London: Hodder and Stoughton, 1973), 53–61. Rhodes cites the reaction of the British Foreign Office to this medieval penalty, captured in its archives: "The Pope seems to be really a full-blown idiot."

13. Monsignor Paschal Robinson to Sir Henry Chilton, July 19, 1929, cited in Kent, op. cit., 86.

14. Rhodes, op. cit., 203–7.

15. Pius's attempt to keep the Vatican out of politics had some signal exceptions, especially his support of Monsignor Ignaz Seipel as prime minister of Austria—an exception he justified because of Seipel's crucial opposition to anti-clericalism. But in other areas, contrary to the popular impression, Pius remained neutral. He did not, for instance, take sides in the Spanish Civil War, though Italian bishops did, to his dismay. Rhodes, op. cit., 113–30.

16. Ibid., 192, 200.

17. Nicholas Cheetham, *Keepers of the Keys* (New York: Scribner's, 1982), 205.

18. This was the kind of warning given LaFarge's father against marrying his Protestant mother.

19. Jerome Murphy-O'Connor, O.P., *Paul: A Critical Life* (Oxford and New York: Oxford University Press, 1996), 339–40.

20. Elaine Pagels, *The Origin of Satan* (New York: Vintage, 1996), 28.

21. John Milton, *De Doctrina Christiana: "exsecratione nobis debita in se translata."*

22. John Henry Newman, "Mental Sufferings of Our Lord in His Passion," in *Discourses to Mixed Congregations* (1849).

I. THE SEARCH FOR THE DOCUMENTS

1. *National Catholic Reporter,* 15 and 22 December 1972 and 19 January 1973.

2. Burkhart Schneider, S.J., "Una enciclica mancata," *Osservatore romano,* 5 April 1973.

3. For which LaFarge worked from 1926 to 1963, the year of his death, and which he edited from 1942 to 1948.

4. *National Catholic Reporter,* 15 and 22 December 1972.

5. In 1972 Walter Abbott was secretary of the Vatican commission on the Bible and Heinrich Bacht was professor of theology in Frankfurt (*National Catholic Reporter,* 15 December 1972, 3–4). Robert Graham, who was interviewed by the *National Catholic Reporter*'s Rome correspondent, Desmond O'Grady (*National Catholic Reporter* 15 December 1972, 8), still directs the section of the Vatican archives devoted to the Second World War.

6. *National Catholic Reporter,* 15 December 1972, 14–15.

7. Jim Castelli, "A Lingering Question," *National Catholic Reporter,* 15 December 1972, 10.

8. A professor of sociology, Zahn is the author of *German Catholics and Hitler's*

Wars: A Study in Social Control (New York: Sheed and Ward, 1962; 2nd ed. 1989).

9. First presented in Berlin on 17 February 1963, Rolf Hochhuth's play *The Deputy* seriously questioned Pius XII's "silence" with regard to Nazi anti-Semitism.

10. Gordon Zahn, "The Unpublished Encyclical—An Opportunity Missed," *National Catholic Reporter* 15 December 1972, 9.

11. *KNA-Nachrichten* (24 December 1972), *Time* magazine (25 December 1972), *Neue Züricher Zeitung* (28 January 1973), *Der Spiegel* (29 January 1973).

12. Begun in 1965; seven volumes had appeared by 1973. This new volume, which inaugurates a third series of works under the general title *The Holy See and the Victims of the War,* covers a period extending from the beginning of Pius XII's pontificate in March 1939 to the end of 1940.

13. *Osservatore romano,* 5 April 1973, 7, in the German weekly edition.

14. Braun (1910–1981) was one of the most fervent and generous of those in France working toward Judeo-Christian rapprochement. Starting in 1941, he served as chaplain in the concentration camps (Gurs Rivesaltes, Noé, Vernet, etc.) where thousands of Spanish republicans, anti-fascists, and German Jewish refugees were interned, and he helped save many of them in collaboration with the Amitiés chrétiennes (with Germaine Ribière, Abbé Glasberg, and Father Chaillet, under the patronage of Cardinal Gerlier, Pastor Boegner, and the Jewish consistory). In 1944 he was the co-founder of International Catholic Aid. He was also the founder and editor-in-chief of *Rencontre. Chrétiens et Juifs* (1967–1982).

15. Georges Passelecq's personal archives.

16. Father Robert Bosc, S.J., wrote the obituary on John LaFarge that appeared in *Informations catholiques internationales,* no. 207, 1 January 1964, 32.

17. Georges Passelecq's personal archives. Original in French. Enclosed with this letter was a copy of Burkhart Schneider's article that appeared in the *Osservatore romano* a year and a half earlier (see note 2).

18. Georges Passelecq's personal archives.

19. Johannes H. Nota, S.J., "Edith Stein und der Entwurf für eine Enzyklika gegen Rassismus und Antisemitismus," *Freiburger Rundbrief,* 1975, 35–41; republished in *Internationale Katholische Zeitschrift,* no. 5 (1976), 154–66.

20. Quoted by Teresia Renata de Spiritu Sancto in *Edith Stein* (Nuremberg: Glock and Lutz, 1952). Jewish by birth, Edith Stein converted to Catholicism in 1922 and entered the Carmelite convent in Köln in 1933. After Kristallnacht (November 1938) she took refuge in the Carmelite convent of Echt, in Holland, where the Nazis arrested her in August 1942. She died in Auschwitz a few weeks later and was beatified in 1987.

21. Nota, op. cit., 36.

22. Ibid.

23. Ibid., 38. "During these years," he went on, "I have personally had an opportunity to meet German Jesuits who had much better things to say about Israel"—for example: Erich Przywara, Wilhelm Klein, Gustav Closen, Augustin

Bea. Father Nota also names Francisca Van Leer and Martin Wijnhoven, and expresses his surprise that Desbuquois had not introduced LaFarge and Gundlach to the thought of Charles Péguy, Léon Bloy, or Jacques Maritain. See Nota, op. cit., 38–40.

24. Discussions in July 1987 with Rabbi Leon Klenicki, director of the Department of International Affairs of the Anti-Defamation League of B'nai B'rith; Rabbi Marc H. Tannenbaum, director of the International Relations Department of the American Jewish Committee; and Dr. Eugene Fischer, secretary of the American Episcopal Committee on relations with Judaism.

25. Telephone conversations on 5 August 1987, with Ms. Jean Blake, then assistant to the editor of the *National Catholic Reporter,* and with Jim Castelli.

26. Personal archives of Bernard Suchecky.

27. Letterhead: *Archivum Romanum Societatis Iesu.* Letter sent to B. Suchecky by J. Nota. Original in French.

28. St. Paul University, Ottawa, Ontario. Edward Stanton, an American Jesuit, was born in Boston in 1916 and taught at Boston College, a Jesuit institution.

29. Chap. 5, 93–154.

30. He adds, however, that "on 22 December 1970, the author wrote to His Holiness Pope Paul VI to ask his permission to use these texts. On 28 January, His Excellency J. Benelli, replied that 'as for your desire to use for your doctoral dissertation extracts from the text on racism prepared by the late Father John LaFarge, I am happy to inform you that you are free to do so' " (Ibid., 180–81). Moreover, in the acknowledgments preceding his dissertation, Stanton writes: "I also thank Father Robert Graham, S.J., [. . .] who read and commented on the section devoted to John LaFarge's draft encyclical for Pius XI, and to Pope Paul VI for having allowed me to use this document" (Ibid., ii).

32. *Gustav Gundlach S.J. (1892–1963). Repräsentant und Interpret der katholischen Soziallehre in der Ära Pius XII. Historische Einordnung und systematische Darstellung.* (Münster, 1973). Published in *Abhandlungen zur Sozialethik,* vol. 9 (Munich, Paderborn, and Vienna: Ferdinand Schöningh, 1975).

32. Ibid., 76, n. 22.

33. Ibid., 627.

34. Ibid., 79–80.

35. The founder of this Katholische Sozialwissenschaftliche Zentralstelle was precisely Gustav Gundlach himself, whose own papers constituted the first collection of documents deposited at this institution! See *Pro iustitia in mundo, Katholische Sozialwissenschaftliche Zentralstelle, Mönchengladbach, 1963–1968* (Köln: J. P. Bachem, 1988), 15f.

36. "Along with the microfilm is a list of the microfilm's contents and copies of my correspondence with Prof. Johannes Schwarte—to whom I also sent a copy of the same microfilm which you have just received." Letter from Thomas Breslin

to B. Suchecky, dated Miami, 20 November 1987. Breslin's letter to Schwarte is dated Charlottesville, 23 February 1973.

37. Viz: a text in French consisting of 119 typed pages entitled *Humani Generis Unitas* (with annotations in LaFarge's hand); a text in English consisting of ninety-nine typed pages, covered with strikeouts and handwritten corrections. The passages not struck out correspond, exactly, to the French text. At the top of the first page there is a handwritten note by LaFarge beginning: "The Unity of the human race..." There is also part (or the totality) of the correspondence between LaFarge and his superiors in New York and Rome, from June to September 1938. These various letters, handwritten or typed, are in English or French; six (fifteen typed pages) are in German, from Gundlach in Rome to LaFarge in New York. The first letter is dated 16 October 1938, the last 30 May 1940. There are several news clippings (from the *New York Times* and *Osservatore romano*) dating from summer 1938 to summer 1940.

38. Paul Droulers, *Politique sociale et christianisme: Le Père Desbuquois et l'*Action populaire, vol. 2, "Dans la gestation d'un monde nouveau (1919–1946)" (Paris: Editions ouvrières, 1981), 37, n. 110.

39. Personal archives of B. Suchecky. Original in German.

40. Personal archives of B. Suchecky. Original in German.

41. Personal archives of B. Suchecky. Original in German.

42. Personal archives of B. Suchecky. Original in French.

43. Nevertheless, on 31 October 1939, Father Vincent P. McCormick, the rector of the Gregorian University, had written to John LaFarge: "Your document came through without difficulty and is resting in our archives" (see chap. 5). Was it subsequently destroyed there? Or was it transferred to other archives? Or later returned to LaFarge?

II. THE COMMISSIONING OF *HUMANI GENERIS UNITAS*

1. Request for funding, 11 April 1938, microf. 3.

2. Letter from LaFarge to Talbot, London, 7 May 1938, microf. 5; memorandum dated Paris, 3 July 1938, microf. 13.

3. John LaFarge, *The Manner Is Ordinary* (1954; rpt., New York: Doubleday, 1957), 236.

4. On his father's side he was descended from Breton nobility (his paternal grandfather had served under Napoleon); on his mother's side he was a direct descendant of Benjamin Franklin. His brother Grant, a friend of Theodore Roosevelt, and his uncle George were the co-designers of the Cathedral of St. John the Divine in New York City. For all the following discussion, in addition to *The Manner Is Ordinary*, we have made use of the following sources: J. LaFarge, autobiographical notes, microf. 1 and 2; J. LaFarge, *Interracial Justice* (New York: America Press, 1937; rpt., 1942 as *The Race Question and the Negro*); the doctoral

dissertation by Edward Stanton; *John LaFarge's Understanding of the Unifying Mission of the Church . . .* , cited in chap. 1; and Robert Bosc's obituary notice on LaFarge in *Informations catholiques internationales,* no. 207, 1 January 1964, 32.

5. He eventually mastered French, German, Spanish, Portuguese, Italian, Russian, Polish, Czech, Slovak, Danish, Dutch, Esperanto, Swedish, Icelandic, Latin, Greek, Hebrew, Syrian, Aramaic, and Galilean! Stanton, op. cit., 13.

6. Ibid., 187.

7. LaFarge in *America* in 1931, quoted by Stanton, op. cit., 117–19.

8. LaFarge, quoted by Stanton, op. cit., 107–9.

9. LaFarge, *Interracial Justice,* vi.

10. Ibid., 12, 14.

11. Ibid., 18–19, 24.

12. Ibid., 59.

13. Ibid., 59–60.

14. Ibid., 60–65. Here it must be understood that "the essential human rights of Negroes do not appertain to them as Negroes, but simply as members of the human family. Human rights are not Negro rights, any more than they are white rights or red-haired persons' rights. They flow from the essential constituents of our nature, not from its accidental characteristics. Negro insistence on human rights as *Negro rights* can only have the effect of provoking white insistence upon supposed 'white people's rights,' which are equally baseless." Ibid., 79.

15. *Interracial Justice,* 78–79.

16. LaFarge, *The Manner Is Ordinary,* 219.

17. Letter from LaFarge to Talbot, Paris, 15 May 1938, microf. 6. The son of Thomas Masaryk, former president of the republic (1918–1935), Jan Masaryk resigned his post of ambassador to London to protest the Munich accords. After the "Prague coup" of February 1948, his body was found beneath the windows of his office at the foreign ministry in Prague. Suicide? Assassination?

18. Letter from LaFarge to Talbot, 17 May 1938, microf. 8. The correspondence sent by LaFarge to Talbot all through his travels in Europe bears witness to his militant commitment against the "Reds" and his quite strong sympathies for Franco.

19. One of the editors of *America.*

20. Letter from LaFarge to Talbot, Paris, 17 May 1938, microf. 8.

21. "Let us pray for each other."

22. Microf. 6 and 7.

23. Postcard dated Coblenz, 20 May 1938. Added and signed, with an arrow pointing to *Oremus,* is: "Code: things are very bad, worse than you imagine." Microf. 11. See also microf. 36.

24. LaFarge, *The Manner Is Ordinary,* 223.

25. Ibid., 224.

26. Ibid., 225.

27. Ibid.

28. Ibid., 226.

29. Ibid., 228.

30. Ibid., 229. The eucharistic congress in Budapest took place 26-30 May 1938.

31. The archbishop's attitude with regard to Ante Pavelic's independent State of Croatia, proclaimed in April 1941, remains very controversial. In 1946, it caused him to be sentenced to sixteen years at hard labor by the Zagreb popular tribunal. In 1954, LaFarge described him as a zealous defender of religion, law, and justice, a convinced anti-racist; "I recalled the language he spoke in the face of Nazi conquerors of Yugoslavia and their Ustashi allies" (*The Manner Is Ordinary*, 230-31). More recently, a French historian claimed that "if Mgr. Stepinac did not wish to condemn the Croatian state, [. . .] and if he felt obliged to criticize only its acts, this was not in any way out of sympathy for any form of totalitarianism, but in order not to undermine the institution which seemed to him, with respect to and against everything, necessary to his nation's independence" (Xavier de Montclos, *Les Chrétiens face au nazisme et au stalinisme. L'épreuve totalitaire, 1939-1945* [Paris: Plon, 1983], 174).

32. LaFarge, *The Manner Is Ordinary*, 231.

33. Letter from LaFarge to Talbot, Rome, 8 June 1938, microf. 13. However, in a cable sent to Talbot in Rome on 4 June, Father John Delaney, S.J., another American Jesuit, explains: "Father LaFarge arrives this afternoon. I shall meet him at the station." Microf. 14.

34. LaFarge, *The Manner Is Ordinary*, 232.

35. Ibid., 233.

36. Letter from LaFarge to Talbot, Rome, 8 June 1938, microf. 13.

37. Ibid.

38. LaFarge, *The Manner Is Ordinary*, 234.

39. Admission ticket, 22 June 1938, microf. 16.

40. LaFarge, *The Manner Is Ordinary*, 235.

41. *"Dites tout simplement ce que vous diriez si vous étiez Pape, vous-même."* Underlined, and in French in the original text. LaFarge's handwritten addition inserts "à tout le monde" after the word "diriez": "what you would say to everyone."

42. Underlined, and in French, in the text. LaFarge's handwritten addition: "emphasizing the words."

43. Handwritten addition: "It will be most carefully passed on, of course, by V.R. Fr. General."

44. Father Zacheus Maher was the American assistant to the Father General; Father Vincent McCormick, the rector of the Gregorian University; Father Phillips, the provincial of New York, and Father d'Ouince, the provincial of Paris; Father Killeen was the superior general's American substitute and "the two men whom I was asked to consult" are Fathers Gundlach and Desbuquois.

45. Memorandum from LaFarge to Father Murphy, dated Paris, 3 July 1938, microf. 18.

46. In French in the text. Comment made by H. Bacht to T. Breslin, *National Catholic Reporter,* 15 December 1972, 8.

47. Handwritten addition: "interracial justice."

48. No date; on stationery with the letterhead "Pontificia Università Gregoriana, Piazza della Pilotta—Roma 101," with "AMDG" at the top; in French, underlined in the text Microf. 19.

49. Where his host was his "friend, Father Albert Le Roy, S.J., who had been for some time a Vatican delegate to the International Labor Office." LaFarge, *The Manner Is Ordinary,* 238.

50. Note from LaFarge to Murphy, 3 July 1938, microf. 18.

III. THE COMPOSITION OF *HUMANI GENERIS UNITAS*

1. LaFarge, *The Manner Is Ordinary,* 238.

2. Sources: Paul Droulers, S.J., *Politique sociale et christianisme. Le Père Desbuquois et Action populaire,* vol. I, *Débuts: Syndicalisme et intégristes (1903–1918);* vol. II, *Dans la gestation d'un monde nouveau (1919–1946)* (Paris and Rome: Gregorian University Press, 1969, 1981). Johannes Schwarte, *Gustav Gundlach S.J. (1892–1963), Repräsentant und Interpret der katholischen Soziallehre in der Ära Pius XII: Historische Einordnung und systematische Darstellung.* Doctoral dissertation, Münster, 1974; published in *Abhandlungen zur Sozialethik,* Band 9 (Paderborn and Munich: Schöningh, 1975). Anton Rauscher, *Gustav Gundlach, 1892–1963* (Paderborn and Munich: Schöningh, 1988). Anton Losinger, "Gerechte Vermögensverteilung. Das Modell Oswald von Nell-Breunings," *Abhandlungen zur Sozialethik,* Band 34 (Paderborn and Munich: Schöningh, 1994).

3. Born in 1869. Entered the novitiate of the Society of Jesus in 1889. Died in 1959.

4. Born in 1892, ordained as a priest in 1924, died in 1963. His novitiate, which he began with the Jesuits of Tisis in 1912, had been interrupted by the war. "Anyone who has known the front," he later wrote, "and the wretchedness of the military hospitals will no longer be a skeptic in epistemology; for him, the reality of the external world is obvious." Quoted by Schwarte, op. cit., 17.

5. Schwarte, op. cit., 20.

6. Ibid. Father Leiber's name will appear again, in connection with *Mit Brennender Sorge* and *Humani Generis Unitas.* He entered the Society of Jesus in 1906 and was ordained a priest eleven years later. He held the chair of Church history at his order's study center in Valkenburg from 1923 to 1929, and subsequently held the same chair at the Gregorian University in Rome. See Carlo Falconi, *Le Silence de Pie XII* (Monaco: Le Rocher, 1965), 87, n. 26.

7. Later, Gundlach castigated "these groups that were throwing around the con-

cepts of 'community,' 'authority,' 'direction'—which sound particularly good to Catholic ears. The anti-intellectual emotionalism of the youth movement, the historicist conviction that Solidarism broke with the 'natural unified line of social Catholicism,' the liturgicist and supernaturalist devaluation of natural law, [. . .] all undermined the foundations of the Weimar democracy on Catholic terrain, and was one day to provide grist for the mill of Hitler's 'national unification.' Gustav Gundlach, "Meine Bestimmung zur Sozialwissenschaft," unpublished autobiographical notes, Rome, 23 February 1962, quoted by Schwarte, op. cit., 30.

8. Founded in 1890, the Volksverein had continually worked toward the recognition of Catholics' place in the German Empire and later in the republic. The Königswinterer Kreis was founded in 1930 and included among its members eminent representatives of the Catholic social movement, experts in economics, social sciences, and theology such as Theodor Bauer, Götz Briefs, Paul Jostock, Rudolf Kleibach, Oswald von Nell-Breuning, Heinrich Rommen, and Joseph Van der Velden (the future bishop of Aachen; at that time general director of the Volksverein). See O. von Nell-Breuning, S.J., "Der Königswinterer Kreis und sein Anteil an Quadragesimo Anno," *Soziale Verantwortung* (Berlin, 1968), quoted by Losinger, op. cit., 23.

9. Quoted by Schwarte, op. cit., 29–32.

10. Quoted by Schwarte, op. cit., 39, 40–42.

11. Droulers, op. cit., vol. 2, 153.

12. Ibid., 153–55.

13. Droulers, op. cit., 333, n. 100.

14. Ibid., 196–98.

15. In fact, Gundlach's ideas were chiefly stated later on, through the social doctrine of Pius XII. It was Gundlach who conceived the drafts of Pius XII's speeches and declarations, as well as his Christmas addresses, which became famous, even though this pope did not publish a single specifically social encyclical. Rauscher, op. cit., 7.

16. Schwarte, op. cit., 51–53.

17. *Staatsvolk* in the original.

18. *Volksgemeinschaft* in the original.

19. This decree will be discussed in chap. 5.

20. *Lexikon für Theologie und Kirche,* vol. 1, 2d ed. (Freiburg-im-Breisgau: Herder, 1930), 504–5.

21. Sources: Johannes Schwarte, op. cit., 66–71; Guenter Lewy, *L'Église catholique et l'Allemagne nazie* (Paris: Stock, 1964), 186; Alain Fleury, *"La Croix" et l'Allemagne* (Paris: Cerf, 1986), 287–90; Desmond O'Grady, "Pius XI—'Complex and Imperious,'" *National Catholic Reporter,* 15 December 1972; *La Documentation catholique,* vol. 39, no. 870 (20 April 1938), 451–74.

22. *La Documentation catholique,* loc. cit., 453.

23. Ibid., 453.

24. "Ordinarily all the Prussian bishops and the bishops of the Upper Rhineland took part. The archbishop of Munich and Freising represented the Bavarian bishops (organized within the framework of the Freising conference) and thus conferred a national character on the assembly." Lewy, op. cit., 24.

25. The English press, for instance, called Cardinal Innitzer "the Heil-Hitler Cardinal." See *La Documentation catholique,* loc. cit., 24.

26. *La Documentation catholique,* loc. cit., 55.

27. Journal of the S.S.

28. *La Documentation catholique,* loc. cit., 456–68.

29. Quoted in *La Documentation catholique,* loc. cit., 459.

30. Schwarte, op. cit., 71, quoting Gundlach, *Meine Bestimmung zur Sozial-wissenschaft,* 8.

31. Dated 6 April 1938, reproduced in the German edition of the *Osservatore romano* for 7 April and in the Italian edition for 8 April. Quoted here from *La Documentation catholique* for 20 April 1938, loc. cit., 469.

32. In two similar telegrams, written in Latin and coming from the Provincial of the Jesuits in Prague and the Rector of the Jesuits in Maastricht, themselves warned by the prelate Hermann Josef Schmitt, secretary general of the Reichs-verband der katholischen Arbeitervereine. Schwarte, op. cit., 71.

33. During the weeks following 12 March, 79,000 people were arrested in the city of Vienna alone. Social Democrats, Social Christians, monarchists, and Austrian nationalists were prevented from campaigning freely; and communists were out-lawed. The voting booths were arranged in such a way that the choices made by voters could not escape the view of the electoral officials, who consisted of Austrian Nazis. See William L. Shirer, *The Rise and Fall of the Third Reich* (New York: Simon and Schuster, 1960), 337.

34. "I spent the summer of 1938 working very hard, in the heat of the Parisian suburbs. The work consisted of preparing, along with others, a document that was to serve as the basis for an encyclical of Pius XI. The pope wished to set forth systematically the point of view of the Church's social doctrine with respect to the State, the Nation, and Race." *Meine Bestimmung . . . ,*" 8.

35. Letter from Heinrich Bacht, 5 March 1973, to Schwarte, who quotes it in his dissertation, 78–79.

36. Handwritten note in the upper left corner.

37. No signature; letter from Talbot to LaFarge, 13 July 1938, microf. 22. Original in English.

38. Murphy to Talbot, handwritten note, 18 July 1938, microf. 24. Original in English.

39. See this address in chap. 5.

40. Ledochowski to LaFarge, Naples, 17 July 1938, microf. 27.

41. Cable from LaFarge to Talbot, Paris, 21 July 1938, microf. 26. Original in English.

42. Talbot to Murphy, 22 July 1938, microf. 25. Original in English.

43. Ledochowski to LaFarge, Naples, 26 July 1938, microf. 29.

44. Letter from LaFarge to Talbot, Paris, 5 August, 1938, microf. 31.

45. In French in the text.

46. LaFarge to Talbot, Paris, 11 August 1938, microf. 32. Original in English.

47. In a letter dated New York, 13 August, Talbot informed LaFarge that "we have not published your article on Germany because it seemed too favorable. In your kindness, I think you have depicted the conditions imposed on Catholics as far better than they are." Microf. 33.

48. LaFarge to Talbot, Paris, 23 August 1938, microf. 36. Original in English.

49. Ledochowski to LaFarge, Frascati, 31 August 1938, microf. 34.

50. Ledochowski to LaFarge, Frascati, 1 September 1938, microf. 37.

51. LaFarge to Talbot, Paris, 2 September 1938, microf. 38. Original in English.

52. LaFarge to Talbot, Paris, 18 September 1938, microf. 39. Original in English.

53. LaFarge, *The Manner Is Ordinary*, 237.

54. Cf. Schirer, op. cit., 398. Shirer, who was in the Sportspalast for Hitler's speech, gives a description of it very similar to LaFarge's.

55. Edvard Beneš (1884–1948) succeeded Thomas Masaryk as president of Czechoslovakia in 1935. He resigned after the Munich accords and went to live in Chicago. After he returned to Prague in 1945, he formed a coalition government. Yielding to communist pressure, in February 1948 he legalized the "Prague coup."

56. LaFarge, *The Manner Is Ordinary*, 237–38. In the last letter he had sent LaFarge, dated 29 September, Talbot reported: "This week we are all speculating, as from afar, on the detonations through all of Europe. While none of us believe that war will be declared on Saturday, we are apprehensive. It seems that war is inevitable and if it does not break out immediately, it must come eventually, and that will be the end, probably, of European civilization [. . .]. Microf. 40.

57. Microf. 42.

58. "War clouds were shaping up and I anxiously scanned the news. One afternoon, after lunch, when we were sitting in the Fathers' recreation room in the rue Monsieur, the telephone rang in the adjoining office of the Superior. In a few minutes he informed us that there would be no war. 'M. Daladier and M. Chamberlain have conferred with Hitler and Mussolini in Munich and all will be well.' My passage home was now assured." LaFarge, *The Manner Is Ordinary*, 243.

IV. WHAT HAPPENED TO THE DRAFT?

1. All written in German.

2. Father Vincent P. McCormick, rector of the Pontifical Gregorian University.

3. E[ure] H[ochwürdigkeit], that is, "Your Reverence."

4. The Borgo Santo Spirito, address of the general house of the Jesuits in Rome.

5. Father Ledochowski, superior general of the Jesuits.

6. The name means "Fisher" in German: an allusion to the "fisher ring" the pope wears. In other words, "Mr. Fischer" is Pius XI.

7. Letter from Gundlach to LaFarge, Rome, 16 October 1938, microf. 41.

8. Letter from Killeen to LaFarge, 27 October 1938, microf. 43. Original in English.

9. D. Mondrone, S.J., "Il Padre Enrico Rosa D.C.D.G. In Memoriam Patris," *La Civiltà cattolica,* vol. 4, quad. 2124, 9 December 1938, 481–96. The "Sphinx of modernism" to whom the author alludes is Ernesto Buonaiuti, whom Father Rosa opposed, going so far as to ask for his excommunication.

10. Giuseppe De Luca in the *Osservatore romano* for 27 December 1936, quoted by Mondrone, op. cit., 490–91.

11. On this subject, the microfilm contains two articles clipped from the *New York World-Telegram* for 28 November and the *New York Times* for 29 November: "Pope Pius XI, who was near death on Friday, resumed almost normal activity today and was reported to be planning an encyclical on world problems. [. . .] Reports that he would soon issue an encyclical were based chiefly on the belief that the Pope was convinced that another series of heart attacks similar to Friday's would prove fatal. It was believed, therefore, that he was anxious to reaffirm his position on various world problems, such as his condemnation of armed conflicts and Communism and his pleas to leading statesmen to co-operate for peace." *New York World-Telegram,* 28 November 1938, microf. 45. "Vatican sources indicated preparation of an encyclical, which Italian circles for some time have reported the Pope to be working on, might have been delayed by his illness. Italians last week expressed the belief that the Pope was preparing an encyclical, an allocution or the calling of a consistory to fill five vacancies in the College of Cardinals when he was stricken last Friday. [. . .]" *New York Times,* 29 November 1938, microf. 46.

12. We return to this subject in chap. 5.

13. Probably Father Robert Leiber, S.J.

14. Mussolini.

15. See chap. 5.

16. Gundlach is probably referring to the anti-Semitic violence fomented by the Nazi regime during the night of 9 November 1938 (Kristallnacht). Neither the German bishops nor the Vatican made the slightest protest.

17. We have not been able to determine the identity of the American bishop to whom Gundlach refers.

18. Letter from Gundlach to LaFarge, Rome, 18 November 1938, microf. 44.

19. Letter from Father Zacheus J. Maher to LaFarge, Rome, 3 January 1939, microf. 47. Original in English.

20. That is, the general of the Jesuits.

21. A law passed in October 1938 gave foreign Jews living in Italy six months to leave the kingdom and its colonial dependencies.

22. Letter from Gundlach to LaFarge, 28 January 1939, microf. 48.

23. *Admodum reverendus pater noster,* "Our Very Reverend Father," that is, Ledochowski.

24. Pius XII.

25. Pius XI.

26. Respect for authority.

27. Pius XII.

28. The Bishop of Berlin, Mgr. Konrad von Preysing.

29. Comte de Montalembert (Charles Forbes), 1810–1870.

30. Letter from Gundlach to LaFarge, Rome, 15 March 1939, microf. 50.

31. Letter from Maher to LaFarge, Rome, 16 March 1939, microf. 50. Original in English.

32. Jesuit theology students.

33. Letter from Maher to LaFarge, Easter Monday 1939, microf. 52. Original in English.

34. John LaFarge, *The Race Question and the Negro: A Study of the Catholic Doctrine on Interracial Justice* (New York: Longmans, 1943).

35. J. LaFarge, "Racism," *New Catholic Encyclopedia* (Washington: McGraw-Hill, 1967), XII: 54–60. See particularly 57 to 59.

36. That is, between the pope and Ledochowski.

37. Ledochowski's.

38. Gundlach presumably is alluding to the statement made on 14 April 1939 by the president of the United States, Franklin Delano Roosevelt. Let us briefly put it in its context. After the beginning of Pius XII's pontificate, events had moved very quickly and tension had escalated in Europe. After the easy conquest of Austria and the Sudetenland in April and October 1938, Hitler invaded the rest of Czechoslovakia on 15 March 1939 and seized the Lithuanian territory of Memel on 23 March. Breaking with the attitude he had adopted up to that point, Chamberlain then declared to the House of Commons on 31 March that "Great Britain and France will provide the Polish government with all the aid in their power" in the event that Poland was attacked and resisted. The next day, Hitler stated that "Germany has no hostile intentions toward other peoples," but on 3 April he secretly ordered his generals to be prepared to "eliminate definitively, if necessary, any threat proceeding from Poland [. . .] at any time from 1 September on." On 7 April, Mussolini occupied Albania. On 13 April, France and Britain responded by giving their guarantee of protection to Greece and Romania. On 15 April an appeal from President Roosevelt reached Rome and Berlin asking the Axis powers to give assurance that they would not attack or invade the territory of a series of independent nations, among which were Poland, the Baltic states, the USSR, Denmark, Belgium, France, and Great Britain. Hitler reacted on 28 April in an extremely brutal and ironic discourse before the Reichstag, which nevertheless carefully avoided answering the precise question he had been asked by the president of the United States. See William Shirer, op. cit., 471ff.

39. Weichsel=Vistula; thus, the reference is to Poland.

40. Berlin.

41. Letter from Gundlach to LaFarge, Rome, 10 May 1939, microf. 53.

42. The Soviets intervened only on 17 September, invoking as a pretext the necessity of protecting the Ukraine and Byelorussia from the German menace.

43. *New York Times,* 17 October 1939, microf. 52.

44. Let us also note that one of the French editions of *Summi Pontificatus* was published by *Action populaire,* that it bears the *Nihil obstat* "G. Desbuquois, Vanveis, die 2a Decembris 1939," and that it is copiously annotated by Desbuquois himself. See *Action populaire,* "L'Encyclique *Summi Pontificatus,* 20 octobre 1939. Traduction française avec table analytique et commentaires" (Paris: Éditions Spes, 1939).

45. Letter from Vincent McCormick to LaFarge, Rome, 31 October 1939, microf. 56. Original in English.

46. Lucifer's banner.

47. Letter from Gundlach to LaFarge, Rome, 30 May 1940, microf. 57.

V. A FEW SUPPLEMENTARY DOCUMENTS CONCERNING *HUMANI GENERIS UNITAS*

1. The best-known are: The Congregation of the Priests and Nuns of Our Lady of Zion (1852), the Arch-brotherhood of Prayers for the Return of the People of Israel (1905), and its Anglo-American branch, the Catholic Guild of Israel (1917).

2. The article "Amici Israel" in *Lexikon für Theologie und Kirche* (1930) gives the date 6 June 1926.

3. *Pax super Israel* (1926, 4 p.); *Opus sacerdotale: Amici Israel* (1926, 2 p.); *Status Operis* (1927, 4 p.), *Pax super Israel* (I, 1927, 36 p.; II, June 1927, 31 p.; III, January 1928, 18 p.). See *Nouvelle Revue théologique* 40 (July, 1928): 533–35.

4. In Latin in the *Nouvelle Revue théologique,* pp. 532–33. In French in René Laurentin, *l'Église et les juifs à Vatican II* (Tournai: Casterman, 1967), 104–5.

5. *Nouvelle Revue théologique,* 537.

6. On the Church and Nazism, see especially Guenter Lewy, *l'Église catholique et l'Allemagne nazie* (Paris: Stock, 1965), and, for a different point of view, several articles by Jean-Marie Mayeur, in Jean-Marie Mayeur, Charles Pietri, André Vauchez, and Marc Venard, *Histoire du Christianisme des origines à nos jours* (Paris: Desclée-Fayard, 1990), 12: 318f., 574–86.

7. G. Lewy gives many examples of this all through his book.

8. And this took place with the agreement of the German Church hierarchy and the Vatican. See G. Lewy, op. cit., chap. 4, "La grande réconciliation," 91f.

9. The Nuremberg laws date from September 1938.

10. The Vatican secretary of state had brought together all the components with

the help of his German co-workers, Mgr. Ludwig Kaas, the Jesuit priests Robert Leiber, Augustin Béa, and H. (?) Heinrich, regularly submitting the form and content of the text to the pope. When the draft was completed, it was also submitted to Cardinals Beltram, Faulhaber, and Schult, as well as to the bishops of Berlin and Münster, who were called to Rome for the purpose of reviewing it. Cardinal Faulhaber is supposed to have put on the final touches. See Monsignor Georges Roche and Philippe Saint-Germain, *Pie XII devant l'histoire* (Paris: Lafont, 1972), 68. Let us note in passing that Father Béa (1881–1968), the provincial of the Jesuit province of southern Germany, and later Pius XII's confessor, was to become in 1960 the first president of the Secretariat for Christian Unity. During the Vatican II Council, he was at the center of the polemics and maneuvers around the writing of the text that was finally to become paragraph 4 of the declaration *Nostra Aetate,* always defending the position most favorable to Judeo-Catholic rapprochement. See Stjepan Schmidt, S.J., *Agostino Bea il cardinale dell'unità* (Rome: Città Nuova, 1988).

11. G. Lewy, op. cit., 142.

12. In German: *mit brennender Sorge,* whence the title.

13. *Mit Brennender Sorge,* in *Actes de S.S. Pie XI,* 16 (Paris: Maison de la Bonne Presse, 1937), 7.

14. Ibid., 8.

15. In this case, the 1933 concordat.

16. *Mit Brennender Sorge,* 10–12.

17. Ibid., 49–50.

18. Ibid., 13–16.

19. Ibid., 20–21.

20. Ibid., 21–22.

21. Ibid., 29.

22. Ibid., 36–38.

23. Ibid., 40–41.

24. Ibid., 47–49.

25. Ibid., 27–28.

26. Ibid., 43–46.

27. G. Lewy, op. cit., 14. This author adduces another element in support of his opinion. Following the Nazi government's vigorous protests to the German bishops and the Holy See, according to which the encyclical was a call for opposition to the leaders of the German state and a grave violation of the contractual obligations of the concordat, Cardinal Pacelli, the Vatican secretary of state, sent in turn a note to the German leaders in which he explained that "the Holy See maintains friendly, correct or at least passable relations with States having various constitutional forms and orientations, and avoids interfering in the question of the concrete form of government that a people decides to consider as being most in conformity with its nature and its needs. So far as Germany is concerned, [the

Holy See] has remained constantly faithful to this principle and intends to continue to be faithful to it." Quoted by G. Lewy, op. cit., 143–44.

28. *Mit Brennender Sorge,* 18–19.

29. Yves de La Brière, "L'histoire religieuse du temps présent: Au dixième anniversaire des Accords du Latran," *Études* 1 (5 February 1939): 389–92. On the same topic, also see Jean-Dominique Durand, "le Christianisme dans l'Europe de la première moitié du XXme siècle: l'Italie," in Mayeur, Pietri, Vauchez, and Venard, op. cit., 371–90.

30. de la Brière, op. cit.

31. Durand, *art. cit.*

32. Rome having been carpeted with banners bearing the swastika, Pius XI had departed ostensibly to protest against what he considered as an infraction of article 1 of the 1919 concordat, by which Italy recognized the "sacred character of the Eternal City, the center of the Catholic world and the goal of pilgrimages," and committed itself to "prevent anything in Rome that might be in contradiction with this character." The pope had thus gone to Castelgandolfo, not "through petty diplomacy," the *Osservatore romano* ironically explained on 2 May, "but simply because the air at Castelgandolfo does him good, whereas the air here harms him." Quoted by *La Documentation catholique* 39 (no. 873, 5 June 1938), 690. On the "sacred character" of Rome, see Andrea Riccardi, *Roma "città sacra"? Dalla conciliazione all'operazione Sturzo* (Milan: Vita e Pensiero, 1979).

33. *La Croix,* 6 May 1938, quoted by *La Documentation catholique.*

34. *Osservatore romano,* 3 May 1938; *La Civiltà cattolica,* "Cronaca contemporanea," III (9–22 June 1938): 83; *La Documentation catholique* 39 (no. 872, 20 May 1938), col. 579. "As early as 3 May, M. Georges Goyau published a summary in *Le Figaro.* On 11 May, *La Croix* published the full text in the form of a letter addressed to His Eminence Cardinal Baudrillart, rector of the Catholic Institute of Paris." See *La Documentation catholique* 39 (no. 873, 5 June 1938): 690.

35. By analogy with the anti-modernist *Syllabus* of 1864. See *La Documentation catholique,* loc. cit.

36. For example, the lectures given at the Catholic Institute of Paris by Cardinal Alfred Baudrillart and Mgr. Bressolles, its rector and vice-rector, respectively, and by four professors, R. d'Harcourt, A. de Lapparent, Y. de La Brière, and E. Seillière, which were later collected in a book titled *Racisme et christianisme* (Paris: Flammarion, 1939). In addition, the studies by Father Pierre Charles, S.J. (Louvain), J. Folliet (Lyons), Father Pierre Lorson, S.J. (Strasbourg), and E. Van Campenhout (Louvain), which appeared in the February 1939 issue of *La Nouvelle Revue théologique* at the Catholic University of Louvain, and were later published under the title *Racisme et Catholicisme* (Paris and Tournai: Casterman, 1939). Finally, we might mention the homilies and speeches given by Cardinal-Archbishops Faulhaber of Munich (6 November 1938), Schuster of Milan (13 November 1938),

and Cerejeira of Lisbon (18 November 1938), to which we shall return later. Of all these actions, only Father Charles's address discussed anti-Semitism as such.

37. Pinchas E. Lapide, *Rome et les Juifs* (Paris: Seuil, 1967), 137.

38. Quoted here after *Il Messaggero* for 15 July 1938, and the complete translation published in *La Documentation catholique* 39 (n. 879, 5 September 1938).

39. *La Documentation catholique*, loc. cit.

40. See chap. 3, n. 40.

41. "Make disciples of all nations" (Matthew 18:19).

42. "I believe in the Holy Catholic Church."

43. *Osservatore romano*, 17 July 1938, translated and published in *La Documentation catholique* 39, 5 September 1938, cols. 1054–1055.

44. Quoted from the *Osservatore romano*, 23 July 1938; translation in *La Documentation catholique*, loc. cit.

45. "Anyone who eats pope will die of it." In French in the original.

46. *Osservatore romano* for 30 July 1938 published on its first page a "very detailed overview" of this declaration.

47. The author refers in fact to the letter of the Sacred Congregation of Seminaries and Universities held on the preceding 13 April, published without comment in "Cronaca contemporanea," *Civiltà cattolica* 3 (9–22 June 1938), 83–84.

48. Unsigned "Cronaca contemporanea," *La Civiltà cattolica* 3, quad. 2115 (29 July 1938), 277–78.

49. In addition, in the issue for 8 July the publication had begun a "rigorously scientific" study by Father A. Messineo, S.J., entitled "Il problema della Nazione." It was published almost at full length in the *Osservatore romano* for 21 July and 13 August 1938, and in toto as "Nation and Race: A study by R. P. Messineo" in *La Documentation catholique* for 5 September 1938 (vol. 39, no. 879). This study inaugurated a practically uninterrupted series of articles by the same author, devoted to the "problem of the nation" (8 July 1938), to "the constitutive elements of the nation and the race" (27 July 1938), to the "nature and essence of the nation" (12 August 1938), to the "nation and the State" (7 October 1938), to the "nation and the State in the hierarchy of social entities" (10 November 1938), to "patriotism, nationalism, internationalism" (9 December 1938), to "the search for a solution: Clarifications and distinctions" (9 January 1939), and so on.

50. Unsigned, "La rivoluzione mondiale e gli ebrei," *La Civiltà cattolica* 4, quad. 1736 (12 October 1922), 111–21.

51. Unsigned, "La questione giudaica," *La Civiltà cattolica* 4, quad. 2071 (25 September 1936), 37–46.

52. Léon de Poncins, *la Mystérieuse Internationale juïve* (Paris: Beauchesnes, 1936), 207–11.

53. Joseph Bonsirven, S.J., *Sur les ruines du temple* (Paris: Grasset, 1928), quoted by *La Civiltà cattolica*, op. cit., 46.

54. Unsigned, "La questione giudaica e il Sionismo," *La Civiltà cattolica* 2, quad. 2087 (28 May 1937), 418–31; "La questione giudaica e le conversioni," 2, quad. 2088 (11 June 1937), 497–510; "La questione giudaica e l'apostolato cattolico," 3, quad. 2089 (23 June 1937), 27–39.

55. Hilaire Belloc, *The Jews* (London: Constable, 1922); Italian trans., *Gli Ebrei* (Milan: Vita e pensiero, 1934).

56. From third article cited in note 54.

57. Unsigned, "Rivista della stampa: La 'Teoria moderna delle razze' impugnata da un acattolico," *La Civiltà cattolica* 3, quad. 2113 (24 June 1938), 62–71. The book in question is Dr. Rudolf Laemmel's *Die Menschlichen Rassen: Eine populär-wissenschaftliche Einführung in die Grundprobleme der Rassentheorie* (Zurich, 1936).

58. A Jewish leader of the Hungarian Communist party and of the short-lived Soviet Republic of Hungary (March–August 1919).

59. M. Barbera, S.J., "La questione dei giudei in Ungheria," *La Civiltà cattolica* 3, quad. 2114 (8 July 1938), 146–53. In 1953, Father Yves Congar, O.P., explained that "the [Hungarian] Catholic bishops accepted the *numerus clausus* established for the access to certain professions and certain schools in Hungary before 1938, where they were members of the Parliament. They were acting as leaders of the nation in a country where the Jewish minority (5.3% of the population) held in various domains (the press, the theater, etc.) virtually all the posts, or, in any case, a role superior to the one that its size would have given it, taking into account its level of culture. This is only one example among many of the questions that might be raised in the political and social domain." Yves Congar, *l'Église catholique devant la question raciale* (Paris: Unesco, 1953), 55.

60. "Un tremendo atto di accusa," *Il Regime fascista,* 30 August 1938, quoted by Enrico Rosa, "La questione giudaica e *La Civiltà cattolica,*" *La Civiltà cattolica* 4, quad. 2119 (22 September 1938), 5.

61. See for example, Enrico Rosa, "La questione giudaica e l'antisemitismo nazionalsocialista," *La Civiltà cattolica* 4, quad. 2024 (13 October 1934), 126–36, and quad. 2025 (26 October 1934), 276–85. In this article Father Rosa proceeded in the same way as in his 1938 article quoted above, that is, by criticizing various Nazi publications that exploited manipulated quotations of the pope or from *La Civiltà cattolica.*

62. "Della questione giudaica in Europa," published in three installments, *La Civiltà cattolica* 14, vol. 9, 5, 385, 641, and 1890. See E. Rosa, op. cit., 6.

63. In the second part, which is too long to be quoted here, Father Rosa engaged in a long reflection, which is just as interesting and instructive, concerning the manner in which the "anti-Catholic trend" within the Italian Risorgimento had led to the "degeneration of its initial inspiration, which was fundamentally Christian in origin," and to the role played by the Jews in this "degeneration."

64. See chap. 3, n. 20.

65. All these decrees are reported, without comment, in the "Cronaca contemp-

oranea" in *La Civiltà cattolica* 3, quad. 2116 (12 August 1938), 78; 3, quad. 2118 (9 September 1938), 567; 4, quad. 2124 (9 September 1938), 567; 1, quad. 2125 (31 December 1939), 91; 2, quad. 2135 (27 May 1939), 475–78; 2, quad. 2136 (10 June 1939), 569–70; and so on.

66. "Deign to look upon this offering with a favorable countenance, to accept it as you have accepted the gifts of your child, the righteous Abel, and the sacrifice of our patriarch Abraham, and the one your archpriest Melchizedek made to you. . . ." Cf. Genesis 14:18; Psalms 109:4; Hebrews 7:1–15.

67. Galatians 3:16.

68. The complete text was published in *La Libre Belgique* for 14 September 1938, and reproduced in *La Documentation catholique* 39, no. 885 (5 December 1938), cols. 1459–1460. See also René Laurentin, *l'Église et les Juifs à Vatican II,* 45–46, and especially 107–9.

69. In the introduction to his article in *La Libre Belgique,* Mgr. Picard pointed out that "the text we are offering has no official character. [. . .] We would not have made it public had not the Holy Father asked us to do so."

70. In Paris, on 7 November 1938, a young Polish Jew, Herschel Grynzpan, shot an official at the Germany Embassy, Ernst von Rath, who died at 9 A.M. on 9 November. Around 10 o'clock that night, Goebbels, after having discussed the matter with Hitler, ordered the Nazi party's local organizations to unleash twenty-four hours of anti-Jewish terrorism all over the Reich. The outcome: 91 Jews murdered and 20,000 more sent to concentration camps during the following days, 267 synagogues destroyed, hundreds of Jewish cemeteries desecrated, thousands of commercial establishments and private apartments belonging to Jews vandalized and pillaged. In all, one billion marks' worth of destruction, a sum that the German Jewish community had to pay as an additional punishment . . . and to prevent German insurance companies' having to pay for the damage.

71. In France, *La Croix* broke, according to Alain Fleury, with "the old resentments kept alive up to that point by the paper's anti-Semitic tradition," and expressed its pity and sympathy for the victims, not without first reminding its readers that "we are not ignorant of the role played by some of them in the bloody Bolshevik revolution; but their wretchedness in the Reich makes us forget all other aspects of this painful question" (*La Croix,* 27–28 November 1938). All the same, Fleury notes, "apart from the immediate reactions, which were usually anonymous and published in the inside pages, *La Croix* did not directly or 'officially' condemn (as an editorial by Father [Léon] Merklen, [director of *La Croix*], might have done, for example) the Nazis' anti-Semitic persecution, on the occasion of the pogroms of November 1938." Alain Fleury, *"La Croix" et l'Allemagne, 1930–1940* (Paris: Cerf, 1986), 324–25. *Études* did not take an official position, either, although Yves de La Brière denounced in its pages the "abominable and inhuman violence that German anti-Semitism has repeatedly perpetrated [. . .]. Hitler's Germany has aroused against itself the indignation, indeed the exasperation, of the whole

civilized world, by the monstrous nature of its own vindictive acts, both governmental and popular, whose exorbitant nature it does not seem to discern, even
after the fact. This is a flagrant moral disgrace to which the German empire has
fallen heir [. . .]." Yves de La Brière, "Histoire religieuse du temps présent: Racisme et droit matrimonial," *Études* 238, 4 (5 December 1938), 665.

72. Particularly in Germany, where the silence of the hierarchy is all the more
cruelly underscored by the frequently cited words of compassion uttered by the
dean of Lichtenberg, who in his Berlin church on the evening of 10 November
called on his parishioners to pray "for the priests in the concentration camps, for
the Jews, for the non-Aryans," adding, "What happened yesterday, we know; what
will happen tomorrow, we do not know; but we are witness to what is happening
today; right nearby [this church] the synagogue is in flames, and it is also a house
of God." Konrad Repgen, "Judenpogrom, Rassenideologie und katholische Kirche
1938," *Kirche und Gesellschaft,* no. 152/153 (Mönchengladbach, 1988): 10–11.

73. For all the following quotations, see *La Documentation catholique* 39, no. 886
(20 December 1938), 1481–1510.

74. *La Documentation catholique* gives only the date "November 1938."

75. In Colossians 3:10–11, Paul proclaims: "[you have] put on the new nature,
which is being renewed in knowledge after the image of its creator. Here there
cannot be Greek or Jew, circumcised and uncircumcised, barbarian, Scythian, slave,
free man, but Christ is all, and in all."

76. Konrad Repgen, op. cit.

77. Concerning Kristallnacht, see *Osservatore romano,* 11–18, 20, 23, 24, 26, and
27 November and 3, 16, 21, and 24 December 1938. For the cardinals' statements,
see *Osservatore romano,* 18, 19, and 24 November; see also *La Documentation catholique,* 20 December 1938.

78. This latter quotation is drawn from Cardinal Schuster's speech quoted above.

79. *La Civiltà cattolica* reproduces this article in its entirety; cf. "Cronaca contemporanea," 4, quad. 2123 (25 November 1938), 471–74. In France, this question was discussed three times on the first page of *La Croix,* and it provoked, on
16 November, an editorial by Father Merklen pointing out, in the same terms as
those used by the *Osservatore romano,* that it was a "question of principle of capital
importance" (Alain Fleury, op. cit., 325). In *Études,* Yves de La Brière also followed
very closely the developments in the *Osservatore romano,* before concluding on a
conciliatory note: "Italian cleverness will not find it difficult to discover a new
formula or a more nuanced plan of action for the decree of 10 November. [. . .]
It is with all their hearts that the friends of Italy, like obedient sons of the Holy
See everywhere in the world, hope that in this matter and in all litigious matters
the spirit of concord and collaboration, which is more than ever postulated by
imperious motives of supreme wisdom, will be strengthened." Yves de La Brière,
"l'Histoire religieuse du temps présent. Racisme et droit matrimonial," *Études* 238,
4 (5 December 1938), 670–72.

80. Wound (Latin).

81. That is, members of Protestant and Orthodox sects.

82. See John LaFarge, op. cit., chap. 14: "Social Equality and Intermarriage."

83. The speech in question is the one given on 13 November 1938 by Cardinal Schuster, which we mentioned above.

84. An allusion to Hitler's trip to Rome in the spring of 1938, also mentioned above.

85. *Osservatore romano,* 25 December 1938. "Faithful and complete" translation in *La Documentation catholique* 40, no. 889 (20 January 1939), 67–72.

86. Account in the *Osservatore romano,* 19 January 1939; full French translation in *La Documentation catholique* 40, no. 891 (20 February 1939), under the title "l'Église, le racisme et le problème juif," 243–46.

87. Cardinal Eugène Tisserant was at the time the prefect of the Congregation for the Eastern Church. These remarks are reported, without indicating the sources, by the *National Catholic Reporter,* 15 December 1972, 13.

88. John XXIII's future secretary of state.

89. *National Catholic Reporter,* 22 December 1972, 3, 4.

90. *La Documentation catholique,* which we are quoting here, explains: "On 26 January last [1959], visiting the Secretary of State, His Holiness John XXIII had had occasion to see, in the secret archives, the manuscript of the speech that Pius XI was to give on 10 February 1939, the day of his death, before the bishops of Italy. For the first time in his pontificate, he had called them all to the Vatican, before the great ceremony that was to take place the next day at St. Peter's for the tenth anniversary of the Lateran accords. It is not without emotion that one will read, in this letter addressed by His Holiness John XXIII to the bishops of Italy, long extracts from this speech[...]." "The remainder of this manuscript, John XXIII said in this letter, deserved to be screened from any profane or indiscreet inspection. Many extravagant hypotheses were framed at that time concerning the final manifestations of a thought and a sensibility that, for anyone acquainted with the spiritual superiority of Pius XI, could only be elevated and very noble. But the circumstances of these weeks, which were not exempt from bitterness for the old pontiff, would certainly make it understandable that he expressed himself in phrases and in a tone of an all-too-justified resentment." *La Documentation catholique* 56, no. 1298 (1 March 1959), 257–64, quoting the *Osservatore romano* for 9–10 February 1959.

91. See chap. 3, n. 46.

VI. CONCLUSION

1. Émile Poulat, *Catholicisme, démocratie et socialisme,* op. cit., 475. On this subject, see also Jean-Marie Mayeur, "Trois papes: Benoît XV, Pius XI, Pius XII,"

in Jean-Marie Mayeur, Charles Pietri, André Vauchez, and Marc Venard, op. cit., (in chap. 5, n. 6), 13–44.

2. Émile Poulat, op. cit., 63–64.

3. "This love for one's country and one's race [*gens,* in Latin], which is a powerful source of many virtues and acts of heroism when it is governed by Christian law, nonetheless becomes a source of numerous injustices and iniquities if, transgressing the rules of justice and law, it degenerates into immoderate nationalism." Pius XI, *Ubi Arcano Dei,* 23 December 1922, quoted by Mayeur, op. cit., 22.

4. This had already been Pius X's motto: "*Instaurare omnia in Christo.*" Mayeur, op. cit., 22–23.

5. Virtually the same arguments concerning the unity and diversity of humanity are found in LaFarge's *Interracial Justice.*

6. See the letter from Father Killeen to LaFarge, 27 October 1938; chap. 3, n. 8.

7. We have seen in chapter 5 that the *Osservatore romano* for 14–15 November 1938, in an article on "the very recent legislative decisions concerning marriages" was to take up the same question in the same spirit.

8. Jules Isaac, *L'Enseignement du mépris* (Paris: Fasquelle, 1962).

9. Gordon Zahn, "The Unpublished Encyclical—An Opportunity Missed," *National Catholic Reporter,* 15 December 1972, 9.

10. That is, paragraphs 72–93 of *Humani Generis Unitas.* See Pius XII, "Lettre encyclique *Summi Pontificatus* aux patriarches, primats, archévêques et autres Ordinaires en paix et communion avec le Siège apostolique," 20 October 1939, in *La Documentation catholique* 40 (5–20 December 1939), pp. 1251–75. The passages similar to those in *Humani Generis Unitas* go from page 1259 to page 1262.

FOREWORD TO *HUMANI GENERIS UNITAS*

1. Probably also a partial translation into Latin, done by Father Heinrich Bacht, S.J., of which we have found no trace. Personal testimony and investigations previous to ours mention it only in passing.

2. Microf. 62.

3. An additional note written in French and typed on a separate sheet is placed at the very end of this "long" English version:

"c) We have created, or invented, for the purpose, *two new expressions* TOTALITY OF EXTENSION, and TERRITORIAL NATIONALITY.

"By Totality of extension (in contrast with intension), we mean more or less what the Holy Father has already indicated in speaking of objective Totalitarianism (in contrast with subjective). The *Totality of intention* is only *the full expression of being itself.* The state, for example, which is a totality of intention [*sic*], perfectly and completely fulfills its duty as a state; in actuality it is fully what is must be in accord with its nature. The totality of extension, on the other hand, is the extension of its activities to areas or to interests beyond its proper functions; it is Totalitarianism per se, the intrusion of the state into matters that are foreign to its nature and its rights. (N.B., for the opportunism of the Encyclical, that this totality [word struck out] of extension is not at all limited to today's so-called totalitarian states, but is found more or less everywhere, for example in public education. The creation of this word gives the Church a new weapon in the battle for freedom of conscience and the freedom of Christian education.

"It is very difficult to find an exact expression, outside of German, for the words *Volk* and *Volkstum*. In French, and in several other modern languages, the word 'peuple' (*people, popolo*) does not seem to express the idea with sufficient precision. The distinction between territorial nationality (*Volkstum*) and nation proposed here is very commonly accepted by modern authors, although the expression 'territorial nationality' is proper to the Encyclical.

"d) The treatment of the question of intermarriage between the races from a moral point of view, without limiting the essential liberties of the human Person and the freedom of the Church in this area, but also without encouraging imprudent and harmful practices, makes use of distinctions that have found much favor among several bishops who have devoted special attention to this subject."

4. An internal analysis of the contents and literary styles, handwritten annotations and deletions, typing, etc., and an external analysis of testimony by specialists and by Gundlach's collaborators (Stanton cites the correspondence of the Jesuit fathers Burkhart Schneider, d'Ouince, Anton Rauscher, and Robert Graham). See *Authorship of the Text*, 186–94.

5. Stanton, op. cit., 192–93.

6. See the discussion of Gundlach's previous writings, chap. 3.

7. Letter from H. Bacht, dated 5 March 1973, to Schwarte, who cites it in his dissertation, 78–79.

8. Rauscher, cited by Schwarte, op. cit., 79.

9. Droulers, op. cit., 336–37.

10. Stanton, op. cit., 189–90.

HUMANI GENERIS UNITAS

1. "Thus the marvelous power of the Church to protect and maintain the civil and political liberty of peoples has always shown forth. The balance of rights, like true fraternity among men, was first proclaimed by Jesus Christ; but his voice was echoed by that of his apostles, who declared that there was neither Jew, nor Greek, nor Barbarian, nor Scythian, but all men are brothers in Christ." Leo XIII, *Libertas*.

2. See the condemned proposition XXXIX in Leo XIII, *Quanta cara*: "The state, as the origin and source of all rights, enjoys a right that is not circumscribed by any limit."

3. Leo XIII, *Quod Apostolici,* I:32: "The Church constantly teaches to the multitude this apostolic principle: *there is no power that does not come from God, and those that exist were established by God.*"

4. Just as once under Liberalism, today Our Predecessor's words have proven true: "And in reality, if unaided human reason alone judges between good and evil, good is suppressed along with evil . . . In public affairs, authority is divorced from the true and natural principle from which it derives its power to provide for the common good." Leo XIII, *Libertas.*

See *Ubi arcano,* "Paying God sovereign homage, the Church recognizes that it is from Him that authority and its rights derive."

5. *Caritate Christi.*

6. *De Civitate Dei,* Lib. XIX, c. 17.

7. *De moribus Eccl.,* Lib. I, c. 30 (*Patrologia Latina,* vol. 32, c. 1336).

8. *De moribus Eccl.,* Lib. I, c. 30.

9. *De moribus Eccl.,* Lib. I, c. 30.

10. *Politics,* 3:16, 1287a.

11. *De Leg,* 1:2, c. 4.

12. *Ep.* 21, M.P.Z. XXII, 1029.

13. *De Sermone Domini in monte,* I, 2.

14. Romans 11:15.

15. *De mor[ibus] Eccl.,* Lib. I, c. 30.

16. Sancti Leonis Papae, *Sermo de Pass. Domini.*

Bibliography

ARCHIVES

LaFarge, John. *Humani Generis Unitas* and associated documents, a microfilm received in December 1987 from Professor Thomas Breslin, who made it in 1969 while he was inventorying the LaFarge archives at Loyola Seminary in New York City

Gundlach, Gustav. *Societas Unio*, 89 typed pages, Gustav Gundlach archives at the Katholische Sozialwissenschaftliche Zentralstelle, Mönchengladbach, Germany

ENCYCLICALS

Pius XI. *Quadragesimo Anno*, 1931; *Mit Brennender Sorge*, 14 March 1937; *Divini Redemptoris*, 19 March 1937

Pius XII. *Summi Pontificatus*, 20 October 1939. French translation, with analytical table of contents and commentaries, Paris: SPES, 1939 (on the cover: *Action populaire*; on the flyleaf: *Nihil obstat*, G. Desbuquois, S.J., December 1939)

DOCTORAL THESES

Schwarte, Johannes. *Gustav Gundlach, S.J. (1892-1963), Repräsentant und Interpret der katholischen Soziallehre in der Ära Pius' XII. Historische Einordnung und systematische Darstellung.* Doctoral thesis in theology, Faculty of Catholic Theology, Westfälischen Wilhelms-Universität, Münster, 1974; *Abhandlungen zur Sozialethik*, ed. Wilhelm Weber and Anton Rauscher, vol. 9. Munich, Paderborn, and Vienna: Ferdinand Schöningh, 1975

Stanton, Edward, S.J. *John LaFarge: Understanding of the Unifying Mission of the*

Church, Especially in the Area of Race Relations. Doctoral dissertation, St. Paul's University, Ottawa, Canada, 1972

ARTICLES

"Amici Israel." In *Lexikon für Theologie und Kirche*, 2nd ed., rev., vol. 1, col. 361. Freiburg im Breisgau: Herder, 1930

Gundlach, Gustav. "Antisemitismus." In *Lexicon für Theologie und Kirche*, 2nd ed., vol. 1, cols. 504–505. Freiburg im Breisgau: Herder, 1930

LaFarge, John, S.J. "Racism." In *New Catholic Encyclopedia*, vol. 12, pp. 54–60. New York: McGraw-Hill, 1967

Nota, Johannes H., S.J. "Edith Stein und der Entwurf für eine Enzyklika gegen Rassismus und Antisemitismus." *Freiburger Rundbrief*, 1975, pp. 35–41

Schneider, Burkhart, S.J. "Una enciclica mancata." *L'Osservatore romano*, 4 April 1974

PERIODICALS

L'Action populaire
America
Cité chrétienne
Civiltà Cattolica
Commonweal
Der Spiegel
La Documentation catholique
Informations catholiques internationales
KNA-Nachrichten
The Month
National Catholic Reporter
Neue Züricher Zeitung
La Nouvelle Revue théologique
L'Osservatore romano
Sens
Stimmen der Zeit
Time

BOOKS

Bonsirven, Joseph, S.J. *Sur les ruines du Temple.* Paris: Grasset, 1928

Bressolles (Mgr.), Robert D'Harcourt, Yves de la Brière, Albert de Lapparent, and Ernest Seillierre. *Racisme et Christianisme.* Preface by Cardinal Baudrillart. Paris: Flammarion, 1939

Charles, Pierre, S.J., Joseph Folliet, Pierre Lorson, S.J., and Ernest Van Canınpenhout. *Racisme et catholicisme*. Paris and Tournai: Casterman, July, 1939. First published in *La Nouvelle Revue théologique*, February 1939

LaFarge, John, S.J. *Interracial Justice*. New York: America Press, 1937. 2nd ed., *The Race Question and the Negro. A Study of the Catholic Doctrine on Interracial Justice*. New York: Longmans, Green, 1943

MEMOIRS

Engel-Janosi, Friedrich, S.J. *Vom Chaos zur Catastrophe: Vatikanische Gespräche 1915 bis 1938*. Vienna: Harold, 1971

Gundlach, Gustav, S.J. *Meine Bestimmung zur Sozialwissenschaft*. Typed autobiographical notes, Rome, 23 February 1962. Quoted by J. Schwarte, op. cit.

LaFarge, John, S.J. *The Manner Is Ordinary*. New York: Harcourt, 1954

Muckermann, Friedrich, S.J. *Im Kampf zwischen zwei Epochen. Lebenserinnerungen*. 3 vols. Mainz: Matthias Grünewald, 1973

Nell-Breuning, Oswald von, S.J. "Der Königswinterer Kreis und sein Anteil an *Quadragesimo Anno*." In *Soziale Verantwortung*, vol. 9. Berlin: 1968

GENERAL STUDIES

Bea, Augustin, Cardinal. *L'Église et le peuple juif*. Paris: Cerf, 1967

Bloy, Léon. *Le Salut par les Juifs*. 1892; rpt. Paris: Mercure de France, 1946

Butturini, Giuseppe. *Alle origine del Vaticano II. Una proposta di Celso Costantini*. Pardenone: Edizione Concordia Sette, 1988

Cahiers Paul-Claudel, no. 7, "La figure d'Israël." Paris: Gallimard, 1968

Confalonieri, Cardinal. *Pio XI visto da vicino*. Turin: Edizione Paoline, 1957

Congar, Yves, O.P. *L'Église catholique devant la question raciale*. Paris: UNESCO, 1953

Conzemius, V. *Églises chrétiennes et totalitarisme national-socialiste. Un bilan historiographique*. Louvain: Publications universitaires de Louvain, 1969

Delpech, François. *Sur les Juifs*. Lyon: Presses universitaires de Lyon, 1983

Droulers, Paul, S.J. *Politique sociale et christianisme. Le père Desbuquois et l'Action populaire*. Paris: Éditions Ouvrières. Vol. 1, *Débuts. Syndicalisme et intégristes (1903–1918)*, 1969; vol. 2, *Dans la gestation d'un monde nouveau (1919–1946)*, 1981

Les Églises devant le judaïsme. Official documents, 1948–1978. Collected, translated, and annotated by Marie-Thérèse Hoch and Bernard Dupuy. Paris: Cerf, 1980

Encyclopedia Judaica, ed. Cecil Roth, art. "Italy," pp. 1134–1135. Jerusalem: Encyclopedia Judaica, 1972; New York: Macmillan, 1972

Ericksen, Robert P. *Theologians under Hitler. Gerhard Kittel, Paul Althaus and Emanuel Hirsch*. New Haven and London: Yale University Press, 1985

Falconi, Carlo. *Le Silence de Pie XII. 1939–1945. Essai fondé sur des documents d'archives recueillis par l'auteur en Pologne et en Yougoslavie.* Trans. Viviana Paques. Monaco: Editions du Rocher, 1965

Flannery, Edward H. *The Anguish of the Jews. Twenty-Three Centuries of Anti-Semitism.* New York and London: Macmillan, 1965

Fleury, Alain. *"La Croix" et l'Allemagne, 1930–1940.* Preface by René Rémond. Paris: Cerf, 1986

Friedlander, Saul. *Pie XII et le IIIᵉ Reich. Documents.* Postface by Alfred Grosser. Paris: Seuil, 1964

Jansen, Hans. *Chriselijke Theologie na Auschwitz.* Vol. 1, *Theologische en Kerkelijke wortels van het Antisemisme.* Gravenhage: Boeckencentrum BV, 1981

Klein, Charlotte. *Theologie und Anti-Judaismus.* Munich: Chr. Kaiser, 1975. Trans., *Anti-Judaïsm in Christian Theology.* Philadelphia: Fortress Press, 1978

Id., "Vatican and Zionism, 897–1964." *Christian Attitudes on Jews and Judaism*, June-July 1974

Id., "In the Mirror of *Civiltà Cattolica.* A Vatican View of Jewry, 1939–62." *Christian Attitudes on Jews and Judaism*, June-November 1975

Lacouture, Jean. *Jésuites.* Paris: Seuil, 1991

Ladous, Régis. *Des Nobel au Vatican.* Paris: Cerf, 1994

Lapide, Pinchas E. *Three Popes and the Jews.* New York: Hawthorn, 1967

Laurentin, René. *L'Église et les Juifs à Vatican II.* Paris: Casterman, 1967

Lewy, Guenter. *L'Église catholique et l'Allemagne nazie.* Paris: Stock, 1965

Losinger, Anton. *Gerechte Vermögensverteilung. Das Modell Oswald von Nell-Breunings. Abhandlungen zur Sozialethik*, vol. 34. Paderborn and Munich: Schöningh, 1994

Lovsky, F. *Antisémitisme et mystère d'Israël.* Paris: Albin Michel, 1955

Lubac (Mgr.) de. *La Résistance chrétienne à l'antisémitisme.* Paris: Fayard, 1988

Marrus, Michael Robert. *The Holocaust in History.* Hanover, NH: University Press of New England, 1987

Mayeur, Jean-Marie, gen. ed. *Histoire du christianisme des origines à nos jours.* Vol. 1, *Guerres mondiales et totalitarisme (1914–1958).* Paris: Desclée-Fayard, 1990

Montcheuil, Yves de. *Spiritualité, théologie et résistance.* Grenoble: Presses universitaires de Grenoble, 1987

Montclos, Xavier de. *Les Chrétiens face au nazisme et au stalinisme.* Paris: Plon, 1983

de Montclos, Xavier, Monique Luirard, François Delpech, Pierre Bolle, et al. *Églises et chrétiens dans la seconde guerre mondiale.* Proceedings of colloquia held in Grenoble, 7–9 October 1976, and in Lyons, 27–30 January 1978. Lyon: Presses Universitaires de Lyon. Vol. 1, *La Région Rhône-Alpes*, 1978; vol. 2, *La France*, 1982

Petit, Jacques. *Bernanos, Bloy, Claudel, Péguy. Quatre écrivains catholiques face à Israël, images et mythes.* Paris: Calmann-Lévy, 1972

Pierrard, Pierre. *Juifs et catholiques français.* Paris: Fayard, 1970

Pontifical Commission on Justice and Peace, *L'Église face au racisme. Pour une société plus fraternelle*, Rome, 10 February 1989. In *Les Grands Textes de la Documentation catholique*, no. 75, supp. to *La Documentation catholique* no. 1979, Paris, 5 March 1989

Poulat, Émile. *Intégrisme et catholicisme intégral*. Tournai and Paris: Casterman, 1969

Id. *Catholicisme, démocratie et socialisme*. Tournai and Paris, Casterman, 1977

Id. *Une Église ébranlée. Changement, conflit et continuité de Pie XII à Jean-Paul II*. Paris and Tournai: Casterman, 1980

Remembering for the Future. Jews and Christians During and After the Holocaust. International Scholars' Conference held in Oxford, 10–13 July 1988. Ed. Yehuda Bauer et al. 2 vols. Oxford and New York: Pergamon Press, 1988

Rauscher, Anton, S.J. *Gustav Gundlach, 1892–1963*. Paderborn and Munich: Schöningh, 1988

Repgen, Konrad. "Judenprogram, Rassenideologie und Katholische Kirche." *Kirche und Gesellschaft*, no. 152/153. Mönchengladbach, 1988

Rhodes, Anthony. *The Vatican in the Age of the Dictators, 1922–1945*. London: Hodder and Stoughton, 1973

Roche, Georges (Mgr.), and Philippe Saint-Germain. *Pie XII devant l'histoire*. Paris: Laffont, 1972

Schmidt, Stjepan, S.J. *Agostino Bea, il cardinale dell'unità*. Rome: Città Nuova, 1988

Shirer, William L. *The Rise and Fall of the Third Reich. A History of Nazi Germany*. New York: Simon and Schuster, 1960

Spiritu Sancto, Teresia Renata de. *Edith Stein*. Nuremberg: Glock und Lutz, 1952

Villey, Michel. *Le Droit et les droits de l'homme*. Paris: Presses Universitaires de France, 1990

Zahn, Gordon C. *German Catholics and Hitler's Wars. A Study in Social Control*. New York: Sheed and Ward, 1962; rpt., Notre Dame, IN: University of Notre Dame Press, 1989

Index